THE FLEXIBLE
WORKPLACE

THE FLEXIBLE WORKPLACE

A Sourcebook of Information and Research

Christine Avery and Diane Zabel

QUORUM BOOKS
Westport, Connecticut • London

Library of Congress Cataloging-in-Publication Data

Avery, Christine.
    The flexible workplace : a sourcebook of information and research / Christine Avery
and Diane Zabel.
        p.   cm.
    Includes bibliographical references and index.
    ISBN 1–56720–189–X (alk. paper)
    1. Hours of labor, Flexible.   2. Part-time employment.   3. Workweek.   I. Zabel, Diane.
II. Title.
HD5109.A94   2001
331.25′72—dc21   00–025461

British Library Cataloguing in Publication Data is available.

Library of Congress Catalog Card Number: 00–025461
ISBN: 1–56720–189–X

First published in 2001

Quorum Books, 88 Post Road West, Westport, CT 06881
An imprint of Greenwood Publishing Group, Inc.
www.quorumbooks.com

Printed in the United States of America

The paper used in this book complies with the
Permanent Paper Standard issued by the National
Information Standards Organization (Z39.48–1984).

10   9   8   7   6   5   4   3   2   1

Contents

Preface

Although there is a large body of literature on the changing nature of work and workplace flexibility, there is no handbook that synthesizes the research on all aspects of this topic. *The Flexible Workplace* is international in scope and pulls together the vast literature on this subject. Chapters explain the concept of flexible work, trace the origin and growth of this workplace trend, and review the research on a range of flexible work arrangements. It identifies aspects of the subject that warrant additional research. This book identifies some useful resources, including books, reports, theses, periodicals, newsletters, videos, and national surveys. It also discusses strategies for locating additional information, including relevant databases, Internet resources, organizations, and search terms.

This book is intended to serve as a handbook for managers, researchers, and students in a wide range of undergraduate and graduate-level courses (industrial/organizational psychology, human resource management, business, sociology, etc.). This important workplace trend is covered in many core and optional human resource management courses and in many courses treating contemporary issues in management.

Workplace flexibility is a topic that is international in scope. Companies in the United States and abroad have become increasingly interested in implementing flexible work arrangements. One of the chapters in *The Flexible Workplace* focuses on companies that have been leaders in implementing flexible work arrangements. It includes examples from both manufacturing and nonmanufacturing settings. It profiles innovative companies in North America, Western Europe, and the United Kingdom.

In addition, we envision this book as a resource for organizations implementing flexible work arrangements, practicing human resource management and personnel managers, and academicians.

ACKNOWLEDGMENTS

We would like to acknowledge the support of the University Libraries at the Pennsylvania State University. In particular, we would like to thank Associate Deans Sally Kalin and Jack Sulzer for their support. Ms. Zabel is grateful to the university for the award of a seven-month sabbatical. The authors would also like to thank our excellent interlibrary loan department for their efforts on our behalf. Most of all we thank our families, especially our children (Zachary, Julian, and Carl).

CHAPTER 1

An Introduction to Flexible Work

The twenty-first century workforce will be more female and more diverse. In addition, there will be increased competition for talented
workers. Since the publication of *Workforce 2000* in 1987, the landmark
report issued by the Hudson Institute, managers have been preparing
for this new workforce by becoming more sensitive to work/family
issues. Industry, both in the United States and abroad, has become
increasingly concerned with the development of family-friendly policies that help employees balance the demands of work and family.
One important type of family-friendly benefit is workplace flexibility
and alternatives to the traditional workweek. Many corporations, however, are developing flexible work arrangements for compelling economic reasons. Permitting employees to telecommute is less expensive
than providing office space. In the United States the 1990 Federal Clean
Air Act and state air-quality standards have induced companies to
offer some type of telecommuting option to their employees. Many
companies are already offering workplace flexibility. Flexible work
arrangements include a range of options: flexible work schedules, compressed workweeks, job sharing, job exchanges, voluntary part-time
work, phased retirement, telecommuting, and home-based work.

Technology has transformed the way we work. Personal computers, fax machines, and other technological innovations have already created the "electronic cottage" as a workplace. Workplace flexibility has not only been adapted to manufacturing settings, but it has also been implemented in the service industries as well as the service professions. Higher education is also beginning to recognize the importance of new ways of working. The Wharton School of Business (University of Pennsylvania) has incorporated work-life issues into its required curriculum (Estess 1996).

How do you define flexibility? Barney Olmsted and Suzanne Smith (1997), coauthors of several leading books on workplace flexibility, offer two definitions of flexibility. From the employer's perspective, they offer this definition: "Flexibility means being able to adjust quickly to changing economic conditions: expanding, contracting, or reallocating labor supply as needed; and improving service in order to become more competitive by increasing productivity and decreasing costs" (p. ix). From the employee's perspective, "Flexibility means being able to adjust work time or workplace when personal needs are in conflict with their current schedule: being able to alter starting and quitting times occasionally; reducing paid work time for a while so they can return to school, start a family, or recover from burnout; attending nonwork functions without being penalized" (p. ix). Catalyst (1998a), an organization that has studied new working patterns for more than three decades, defines alternative or flexible work arrangements as "individually negotiated conditions of employment involving adjustments in the timing, scope, and/or place of work" (p. 3). This introductory chapter traces the origin and growth of this workplace trend. It provides some background on the demographic, economic, and governmental changes that have been an impetus for workplace shifts. The factors behind the movement to make work flexible are also discussed.

THE HISTORY OF WORKPLACE FLEXIBILITY

Simcha Ronen (1981) reminds us that rigid work schedules only developed in the mid-1800s, since most Americans were self-employed or on family farms before this period. Most workers determined their own schedules before industrialization. However, the eight-hour uniform day, the five-day workweek, and fixed starting and finishing times are no longer standard. This deviation from standardized working time began in the 1930s. The W. K. Kellogg Company (the cereal plant located in Battle Creek, Michigan) replaced the traditional three daily eight-hour shifts with four six-hour shifts in order to create work for laid off employees on December 1, 1930. The addition of one entire shift allowed the company to do so. This fascinating experiment has been chronicled by Benjamin Kline Hunnicutt (1996) in a book entitled *Kellogg's Six-Hour Day*. This six-hour day generated much media attention and was supported by workers, government, labor, and the business community. Union demands in the late 1930s and early 1940s and President Roosevelt's executive order mandating a longer work-week (as part of the wartime effort) brought an end to six-hour shifts. The labor union struggled to reestablish the six-hour day after World War II. Some units were able to hold on to six-hour shifts until February 1985, when they were abolished. Hunnicutt pored through archival material and used his own interviews and letters from living Kellogg workers and managers. He found that women were the strongest supporters of a six-hour shift.

In 1930 Kellogg was the world's largest manufacturer of ready-to-eat cereals and employed almost 1,500 workers. Kellogg had been a leader in industrial reform. It was one of the first companies to introduce the eight-hour day and the five-day week. The Kellogg experiment became a national model. Hunnicutt (1996) reported that a 1932 survey of approximately 1,700 business executives indicated that half of all American businesses reduced hours in order to save jobs. Work sharing became a national movement in the United States during the period from 1932 to 1937. Kellogg maintained that employee efficiency and morale increased, accidents and insurance rates improved, and the unit cost of production increased as a result of six-hour days—allowing Kellogg to pay as much for six hours as formerly paid for eight. Kellogg boasted that six-hour days allowed the company to employ 25-percent more workers than in pre-Depression days.

Traditionally, historians argued that labor supported shorter days for economic reasons: to gain higher total wages and to reduce unemployment. However, Hunnicutt (1996, 49) pointed out that some revisionist historians, such as Gary Cross, argue that "leisure" or "freedom from work" was also a factor. Hunnicutt's research indicated that Kellogg workers supported the six-hour day for the same reasons.

Kellogg returned to the eight-hour shifts in February 1943 as a result of Roosevelt's executive order. The six-hour day was restored in 1947 for a majority of Kellogg workers. However, about half of the men employed at Kellogg's were on eight- hour days. The six-hour shifts were typically allocated to women, older men, and disabled workers—a practice Hunnicutt (1996) refers to as "the feminizing of shorter hours" (p. 103). Labor gave up supporting shorter hours in order to concentrate on higher wages. In 1983 Kellogg abolished six-hour days in order to eliminate jobs and benefits attached to positions. The company threatened to move the plant out of state if workers did not vote on eight-hour days companywide.

This idea of sharing work was also supported by Albert Morton Persoff. Persoff's revolutionary book, *Sabbatical Years with Pay: A Plan to Create and Maintain Full Employment,* was published in 1945. In his book, Persoff advocated that every American worker receive a year off with pay every seven years as a strategy to solve the problem of mass unemployment. He described the plan as follows: "Under the plan, each year, one-seventh of all eligible workers will receive a sabbatical year with pay, a leave of absence with pay" (p. 81), and "as each group terminated its sabbatical, it returns to work and the next group of one-seventh of all eligible workers will immediately start its sabbatical year with pay" (p. 82). Persoff believed that as a result of this sabbatical year workers "will acquire a new lease on life, a deep, invigorating and stimulating second breath that will enable them to return to their jobs with more strength and energy, and will" (p. 83). He argued that workers would have the motivation to be productive since the prospect of a year off with pay would be a powerful incentive. In fact, he believed that productivity would rise as a result of this morale-boosting policy. He calculated that "the six-sevenths of the qualifying workers who remain at their jobs will produce the equivalent of total normal production, and at the same time, the one-seventh of the men and women enjoying their sabbatical year will . . . purchase their respective share of the goods and services produced" (p. 90). Persoff projected that workers would not have to put in any more than four additional hours of labor per week in order to achieve this level of productivity. Persoff's radical plan was of course never implemented. Sanctioned time off (paid or unpaid) was almost unheard of outside of academia until the 1950s, when IBM implemented its Personal Leave of Absence program, a program allowing employees to take an unpaid leave of up to three years. In the 1960s labor and industry organized a thirteen-week sabbatical for workers in the steel and aluminum industries in order to avoid layoffs (Rogak 1994).

The dissolution of standard working time is the theme of *Working Time in Transition: The Political Economy of Working Hours in Industrial Nations* (Hinrichs, Roche, and Sirianni 1991). The editors of this volume believe, "Among the pervasive changes that have occurred in recent decades . . . in Western industrial nations, changes in working-time regimes must surely count as one of the most significant" (p. 3). Since the 1950s the length of the working week and length of working life were reduced in Western industrialized countries. The distribution of working hours was altered on a daily and weekly basis. More employees were allowed flexibility in starting and finishing times and part-time employment opportunities became more abundant. Hinrichs, Roche, and Sirianni prophesied that "we may be witnessing the demise of standardized working-time regulations and arrangements that were developed by unions and employees—and often underwritten by governments—over a period of more than a century" (p. 4).

Flextime, the generic term for work schedules that permit flexible starting and quitting times, originated in West Germany. J. Carroll Swart (1978) outlined the history of flextime in *A Flexible Approach to Working Hours*. The publication of this book was significant, since until this time very little had been published in book form, in the United States, about flexible working hours. According to Swart, some credit Christel Kammerer, a West German woman who was a management consultant and political economist, with the origin of the concept of flextime. In the mid-1960s her publications explained the concept of flexible work periods: alternative work arrangements that generally allow employees to decide when to start and finish work and core time, a time period when all of a company's employees are required to be on the job.

Swart (1978) established that the first firm to implement flextime was Messerschmitt-Bolkow-Blohm, a German aerospace company. The company hired Christel Kammerer in the mid-1960s to study the problem of employee tardiness and absenteeism at the company's research and development center at Ottobrunn (near Munich). Employees were having a difficult time arriving by the 7:00 A.M. starting time because of traffic congestion. Kammerer suggested that the company introduce flextime to its employees in 1967. The initial results were positive: Absenteeism dropped by 40 percent, overtime decreased by 50 percent, turnover decreased, tardiness was no longer a problem, and employee morale increased sharply.

Flextime was rapidly adopted in Switzerland. Swart (1978) estimated that in 1977, 40 percent of the Swiss labor force was on flextime, about 30 percent of the West German labor force was on flextime, and about 20 percent of the French workforce was on flextime. Although data were not available, Swart estimated that flextime was rapidly adopted in Scandinavia. In comparison, Great Britain was slow to adopt flextime. According to Swart, the first British experiment with flextime did not occur until 1971. Swart estimated that less than 10 percent of the British workforce was on flextime in 1977. Hewlett Packard first introduced flextime in the United States in 1972 at its Waltham, Massachusetts, plant after using it in its German division.

Flextime grew rapidly throughout Western Europe in the early 1970s. Ronen (1981) has identified the factors contributing to this phenomenon. First, the unemployment rate was very low in much of Western Europe at this time. As a result of a labor shortage, employers adopted alternative work schedules in order to recruit workers. In general, legislation in Europe was less restrictive toward flextime than in the United States. European industry accepted flextime more than U.S. industry.

Interest in telecommuting, a flexible option that allows employees to work at home all or part of their scheduled hours, began in the early 1970s, prompted by the oil crisis in the United States. Jack Nilles, the father of the telecommuting movement, proposed it as a way to reduce energy consumption. In Europe the majority of teleworking (the term generally used in place of telecommuting outside of North America) projects began in the mid-1980s to early 1990s. One exception was the teleworking program ICL Enterprise Systems (a firm in the United Kingdom whose products include software, hardware, and consulting) implemented in 1969 (Korte and Wynne 1996).

Marcia Brumit Kropf (1997) has recently provided a chronological account of research on work/family issues in her history of the national nonprofit organization Catalyst. Catalyst was established in 1962. Originally, work/family research focused on the problems of child care for women with young children. Research has broadened to include studies on both women and men and needs beyond child care. Recent research by Catalyst has focused on the need for organizational change, and family-friendly policies are now studied as business initiatives. Catalyst has studied workplace flexibility since 1968. For the past three decades, Catalyst has helped organizations implement flexible work arrangements.

In 1968 Catalyst published *Part-Time Teachers and How They Work: A Study of Five School Systems*. This was followed by their 1971 study *Part-Time Social Workers in Public Welfare*. The goal of both publications was to provide models for the employment of educated women who did not want to work full time. In the 1970s and early 1980s Catalyst did research on specific flexible work arrangements. In the mid-1980s Catalyst conducted a major study of organizations involved in flexible work arrangements. This was published in 1989 as *Flexible Work Arrangements: Establishing Options for Managers and Professionals*. This was followed by a 1993 study of part-time options, *Flexible Work Arrangements II: Succeeding with Part-Time Options*. In 1995 Catalyst began a comprehensive two-year study of voluntary part-time employment among managers and professionals in four leading U.S. firms. The findings were published in a report entitled *A New Approach to Flexibility: Managing the Work/Time Equation* (Catalyst 1998a).

New Ways to Work is another nonprofit organization concerned with the promotion of workplace flexibility, and emerged around the same time as Catalyst. This organization was established in 1972. New Ways to Work designed the first project in the United States to encourage private-sector experimentation with job sharing, a type of regular part-time work that permits two people to voluntarily share the same full-time position (Olmsted and Smith 1996).

According to Dana Friedman, one of the country's foremost authorities on workplace flexibility, 1987 and 1988 represented a turning point in the development of work/family programs (Miranda and Murphy 1993). Workplace flexibility gained attention as a result of the publication of *Workforce 2000* in 1987. This report documented future labor shortages and an increasingly diverse workforce. The Families and Work Institute is another national nonprofit organization that had led the way in work/family research. Each year, the institute sponsors a national conference on a work/family issue in conjunction with the Conference Board, one of the world's premier business organizations. In the spring of 1993 that conference focused on the business case for workplace flexibility. Representatives from a range of private- and public-sector organizations spoke about their success with a range of flexible work options. A profile of these companies and their work/family programs was published by the Conference Board in 1993 (Miranda and Murphy 1993).

The push for workplace flexibility has moved from being employee driven to employer driven as more employers realize the economic benefits of flexibility. Barney Olmsted (1997), the cofounder of New Ways to Work, describes this evolution. She recently wrote, "In the mid-1970s when New Ways to Work began promoting greater workplace flexibility, it was employees who put on the heat and pioneered the changes." However, she noted, "More recently, concern about the interface between work and family responsibilities has lead to increased employer interest in providing more flexibility in the workplace" (p. 111). In an earlier publication, Olmsted (1995) wrote about the progression of workplace flexibility from accommodation to strategy. Specifically, "During the first decade-and-a-half of their use, flexible work arrangements were considered by most managers to be . . . ways to accommodate a few valued employees" and were "initiated as a result of an ad hoc arrangement between an employee and his or her supervisor" (p. 11). However, this changed by the late 1980s, when "a business case for flexibility started to emerge" (p. 11). There is concrete evidence that flexible work arrangements are being viewed as a business strategy. Olmsted notes, "In more and more firms, managers are being told to exclude the personal reasons that may motivate an employee to ask for a change in schedule and to discuss the request only in terms of business impact" (p. 11). Olmsted argues that this shift from accommodation reinforces the benefits of flexibility to the organization and helps managers decide which employees' requests for flexibility should be supported. In addition, Olmsted points out that "recent research . . . has begun to show that accommodation does not lead to greater flexibility but actually reinforces existing norms" (p. 11).

There are other indications that workplace flexibility has become a major corporate issue. *Working Mother* magazine published its first list of best companies for working mothers in 1986. Companies are eager to make this list, since "landing a spot on one of the high-visibility lists is believed to give a leg up on today's tough recruiting competition" (Stumps 1997, 42). In 1996 *Business Week* published its first rating of family-friendly companies. *Fortune* published its inaugural list of best companies to work for in 1998. Work/life balance is now viewed as an issue for all workers, not just for those with children. Dana Friedman has observed that "the nomenclature of '"work/family" programs has evolved to "work/life" or "life/stages" initiatives, as companies increasingly gear these programs to encompass all employees" (Work/Life Programs Target All Employees 1997, 31).

WORK/FAMILY CONFLICT

How significant an issue is work/family conflict? *Work and Family: Policies for a Changing Work Force* (Ferber, O'Farrell, and Allen 1991) is the title of a report representing the work of twelve experts in the area of work and family. These experts served on the National Research Council's (U.S.) Panel on Employer Policies and Working Families. The purpose of this report was to assess the research on employer policies and working families. The panel also looked at work and family issues in Europe. The panel concluded, "On the basis of experiences in this country and western Europe, employers and unions should consider increasing a variety of options, including part-time work, flexible schedules, and alternative work locations" (p. 4). One of the chapters reviewed the linkages between work and family. Some of the significant findings were that employed women were more vulnerable to stress than employed men since they bear more of the responsibility for child care and housework; employees reported that work interfered with their family and to a lesser extent that family responsibilities interfered with their work; almost 20 percent of workers in the 1977 Quality of Employment Survey (a survey conducted by the U.S. Department of Labor) complained about long work hours; various studies have concluded that excessive work hours are associated with high levels of work/family conflict for both employed men and women; and there is evidence that allowing employees some choices and control over their schedules tended to reduce the negative effects of combining work and home responsibilities.

A 1993 report issued by the Conference Board reported that studies "find that about one-third of employees work less effectively because of child or elder care problems" (Friedman and Brothers 1993, 54). A 1997 survey on absenteeism found that personal illness accounts for more than 25 percent of unscheduled absences—and that "family is-sues" and "personal needs" were the primary reasons for unsched-uled absences (What's Ailing Your Workforce? 1997, 7). Some of the most extensive research on the relationship between work and fami-lies has been conducted by the Families and Work Institute. The insti-tute is conducting the National Study of the Changing Workforce, a longitudinal study on workforce attitudes and preferences, including responses to questions about work/family balance. The study is based on an in-depth, nationally representative survey of approximately 3,400 American workers. One of the issues that the study addresses is how workers manage both work and family obligations.

The first phase of the research was conducted in 1992 and summa-rized in a 1993 report entitled *The Changing Workforce: Highlights of the National Study* (Galinsky, Bond, and Friedman 1993). The 1992 survey was based on telephone interviews conducted with a randomly se-lected national sample of 3,381 employed men and women aged eigh-teen through sixty-four and 337 women with dependent children who were not in the labor force by choice. The following statistical profile emerged: The average worker spent more than forty hours per week working (overtime and commuting bring the hours per week on the job to more than forty-five), 42 percent of workers had experienced downsizing, 42 percent felt burned out, and 47 percent of workers had child- and/or elder-care responsibilities. One of the findings of the 1992 study is that job-to-home spillover is three times as great as home-to-job spillover. That is, "By and large, work problems are more likely to spill over into the home than family problems are to encroach upon work life" (p. 3).

In 1998 the Families and Work Institute released the findings of its 1997 National Study of the Changing Workforce. Like previous insti-tute surveys, it used a nationally representative sample of the U.S. workforce. The 1997 study is based on interviews with approximately 3,000 workers across the United States. The resulting report, titled *The 1997 National Study of the Changing Workforce*, compares responses to data derived from two previous surveys: the 1992 National Study of the Changing Workforce and the Bureau of Labor Department's 1977 Quality of Employment Survey (Bond, Galinsky, and Swanberg 1998). One of the findings is that Americans are working longer hours (an average of forty-seven hours a week for full-time workers), three hours a week longer than twenty years ago (Adler 1998; Lewin 1998; Peterson 1998). More workers (one out of three) bring work home once a week or more since they can't get everything done at work (Jackson 1998a; Peterson 1998). As a result, workers feel that they don't have enough time for their families. Demanding and hectic jobs make it difficult for workers to balance between work and home. Almost one-fourth of women frequently feel stressed out and substantial numbers feel burned out by their jobs (Bond, Galinsky, and Swanberg 1998). Seventy percent of employed mothers and fathers responded that they do not have enough time to spend with their children (Bond, Galinsky, and Swanberg 1998; Lewin 1998; Mann 1998).

One of the major findings was that family-friendly policies impact the bottom line. The study concluded that "employees whose workplaces are supportive and responsive to their needs are the most loyal and are more willing than other workers to work harder than they have to in order to help their employers succeed" (Ginsberg 1998, H7). Ellen Galinsky, one of the authors of the study, stated this simply: "People who have more flexibility will go the extra mile" (p. H7). The study concluded that employers who provide a supportive workplace will have a competitive edge (Bond, Galinsky, and Swanberg 1998). Workplace support was defined to include flexible work arrangements. One encouraging finding was that more workers viewed their workplace as supportive and family friendly (Bond, Galinsky, and Swanberg 1998; Newman 1998; Adler 1998; Gardner 1998). Almost half of all workers are able to choose (within limits) their own starting and quitting times, and 25 percent are able to alter their starting and quitting times on a daily basis (Bond, Galinsky, and Swanberg 1998). Another finding was that fathers are spending more time with their children. During the work week, fathers spend an average of 2.3 hours per workday caring for their children, an increase of half an hour over the last twenty years (Gardner 1998; Kelley 1998; Lewin 1998). They are also spending more time with their children on nonworkdays, 6.4 hours in 1997 compared to 5.2 hours in 1977 (Lewin 1998).

Sylvia Ann Hewlett and Cornell West (1998), with the support of the National Parenting Association, conducted a national survey of parental needs and concerns. The survey, administered by independent pollsters, was carried out the summer of 1996 and targeted American parents whose household income ranged between $20,000 and $100,000. Hewlett and West also conducted a series of focus groups with parents. Their findings are reported in their book *The War Against Parents: What We Can Do for America's Beleaguered Moms and Dads*. The authors found that the overwhelming need was for "time-enhancing workplace policies" (p. 217). Specifically, they found that parents wanted "government and employers to be much more imaginative in creating flexible work arrangements" (p. 217); 90 percent of parents wanted access to flextime, job sharing, compressed workweeks, and benefits for part-time employment; 87 percent of parents wanted legislation guaranteeing three days of paid leave per year so parents could attend parent–teacher conferences, take children to medical or dental appointments, and perform other parenting tasks; 79 percent of parents wanted a law allowing workers to substitute time off for extra pay for overtime; 76 percent of parents wanted a law requiring companies to offer twelve weeks of paid leave following the birth or adoption of a child; and 71 percent of parents wanted legislation allowing employees to trade two weeks pay for an extra two weeks of vacation time annually. Hewlett and West believe that the government should encourage the private sector to develop family-friendly workplaces. They recommend that the government develop a system of tax incentives for companies that offer options such as flextime, compressed workweeks, part-time work with benefits, job sharing, telecommuting, home-based work, career sequencing, and extended parenting leave. They argue that there is already a precedent for this. In some states companies that provide on-site child care are eligible for tax concessions.

THE BENEFITS OF FLEXIBILITY

What other studies have identified the benefits of flexibility? In the landmark study of flexible work arrangements published by Catalyst in 1989, human resource professionals reported these positive outcomes of workplace flexibility: recruitment, retention, increased productivity, and improved morale. However, this study did conclude that "the overwhelming majority of companies have not put any mechanisms into place to evaluate the "success" of such arrangements in terms of their duration, cost and impact on the productivity or morale of the employee or the business unit" (p. xv).

In 1991 the Conference Board published a report synthesizing a 1988 symposium organized by the board on work/family issues and findings from more than eighty other studies. This report concluded that "there is evidence to suggest that work–family programs can improve a company's bottom line" (Friedman 1991, 9). One Wellesley College Center for Research on Women study found that flexibility is associated with greater job satisfaction and reduced work/family stress for all workers, including those without children (Marshall and Barnett 1993). This study, *Family-Friendly Workplaces, Work–Family Interface and Worker Health*, used data from the Adult Lives Project. This project is a longitudinal study of a random sample of 300 Boston-area couples in which both the men and women were employed full time. The sample was limited to couples in which the man was between the ages of twenty-five and forty. Sixty percent of the sample consisted of parents. The sample was predominantly middle class. The purpose of the *Family-Friendly Workplaces* study was to examine the role of workplace benefits and flexibility in the reduction of work/family strain. This study looked at job characteristics that contribute to a family-friendly workplace and explored whether individuals in family-friendly workplaces reported greater job satisfaction, reduced work interference with home life, and less psychological distress. The researchers found that "flexibility is associated with greater job satisfaction and reduced work interference for all workers" (p. 7). Marshall and Barnett concluded that although "job flexibility does not have a significant direct effect on worker's psychological distress," it does have "an indirect effect on psychological distress, through its associations with work interference and job satisfaction" (p. 8). Consequently, "for two-earner couples, job flexibility is associated with job satisfaction and the work–family interface," and indirectly, "job flexibility also impacts worker mental health" (p. 8). The authors stressed that it will become increasingly important to have family-friendly workplaces as the number of dual-earner couples increases.

In 1995 the Conference Board sponsored "Workplace Flexibility in a Global Economy," a conference focusing on the business case for workplace flexibility. Speakers at this conference identified six tangible benefits of workplace flexibility: "productivity gains," "improved customer satisfaction," "reduced absenteeism and turnover," "heightened employee morale," "remuneration methods for survivors of downsizing," and flexibility as a "recruitment tool" (Edelman 1996, 9). Work/Family Directions calculated that every $1 spent on family-friendly benefits yields a $2 savings in direct costs (Swiss 1998). A 1997 review of the literature on flexible work hours identified these benefits as the major advantages of flexible work hours: "lowered stress, increased job enrichment and autonomy, reduced tardiness and absenteeism, and improved job satisfaction and productivity" (Scandura and Lankau 1997, 378).

SOME STATISTICS ON WORKPLACE FLEXIBILITY

How many workers are participating in some form of alternative work arrangement? In 1985 only 12 percent of American workers reported that a flexible work schedule was an option available to them (Marshall 1993). According to the U.S. Bureau of Labor Statistics, this figure increased to 15 percent in 1991 (Olmsted and Smith 1994). The bureau's data indicated that 20 percent of managers, professionals, technicians, and sales workers had flexibility. In contrast, only 10 percent of blue-collar and service workers had flexibility. Workplace flexibility continues to rise as conventional schedules are replaced by flexible schedules. Recent data from the Bureau of Labor Statistics indicate that about 76 percent of full-time employees work conventional schedules, down from 84 percent in 1984 (Chachere 1998). The bureau's data indicate that the use of flextime has more than doubled since

1985. They show that 27.6 percent of American workers had flexible schedules in 1997 compared with 12.4 percent in 1985. Based on these data, *Newsweek* magazine projected that 31.7 percent of American employees will have flexible schedules in the year 2000 (Future of Flextime 1998). In July 1998 the Families and Work Institute released findings from its first "Business Work–Life Study." This national survey examines how 1,057 U.S. companies with 100 or more employees help employees balance work and home responsibilities. Of the companies polled, 68 percent allow employees to periodically adjust starting and quitting times and 24 percent allow workers to change starting and quitting times on a daily basis (Joyner 1998).

Of workers surveyed in the 1992 National Study of the Changing Workforce (a nationally representative study of approximately 3,400 American workers) 29 percent reported that flextime was an option and 24 percent said they were routinely allowed to work at home (Galinsky, Bond and Friedman 1993). A 1994 survey of 1,035 major U.S. employers conducted by Hewitt Associates, a consulting firm, revealed that 66 percent of employers offered flexibility compared to 60 percent in 1993 (Catalyst 1996). LINK Resources, a New York–based market research firm, has been tracking telecommuting and home-based work since 1986. In 1989 LINK estimated that 26.6 million Americans were working at home part of the time (Riley and McCloskey 1997). A recent report released by the Bureau of Labor Statistics confirms this increase in at-home workers. According to this study, 23.3 million Americans worked from home at least part of the time as part of a formal arrangement, brought work home occasionally, or were self-employed in 1997 (Silverstein 1998). The number of at-home workers who receive pay for their work (3.6 million out of these 23.3 million) nearly doubled between 1991 and 1997, an indication that telecommuting has increased as a work option (Coy 1998; Denton 1998; Who Works From Home? 1998).

The trend toward workplace flexibility is not limited to the United States. However, Piotet (1988) has cautioned that it is difficult to statistically compare twelve-hour shifts, part-time work, telecommuting, and other new forms of work across Europe because definitions of these arrangements vary from country to country, and in some cases data are nonexistent or imprecise. In 1985, 12,000 Europeans (from the ten member states of the European Community and Spain and Portugal) were surveyed regarding their attitude toward flexible work (Piotet 1988). Almost one-third of the workers surveyed expressed an interest in reducing their work hours, even if it meant a decrease in income. Employers were also surveyed in various European countries. Flexible work arrangements were viewed positively, primarily as a strategy to better utilize a plant and as a way of adjusting the volume of labor to demand. In 1995 Reed Personnel Services (the leading employment agency in the United Kingdom) and the Home Office Partnership (an independent organization that has introduced flexibility into a range of firms) conducted a survey, covering almost 2 million employees, on changing work patterns in the United Kingdom (*The Shape of Work to Come* 1995). This study found that flexible work arrangements are widespread among employers in the United Kingdom.

One team of researchers calculated that there were 5.89 million telecommuters in the United States (4.8 percent of the U.S. workforce) and 1.27 million teleworkers in the United Kingdom (4.6 percent of the U.K. workforce) in 1993 (Gray, Hodson, and Gordon 1993). FIND/SVP, a New York–based research and consulting firm, estimated that there were 11.1 million telecommuters in the United States in 1997, an increase from 8.5 million in 1995 (Telecommuters by the millions—11 million, to be exact, 1997). This represents an annual growth of 15 percent. FIND/SVP credits two factors: a strong economy and the phenomenal growth of the Internet. FIND/SVP projects that there will be 14 million telecommuters by the year 2000 (Commins 1997). The U.S. Department of Transportation projects that there will be at least 15 million telecommuters by the year 2002 (Seebacher 1998). The Institute for the Study of Distributed Work estimates that there will be 18 million Americans telecommuting by the year 2005 (Himmelberg 1998). However, there are wide discrepancies in the projected number of future telecommuters. For example, it has been estimated that there will be 25 million telecommuters by the year 2000 and more than 90 million telecommuters in the United States by the year 2030 (Riley and McCloskey 1997).

FACTORS DRIVING FLEXIBILITY

What are the demographic factors contributing to the growth of workplace flexibility? One factor is the increase in the number of women in the workforce. In the past twenty-five years the number of women in the workforce has increased dramatically. In 1994 women comprised 46 percent of the total workforce, up from 38 percent in 1970 (Parasuraman and Greenhaus 1997). By 2001 it is projected that 50 percent of all U.S. employees will be women and that 75 percent of all women between the ages of forty-five and sixty will be in the labor force (Estess 1996). Not only have more women entered the workforce, but a growing number of women have moved into the professional and managerial ranks (Perlow 1997). As a result, more women are subjected to work environments that demand long work hours and sometimes unpredictable work hours.

Impact of Women in the Workforce

Since more women are working, dual-career couples have become the norm rather than the exception. Dual-career couples comprise 45 percent of the U.S. workforce (Kate 1998; Catalyst 1998b). Catalyst recently conducted a year-long study of two-income couples in the United States. The purpose of this national study of dual-career marriages was to identify actions corporations can take to attract and retain members of dual-career couples. Catalyst conducted in-depth interviews with both members of twenty-five dual-earner couples. In addition, Yankelovich Partners, on behalf of Catalyst, conducted telephone surveys with 802 randomly selected dual-earner couples. The results of both surveys have been published by Catalyst (1998b) in a report titled *Two Careers, One Marriage: Making It Work in the Workplace*. One of the other important findings was that dual-income couples view their careers as equal in importance and are demanding flexible hours and other forms of career flexibility (Jackson 1998b; Catalyst 1998b). Flexibility was important to both men and women. Of the respondents (almost 1,000 men and women) in the Catalyst study, 85 percent wanted their company to offer flexible hours (as an informal policy) and 63 percent wanted a formal flexible-hours program (Brooks 1998; Kate 1998; Catalyst 1998b). Consequently, Catalyst urged employers to expand opportunities for informal flexibility, since dual-income couples want more control over their daily work lives.

Not only are there more women in the workforce, but there are more women with children in the workforce. In the United States, 62 percent of women with children under the age of six are employed and 75 percent of women with children between the ages of six and seventeen are employed (Parasuraman and Greenhaus 1997). More than half of all mothers return to work by the time their children are one year old (Marshall 1993). Mothers with preschoolers comprise the fastest growing segment of the workforce (Estess 1996).

These demographic trends are not unique to the United States. *The Family-Friendly Employer: Examples from Europe* (Hogg and Harker 1992) profiles twenty-five corporate initiatives in seven European countries (Belgium, Denmark, France, Germany, Ireland, The Netherlands, and the United Kingdom) to help workers balance work/family obligations. The authors found that more women have entered the workforce in the European Community (EC). In the member states of the EC, four out of ten jobs are now occupied by women and there has been a continuous growth in the number of women with young children (defined as children under the age of ten) in the workforce. They noted that the labor-force participation of mothers with young children increased from 42 percent to 49 percent between 1985 and 1990. Another important trend identified by Hogg and Harker is the increase in single-parent households in the EC. In the United States more families are also headed by single parents than in the past. Single-parent families comprise 23 percent of the U.S. workforce (Parasuraman and Green-haus 1997).

Changing Role of Fathers

Fathers are playing an increasing role in the care of children (*Catalyst*). Joseph Pleck has conducted research on the relevance of family-friendly policies to men. His research indicates that there has been a trend toward greater father involvement in child care and housework (Pleck 1994). He found that in one out of five dual-income couples with preschool children, fathers are the primary caregiver. Pleck has shown that by the mid-1980s, men's average share of child care and housework performed by couples was about one-third of the total. This figure was one-fifth two decades earlier. Consequently, Pleck concluded that family-friendly policies are of increasing importance to men.

In 1997 James Levine and Todd Pittinsky published *Working Fathers: New Strategies for Balancing Work and Family*, the first practical guide to creating a father-friendly workplace. Levine is the director of a national project that focuses on developing men's involvement in their children's lives. He also conducts seminars to major corporations on combining work and family. Pittinsky is a researcher at the Families and Work Institute. The authors point out that "books for fathers typically omit attention to the workplace, as if the workplace does not have any impact on them as parents" and that "books about work typically omit attention to men as fathers, as if men leave their parent selves at home when they go to work" (p. 4).

How many working fathers are there in the United States? In 1995 there were more than 25 million fathers in the United States with a child under age eighteen and 96 percent of them were employed (Levine and Pittinsky 1997). How much work/family conflict do men experience? According to Levine and Pittinsky, "When companies have actually surveyed their male employees about work–family conflict—which they have only recently started to do—their level of work–family conflict turns out to be as great as for the female employees" (p. 15). Levine and Pittinsky point out that data from the 1992 National Study of the Changing Workforce also found no significant difference between men and women in terms of work/family conflict in dual-earner families. This comprehensive national survey found that work/family conflict is widespread, and it is reported by fathers and mothers in all socioeconomic groups.

In their response to Arlie Hochschild's (1989) groundbreaking book *The Second Shift*, a book whose premise is that women are responsible for a disproportionate share of housework and child care, Levine and Pittinsky (1997) note that "the domestic gap between men and women has been closing over the last decade" (p. 23). Again, they utilize data from the 1992 National Study of the Changing Workforce. This survey found that employed fathers who work full time put in about six hours a week more at their paid job than employed mothers who work full time. When commuting is figured in, the average working father puts in even more time. Levine and Pittinsky calculated that this amounts to an extra day of paid work a week. Although Levine and Pittinsky concede that men still average less time on housework and child care, they note that men's share of the workload is increasing. Data from the 1997 National Study of the Changing Workforce confirm that men are spending more time on household chores, 2.1 hours on workdays (up from 1.2 hours in 1977), and 4.9 hours on nonworkdays, up from 4 hours in 1977 (Lewin 1998).

Eldercare Responsibilities

While many employees are interested in workplace flexibility as a way to help them balance work and child-care responsibilities, other employees are interested in flexibility to help ease the demands of caring for aging parents and other relatives. Some employees have both child-care and eldercare responsibilities. Adult children of the elderly are often referred to as the "sandwich generation," since they often care for their own children and elderly parents simultaneously (Miller 1981, 419). The 1992 National Study of the Changing Workforce (Galinsky, Bond, and Friedman 1993) found that 7 percent of workers had eldercare responsibilities and the average total amount of care was 11.7 hours per week. Surprisingly, 56 percent of the caregivers were women and 44 percent were men. This survey projected that 18 percent of the workforce will be caring for elders in the next five years, warning that "strong demographic trends virtually guarantee that a growing proportion of men and women in the U.S. labor force will be faced with elder care responsibilities—sometimes on top of child care responsibilities" (p. 62).

A 1993 Conference Board report indicated that "about 8 percent of the average employee population is providing major care to an elderly relative; about 20 percent provide some care," and "about 40 percent of employees expect to assume eldercare responsibilities in the next five years" (Friedman and Brothers 1993, 54). A 1997 publication estimated that 15 percent of adults are responsible for caring for elderly parents and other relatives, and this figure is increasing

(Parasuraman and Greenhaus 1997). Of those surveyed in the 1997 National Study of the Changing Workforce, 25 percent had cared for an elderly relative during the preceding year (Lewin 1998). These workers spent an average of eleven hours a week providing care, with male and female caregivers providing the same amount of care (Lewin 1998; Mann 1998). In a 1997 interview, Dana Friedman projected that 40 percent of Americans will have eldercare responsibilities within the next five years (Work/Life Programs Target All Employees 1997). She noted that this responsibility will be complicated by the fact that one-third of workers will have an elderly relative living in a different city than their own. An increase in the elderly population, and its impact on eldercare responsibilities, is also an important demographic trend in the European Community (Hogg and Harker 1992). It has been estimated that 1 million workers in the United Kingdom take one day off a month to care for children and/or elderly relatives (Welch 1996).

This burgeoning responsibility for eldercare impacts the bottom line. It is estimated that 12 percent of employees quit their jobs because of their eldercare responsibilities (Friedman 1991). A 1997 study released by the Metropolitan Life Insurance Company found that lost productivity from employees caring for elderly relatives and friends cost American business $11 billion a year and that workplace programs such as flexible work schedules and job sharing could reduce this cost significantly (Eldercare Tasks Cost Business $11 Billion a Year 1997; Juggling the Demands of Dependent Care 1997). More than one-third of the caregivers polled in the 1997 National Study of the Changing Workforce had reduced their work hours or took time off to provide care for an elderly relative. Men were just as likely as women to take time off from work or reduce their work hours because of eldercare responsibilities (Lewin 1998).

Aging of Baby Boomers

The aging of the baby boomers is another trend that is impacting the workplace. Some human resource specialists have warned companies that they could face a critical staffing shortage caused by the retirement of baby boomers. Baby boomers represent 52 percent of the U.S. workforce, and this crisis will occur by the year 2011 when the first of the boomers turn sixty-five (Sunoo 1997). This mass exodus of employees could begin even earlier if a large number of boomers decide to retire early. One trend that is already noticeable is that more men have been retiring earlier as more women have joined the workforce (Koenig 1998). Apparently, many of these men feel that their spouses' earnings give them the financial freedom to retire early. Some companies that are thinking ahead are offering phased retirement programs, an arrangement that allows employees to prepare for retirement by scaling back their schedules when they reach a certain age.

Downshifting

Changing attitudes toward work have also been an impetus to experiment with workplace flexibility. Employers have to respond to a growing number of employees who are deliberately attempting to scale back their hours at work. Gerald Celente, director and founder of the Trends Research Institute (based in Rhinebeck, New York), coined the term "downshifting" to describe this voluntary downscaling (Jones and Ghazi 1997a). The institute has been tracking downshifting as a trend since the fall of the stock market in 1987 (Carpenter 1996). Celente believes that downsizing "is going to be the growing trend of the millennium." His institute projects that about 25 percent of Americans "will try to scale back their lives to some degree" in the next decade (Armour 1998, 1B).

A 1997 survey conducted by the Lutheran Brotherhood found that approximately one-third of participants would be satisfied with less, exchanging their current lifestyle for a simpler one with less pay (Armour 1998). Previous surveys indicated that Americans would give up money for time. The 3,400 American workers surveyed in the 1992 National Study of the Changing Workforce (Galinsky, Bond, and Friedman 1993) reported the following allocation of time and energy: 43-percent family and friends, 37-percent job/career, and 20-percent self. However, they indicated that they would prefer the following allocation: 47-percent family and friends, 30-percent job/career, and 23-percent self. The data imply that workers want more balanced lives. Data from the 1997 National Study of the Changing Workforce indicate that workers want to work less. The study indicated that 64 percent of workers reported they would reduce their work hours by an average of eleven hours a week if they could afford to do so, financially or professionally (Study: We Work More, But Don't Want To 1998). Renowned sociologist Juliet B. Schor reported, "70 percent of people earning $30,000 or more per year say that if they had the opportunity they would give up one day's pay in order to get an additional day off each week," and "Even among people earning $20,000 per year or less, half say that they would like the opportunity to give up a day's pay in order to get an extra day off" (Friedman and Brothers 1993, 13).

According to some trend watchers, downshifting "cuts across all age groups and geographic areas, from the slackers of Generation X to seniors living on fixed incomes" (Evenson 1995, C1). Others have characterized downshifters as upper-middle-income professionals with transferable skills who are in the middle of their careers (Patureau

1991). Jennifer Laabs (1996) defines downshifters as "a new breed of workers" who "want to slow down at work, so they can upshift in other areas of their lives" (p. 62). She divides them into two categories: "those who want to break out of the corporate mold, temporarily or permanently, and those who want to work less" (p. 62). A 1997 article in *Newsweek* gave downshifters a new name, "sell-ins" (Marin and Gegax 1997, 72).

Amy Saltzman's 1991 book, *Down-Shifting: Reinventing Success on a Slower Track*, profiles professionals who are career downshifters. The downshifters that Saltzman interviewed represent a variety of occupations (business managers, engineers, doctors, lawyers, journalists, and professors), work environments, and geographic regions. Saltzman created the following classification of downshifters: (1) plateauers (people who turn down promotions and other advancements), (2) backtrackers (people who move down the career ladder intentionally), (3) career shifters (not people who change careers but people who find settings that place less emphasis on the fast track), (4) self-employers, and (5) urban escapees. In addition to slowing down their careers, these downshifters have developed new definitions of success. Although many companies have implemented flexibility and other work/family initiatives, Saltzman concluded that "while a handful of companies have made genuine attempts to confront shifting societal values and address individual needs, the overall assumptions about success and progress in a career remain unchanged" (p. 63).

Stephanie Armour (1998), a reporter for *USA Today*, believes that voluntary downscaling is the result of several trends: baby boomers looking for more balance in their lives, a backlash against corporations that demand longer hours but offer fewer rewards, and a willingness to take economic risks because of a strong economy and the economic security that many households have because of a second wage earner. Downshifting has also taken hold in Britain. The 1997 publication of Judy Jones and Polly Ghazi's (1997b) book *Getting a Life: The Downshifter's Guide to Happier, Simpler Living* is evidence of this movement in Britain. Research by the Henley Centre for Forecasting confirms that significant numbers of people in Britain are interested in voluntary downscaling. The centre has "hard evidence that downshifting is a significant, emerging trend" (Jones and Ghazi 1997a, 1) in Britain. According to a survey conducted by the centre in 1996, 6 percent of Britons voluntarily reduced their income in the past year and another 6 percent of Britons intend to opt for lower earnings in exchange for less work and more balance in their lives (Thynne 1997).

Ian Christie, as associate director at Britain's Henley Centre for Forecasting, defines downshifting in the following ways: "It's taking a deliberate decision to opt out of the culture of consumerism and the career rat race" and "It's about cutting back on purchasing, reducing working hours, and perhaps bailing out of conventional work in search of greater quality of life and control over one's work" (Jones and Ghazi 1997a, 1). Ray Pohl, a leading British sociologist, defines downshifting as "a conscious attempt to live life at a quieter pace in order to spend more time away from employment" (p. 1). Pohl does not believe that the terms "voluntary simplicity" and "downshifting" are interchangeable. He contends that "the two phenomenon are quite distinct" (p. 1). Although both de-emphasize material accumulation, he points out that the practitioners of volunteer simplicity "never joined the rat race" and that this longer-established movement is rooted in the environmental movement (p. 1). In contrast, he argues that "downshifting is a more recent and much more mainstream phenomenon, an expression of the gathering revolt of the 'long hours' culture and aggressive corporatism of the Eighties, and the relentless waves of redundancies that followed" (p. 1).

Corporate Downsizing

Other experts believe that the corporate downsizing of the 1990s contributed to the growth of work/family initiatives (Miranda and Murphy 1993). Fiscal constraints as a result of recessions and layoffs strengthened the case for work/family programs. As a result of downsizing, many workers have assumed broader job responsibilities and heavier workloads. Some corporations have implemented flexibility in order to help workers cope with the stress of longer work hours. In 1996 the Conference Board published a report based on excerpts of speeches delivered at the 1995 Workplace Flexibility Conference, a conference held in New York in September 1995. The conference was cosponsored by New Ways to Work, William M. Mercer Incorporated, Kwasha Lipton, and Coopers Lybrand. One finding was that "companies have found that career development opportunities, alternative work arrangements, and other supportive workplace programs are vital aspects of post-downsizing HR management" and that these initiatives "help not only to alleviate morale problems, but also to attract and retain high quality workers the company must have to thrive and grow again" (Edelman 1996, 8).

Employee Recruitment and Retention

The recruitment and retention of employees is one major employer-driven factor driving workplace flexibility. A 1989 Catalyst study of flexible work arrangements in fifty companies found that retention of valued employees was a major motivator. Of the companies studied,

62 percent cited this as a reason for offering flexible work arrangements. The 1992 National Study of the Changing Workforce found that "quality of life issues figure as prominently as money in workers' definitions of success and in their decisions to take jobs or leave them" (Galinsky, Bond, and Friedman 1993, 16). In this nationally representative survey of more than 3,000 U.S. workers, 60 percent of workers rated "effect on personal/family life" as an important reason for joining their current employer, 46 percent rated "family-supportive policies" as an important reason, and 38 percent rated "control of work schedule" as an important reason (p. 16). This landmark study concluded that "when workers have more autonomy in their jobs and more control over their work schedules they are more satisfied and committed workers" (p. 19).

A study using 160 matched male and female managers employed in small or medium-size organizations found that women who perceived their organization as flexible (specifically, that their organization offered flexible work hours) reported higher levels of organizational commitment and job satisfaction than women who did not perceive their organization to be flexible (Scandura and Lankau 1997). A report published by the Conference Board concluded, "Research shows that companies without work family programs are less successful recruiters and lose more talented people" (Friedman and Brothers 1993, 54). In the early 1990s experts predicted that most industrialized countries would experience a shortage of qualified labor in the next five to ten years (Becker et al. 1993). Because of the tight labor market of the late 1990s, some corporations have adopted telecommuting as a recruiting strategy (Commins 1997). One of the benefits of telecommuting is strategic staffing (Schepp and Schepp 1995). It allows companies to hire the best individual for a job regardless of location. In addition, allowing employees to telecommute can reduce relocation costs.

Productivity

Productivity has become a driving force for flexibility. Absenteeism and turnover reduce productivity. It is estimated that about one-half of annual absences (averaging between seven and nine days a year) may be due to family concerns (Friedman 1991). A 1991 Conference Board report indicates that an estimated 16 percent of new mothers do not return to their jobs after maternity care and an estimated 12 percent of workers quit their jobs because of eldercare responsibilities (Friedman 1991). By reducing turnover, companies reduce recruiting and training costs. Many employees and employers are interested in telecommuting, since it has been associated with increased productivity. Pilot telecommuting programs have shown productivity increases ranging from 10 to 40 percent (Schepp and Schepp 1995). In an article examining the impact of new ways of working on corporate culture, Gail Dutton (1994) found that in Southern California the adoption of flexible schedules, compressed workweeks, and telecommuting as a consequence of the 1994 earthquake changed the corporate culture, "many say for the better—making it more focused, creative and results-oriented by enabling managers to concentrate on managing the results rather than the process" (p. 49).

Development of a Global Economy

A global economy has also been an impetus for workplace flexibility. A global economy requires that business be conducted over more time zones. The demands of a global economy—that is, the need to provide service twenty-four hours a day, seven days a week—has been a critical factor in many companies' decision to implement flexibility. A 1996 Conference Board report noted that workplace flexibility has moved beyond an accommodation made on a case-by-case basis for working mothers, top performers, and other select groups of employees. The report concluded that workplace flexibility "has become an essential part of doing business in a global economy" (Edelman 1996, 8).

Lowering Costs

While many organizations view flexibility as a strategy to improve customer relations in a global economy, many companies at the same time are interested in lowering overhead costs (such as real estate, office space, and parking). Research conducted by Franklin Becker and his associates at Cornell University's International Workplace Studies Program indicates that the average occupancy rate for traditional offices (that is, those with personally assigned workstations) ranges from 30 to 50 percent (Sims, Joroff, and Becker 1996). This average applies to offices in North America, Europe, and Japan. Occupancy levels are even lower for jobs requiring a great deal of customer interaction, such as sales, or in organizations that have implemented telecommuting or cross-functional teams. As a result, companies are spending lots of money on space that is not being used efficiently.

One alternative workplace strategy that has been adopted by some companies to address this problem is the use of non-territorial offices. The term "non-territorial office" was coined by MIT researcher Thomas Allen and means "any space allocation program that does not assign desks or workstations to specific individuals" (Sims, Joroff, and Becker 1996, 39). Variations of this concept include "just-in-time," Andersen Consulting's term; "hoteling," the term coined by Ernst and Young;

"hot desking," a term derived from the U.S. Navy's term to describe bunks used by several sailors on different shifts; and "red carpet," a term coined by Hewlett-Packard (Sims, Joroff, and Becker 1996).

Growth of Information Economy

The growth of the information-based economy, the development of the information highway, the increase in the number of information workers, and advances in computer technology have all contributed to the growth of workplace flexibility, especially telecommuting (Eldib and Minoli 1995; Schepp and Schepp 1995). Technology has been an enabler and driver of the telecommuting movement (Hollister 1995). PCs have become widely available and affordable, along with notebook computers, fast modems, and fax machines. An improved telecommunications infrastructure has also been an enabler. Improvements in telecommunications have resulted in the development of high-speed data links between home and office. Technological developments have made it possible for workers to perform their jobs from remote locations.

Government Support

In the United States there has been government support for telecommuting and other forms of flexibility. The federal government has been a strong advocate for workplace flexibility. In fact, the federal government has been a leader in the area of workplace flexibility. It pioneered the use of flexible work schedules in the 1970s. In 1993 the Family and Medical Leave Act (FMLA) went into effect. This groundbreaking legislation guaranteed American workers at companies with more than fifty employees the right to take up to twelve weeks of unpaid leave in order to care for a child or ill family member. In 1997 President Clinton expanded unpaid leave for federal workers, granting 1.9 million federal employees up to twenty-four hours of unpaid leave annually for family matters and emergencies (Jackson 1997). President Clinton is pressuring Congress to expand the Family and Medical Leave Act to give all workers twenty-four hours of annual unpaid leave for personal reasons (Ginsberg 1997; President Approves 24 Hours 1997). In 1996 President Clinton issued a memorandum to the heads of executive departments and agencies, directing them to implement family-friendly work arrangements in their departments and agencies (Gore 1997). These arrangements were defined to include flexible work schedules, job sharing, career part-time work, telecommuting, and satellite work locations. The Clinton administration has established a goal of getting 60,000 federal employees to telecommute by the end of 1998 and 160,000 by the year 2000 (Zajac 1997). The government (under the direction of the General Services Administration) has established telecommuting centers around Washington, D.C., Atlanta, Chicago, Philadelphia, and other major cities for use by all federal employees (Gore 1997). Government regulations, such as the 1990 Federal Clean Air Act, have also motivated companies to explore telecommuting and other strategies for reducing commuting time. This federal legislation required firms with more than 100 workers to develop plans to reduce automobile traffic. Unfortunately, not all companies complied, enforcement was intermittent, and the law was modified in 1995 to make trip-reduction plans voluntary rather than mandatory (Pristin 1996). However, some states (such as New Jersey, New York, Texas, and California) have passed clean air enactments that have led to an increase in telecommuting initiatives (Eldib and Minoli 1995).

Environmental Reasons

Telecommuting has not only been a response to environmental concerns such as compliance with air quality standards. It has also been used as a strategy to alleviate problems caused by natural disasters (earthquakes, hurricanes, floods, and blizzards) and special events (such as the 1996 Olympics in Atlanta). Telecommuting can help companies recover from disasters. Many companies in California developed work centers and telecommuting policies in the 1990s as a result of a series of earthquakes in the late 1980s and early 1990s. This also happened in Florida following the 1993 hurricane. There was a "telecommuting boomlet" in Southern California following the January 1994 earthquake (Silverstein 1994). Pacific Bell conducted a survey in the autumn of 1994 and found that nine out of ten Californians who began telecommuting after the January earthquake were still telecommuting on a regular basis (Schrage 1995). However, others concluded that telecommuting made "only modest gains after the earthquake" and that organizations have been slow to adopt it as a permanent strategy (Silverstein 1994).

The 1996 Olympics in Atlanta present an interesting case study in telecommuting. BellSouth estimated that 200,000 workers telecommuted for part of the time during the Olympic Games (Sadowsky 1997). Many firms also instituted flextime policies. While many companies abandoned flexible schedules, telecommmuting, and home-based work after the Olympics, several major Atlanta employers still have telecommuting programs in place (Kempner and Quinn 1996). The list includes AT&T, Hewlett-Packard, Holiday Inn, BellSouth Telecommunications, and federal, state, and local government agencies such as the General Services Administration, the Georgia Department of Transportation, and Fulton County (Sadowsky 1997).

Increasing Labor Pool

Organizations have also been motivated to adopt telecommuting as a strategy to utilize new groups of workers, such as the disabled (Eldib and Minoli 1995). Alan Roulstone's (1998) groundbreaking book, *Enabling Technology: Disabled People, Work and New Technology*, explores the potential of telecommuting and home-based work for disabled people. Other untapped U.S. labor markets that companies hope to gain access to by offering telecommuting as an option include stay-at-home mothers, rural residents, and the elderly (Himmelberg 1997). In addition, some companies have viewed telecommuting as a recruitment tool for Generation Xers, since it appeals to this group's interest in technology (Schepp and Schepp 1995). Companies have also realized that telecommuting can be used as a tool to access global labor markets (Himmelberg 1997). A recent article in the *New York Times* referred to this phenomenon as "global telecommuting" (Myerson 1998, sec. 4, p. 4). It is increasingly common for U.S. companies to hire overseas programmers, since there is a shortage of programmers in the United States. American companies have found that exporting this work is cost effective, since the salaries for programmers and other computer specialists are generally much lower in India, the Philippines, South Africa, and other regions of the world. In fact, Bangalore has been called the "Silicon Valley of South Asia" (sec. 4, p. 4).

BARRIERS TO FLEXIBILITY

While there are many employer and employee factors driving workplace flexibility, there are also many obstacles to flexibility. In a 1989 Catalyst study involving three types of flexible work arrangements (part-time work, job sharing, and telecommuting) in fifty companies, 41 percent of the human resource professionals interviewed cited resistance (at least initially) to flexible work arrangements by middle managers. A common concern reported by managers was that granting an employee a flexible arrangement would set a precedent and open a "floodgate" of requests. This was not a problem in any of the companies Catalyst studied. A British expert on workplace flexibility has noted that almost all "studies into the introduction of new ways of working point to middle management as a major point of resistance within organisations" (Murphy 1996, 65).

Kathleen Christensen has identified several barriers to flexibility: resistance by top management, union resistance, resistance by supervisors who perceive difficulty in managing employees on flexible schedules, and nonparticipating employees who are resentful of those on flexible schedules (Flexible Work Schedules 1990). Many experts believe that the prominent reason why one workplace is more flexible than another is culture. In a study on the impact of family-friendly policies on the glass ceiling, Debra Schwartz (1994) found "strong evidence that supervisor attitudes and company culture influence both employee use of work–family policies, especially leaves and flexible work arrrangements, and the repercussions that result for making use of these policies" (p. 3). In her review of the literature, Schwartz noted that prior research "suggests that use of leaves and flexible arrangements is relatively low and attributes this to the widespread existence of concerns about career damage" (p. 18). She concluded that "traditional beliefs about the nature of work persist" (p. 27), notions that committed professionals work full-time, put in long hours in the office, and are available to work at all times. This same concern was voiced by Virginia O'Brien in her 1998 book *Success On Our Own Terms: Tales of Extraordinary, Ordinary Business Women*. O'Brien found that cultural attitudes were the biggest obstacle to workplace change and that while many firms offer a range of flexible work options, "they are not always fully utilized because individual managers do not support them and employees fear negative consequences" (p. 171).

In reviewing the body of literature produced by Catalyst, Marcia Brumit Kropf (1997) has identified six categories of obstacles to flexibility: policy barriers, obstacles created by work definitions, obstacles created by information and reporting systems, managerial barriers, cultural barriers, and obstacles caused by myths and misconceptions surrounding alternative work options. Policies are often ad hoc, inconsistent, and dependent upon individual managers, since many organizations lack formal written policies. Work continues to be defined in terms of hours in the workplace. Many companies use a head-count system that penalizes workers working part time or sharing a job. Traditional management uses line-of-sight supervision. Organizations reward employees who put in long hours. Some managers are afraid to allow flexible work arrangements for fear that everyone will want a flexible schedule. Kropf believes that future research on work/family issues will focus on overcoming these barriers.

One of the most troubling studies of the barriers to flexibility is contained in Arlie Russell Hochschild's (1997) book *The Time Bind: When Work Becomes Home and Home Becomes Work*. This book is based on her study of a company that was ranked as one of the most family-friendly companies in the United States. Hochschild does not reveal the company's real name, she gives it the fictitious name of Amerco. The management of this company approached Hochschild for help, since they wanted to find out why they were losing professional women at a greater rate than professional men. The company had a range of work/family programs, including flextime, job sharing, and part-time work. Hochschild spent three summers between 1990 and 1993 studying the company. She interviewed 130 employees from all levels. She also followed six families around on a typical workday. The company's family-friendly policies were relevant to many employees. Half of the employees reported that they needed help balancing work with family. Hochschild found that although the company's policies allowed employees to cut back their hours, almost no one did. She found that "programs that allowed parents to work undistracted by family concerns were endlessly in demand, while policies offering shorter hours that allowed workers more free or family time, languished" (p. 25).

Another of Hochschild's (1997) startling findings was that Amerco employees with young children worked longer hours than those employees without children. Why didn't these working parents take the opportunity to reduce their hours at work? Hochschild rejected the explanation that working parents at Amerco couldn't afford to reduce their hours. She found that the majority of Amerco employees did not even take all of the paid vacation days they had accrued. Also, those Amerco women who earned more were less interested in working part time than those Amerco women who earned less. Hochschild also dismissed the rationale that workers were reluctant to reduce working hours because they feared downsizing and layoffs. Amerco workers were not fearful of losing their jobs. Support of middle management was also not an obstacle. Hochschild found that receptive managers received the same number of requests to participate in any of Amerco's flexible options as resistant managers. Amerco workers were not applying and being turned down. Rather, few Amerco employees requested permission to participate in these options. Hochschild's stunning conclusion was that to some Amerco employees, "home had become work and work had become home" (p. 38). She argued that work is valued and home is not, speculating that most people prefer to spend more time on tasks that are appreciated. As a result, workers feel more competent at work than at home.

Another interesting case study that sheds light on barriers to flexibility is Leslie Perlow's (1997) four-year study of product development engineers at a Fortune 500 company (given the fictitious name of Ditto). This study is recounted in her fascinating book, *Finding Time: How Corporations, Individuals, and Families Can Benefit from New Work Practices*. Product engineers at Ditto typically take three to five years to develop a new product. Perlow studied engineers' use of time in-depth (chronicling how several engineers spent their time in and out of the office) and the effects of work on engineers themselves, their families, and the corporation. The group of engineers that Perlow studies was under pressure to develop a color laser printer and get it to market as soon as possible.

Perlow (1997) found that the work culture awarded long hours. It was not atypical for engineers to work eighty or more hours per week because of the pressure to put in long hours and the fear of being terminated as a result of layoffs. Perlow analyzed daily logs kept by software engineers to determine how much time engineers spent on individual technical problem solving, referred to as "real engineering" (p. 76), compared to time spent interacting with others. She found that engineers did not have enough time for "real engineering" because of constant interruptions in the course of a day. While it is important for engineers to interact, Perlow found that the majority of interactions could be planned and it would be beneficial if these interactions between engineers, managers, and staff were planned rather than spontaneous. Perlow concluded that this "pervasive pattern of interruptions . . . perpetuates the crisis mentality . . . and in turn, reinforces the assumption that long hours and a willingness to accommodate to the demands of the work are necessary to succeed" (p. 95). The result is what Perlow termed a "vicious work time cycle," which in turn is "a major impediment to corporate productivity" (p. 95).

Ditto had a wide range of flexible options available to help employees. Ditto had also been on *Working Mother's* list of the 100 best companies for working women. However, Perlow (1997) found engineers resistant to using flextime, telecommuting, job sharing, or part-time work for fear that doing so would hinder their career advancement. Perlow conducted an experiment with engineers to see if there was a way to achieve a less disruptive way of working. The first phase of the experiment involved the use of uninterrupted blocks of quiet time (before noon) three days a week. Almost 60 percent of the engineers who participated in this forced quiet time experiment reported increased productivity. During the second phase of this experiment, Perlow tried to optimize interaction time, setting aside blocks of time for interaction (between 11:00 A.M. and 3:00 P.M.) as well as quiet time (before 11:00 A.M. and after 3:00 P.M.). She found that this phase was less successful and that some engineers found this arrangement too restrictive. The third and final phase of Perlow's experiment was a repeat of the first phase, imposed quiet time three days a week until noon. More than two-thirds of the engineers reported that this forced quiet time increased their productivity. Perlow inferred that quiet time is "possible and desirable," but that "too much quiet time or too rigid a structure may be counterproductive" (pp. 127–128).

Based on this experiment, Perlow (1997) believed that the "work process could be made more efficient and effective" (p. 130). However, this "will require a shift from a system that rewards individual heroics and long hours to a system that rewards individuals' contributions . . . without the accompanying emphasis on visible hours" (p. 130). The purpose of Perlow's research "was not to look for ways to make knowledge workers more efficient but to understand how they use their time at work and whether they need to work such long hours" (p. 133). She found that "inefficiencies at work contribute to extra, unnecessary hours of work," and that "at least in certain work settings, if the way time is used were altered, more work could get done in less time, leaving more time for other things" (p. 134).

CONCLUSION

Workplace flexibility is a topic that is international in scope. Companies in North America, Western Europe, and the United Kingdom have become increasingly interested in implementing alternatives to the traditional eight-hour day and five-day workweek. Several factors have contributed to the development and growth of this workplace trend. These factors include the need to retain and recruit talented workers, the attempt to balance work and family obligations, the passage of family-friendly legislation, corporate downsizing, the rise of a global economy, the high cost of office space, and the need to reduce employee commuting time because of air-quality standards.

Chapter 2 reviews the literature on a range of flexible scheduling options, including flextime, compressed workweek, job sharing, voluntary part-time work, leaves, and phased retirement. It examines the characteristics of flexible workers and the characteristics of flexible jobs. The advantages and disadvantages of each of these arrangements are outlined. The barriers to specific options are discussed. Chapter 3 focuses on telecommuting. It discusses the pros and cons of telecommuting and barriers to its implementation. It provides a profile of telecommuters and a profile of the organization most likely to offer this option. Chapter 4 looks at some companies that have been leaders in implementing flexible work arrangements. It includes examples from both manufacturing and nonmanufacturing settings. This chapter identifies some innovative companies in North America, Western Europe, and the United Kingdom. Chapter 5 discusses the future of workplace flexibility. It looks at newly emerging workplace options, such as paid time off, leave banks, and annual hours contracts. It also discusses unresolved issues relating to flexibility, such as equity, training, promotion opportunities, and access to benefits. Chapter 6 identifies some useful resources for the flexible worker, the organization seeking to implement flexibility, and students and researchers studying workplace flexibility. Chapter 7 identifies strategies for locating information. The book concludes with a glossary of terms and indexes of names, titles, and subjects.

REFERENCES

Adler, M. 1998. Report on the Family and Work Institute's most recent national study of the changing workforce. *NPR Morning Edition* [on-line]. Lexis-Nexis Academic Universe/General News Topics/Transcripts. [cited 15 April 1998].

Armour, S. 1998. Jumping off the fast track, downshifters choose less stress over success. *USA Today*, 9 April, B1.

Becker, F., A. J. Rappaport, K. L. Quinn, and W. R. Sims. 1993. *New working practices: Benchmarking flexible scheduling, staffing and work location in an international context.* Ithaca, N.Y.: Cornell University, International Workplace Studies Program.

Bond, J. T., E. Galinsky, and J. E. Swanberg. 1998. *The 1997 National Study of the Changing Workforce.* New York: Families and Work Institute.

Brooks, N. R. 1998. Balancing act/work & careers: Two-career couples just want some workplace flexibility, study shows. *Los Angeles Times*, 8 February, D5.

Carpenter, S. L. 1996. Quite simply: Fed up with the fast track, these "downshifters" are making do with less and enjoying life more. *Times-Picayune*, 4 June, F1.

Catalyst. 1968. *Part-time teachers and how they work: A study of five school systems.* New York: Catalyst.

———. 1971. *Part-time social workers in public welfare.* New York: Catalyst.

———. 1989. *Flexible work arrangements: Establishing options for managers and professionals.* New York: Catalyst.

———. 1993. *Flexible work arrangements II: Succeeding with part-time options.* New York: Catalyst.

———. 1996. *Making work flexible: Policy to practice.* New York: Catalyst.

———. 1998a. *A new approach to flexibility: Managing the work/time equation.* New York: Catalyst.

———. 1998b. *Two careers, one marriage: Making it work in the workplace.* New York: Catalyst.

Chachere, D. R. 1998. A flexible workplace. *St. Louis-Dispatch*, 17 March, B7.

Commins, P. 1997. Survival guide/small fix-its for work's frustrations/telecommuting gets new push. *Newsday*, 13 October, C2.

Coy, P. 1998. Home sweet office: At-home workers are on the rise. *Business Week*, 6 April, 30.

Denton, J. 1998. Telecommuting grows as work option. *Daily Oklahoman*, 26 April, 4.

Dutton, G. 1994. Can California change its corporate culture? *Management Review* 83 (6): 49–54.

Edelman, K. A., ed. 1996. *Building the business case for workplace flexibility: A conference report.* Report no. 1154-96-CH. New York: The Conference Board.

Eldercare tasks cost business $11 billion a year, workplace programs can bring significant reduction. 1997. *Employee Benefit Plan Review* 52 (3): 35.

Eldib, O., and D. Minoli. 1995. *Telecommuting.* Boston: Artech House.

Estess, P. 1996. *Work concepts for the future: Managing alternative work arrangements.* Menlo Park, Calif.: Crisp.

Evenson, B. 1995. Enough is enough: Voluntary downshifters trade in everything for the simple life. *The Ottawa Citizen,* 15 October, C1.

Ferber, M. A., B. O'Farrell, and L. R. Allen, eds. 1991. *Work and family: Policies for a changing work force.* Washington, D.C.: National Academy Press.

Flexible work schedules. 1990. *Supervision* 51 (6): 3.

Friedman, D. E. 1991. *Linking work–family issues to the bottom line.* New York: The Conference Board.

Friedman, D. E., and T. Brothers, eds. 1993. *Work–family needs: Leading corporations respond.* New York: The Conference Board.

Future of flextime. 1998. *Newsweek,* 15 June, 14.

Galinsky, E., J. T. Bond, and D. E. Friedman. 1993. *The changing workforce: Highlights of the national study.* New York: Families and Work Institute.

Gardner, M. 1998. Dads put more time into home life, new survey shows. *Christian Science Monitor,* 16 April, 8.

Ginsberg, S. 1997. To some employers, an expanded family leave act won't fly. *Washington Post,* 23 March, H6.

———. 1998. Raising corporate profits by reaching out to families; study shows company supports programs boost worker productivity, loyalty, and rank as biggest factor in job satisfaction. *Washington Post,* 19 April, H7.

Gore, A. 1997. *Turning the key: Unlocking human potential in the family-friendly federal workplace: A status report on federal workplace family-friendly initiatives.* Washington, D.C.: GPO.

Gray, M., N. Hodson, and G. Gordon. 1993. *Teleworking explained.* Chichester, England: Wiley.

Hewlett, S. A., and C. West. 1998. *The war against parents: What we can do for America's beleaguered moms and dads.* Boston: Houghton Mifflin.

Himmelberg, M. 1997. NCR adapts to rules of the road on its telecommuting highway. *Orange County Register,* 10 November, D14.

———. 1998. Telecommuters don't get proper training, equipment for the job, at work. However, a survey of such workers indicates they feel more productive. *Orange County Register,* 7 May, C2.

Hinrichs, K., W. Roche, and C. Sirianni, eds. 1991. *Working time in transition: The political economy of working hours in industrial nations.* Philadelphia: Temple University Press.

Hochschild, A. R. 1989. *The second shift: Working parents and the revolution at home.* New York: Viking.

———. 1997. *The time bind: When work becomes home and home becomes work.* New York: Henry Holt.

Hogg, C., and L. Harker. 1992. *The family-friendly employer: Examples from Europe*. New York: Daycare Trust, in association with Families and Work Institute.

Hollister, N. 1995. *The mobile office: Towards the virtual corporation*. London: Financial Times Telecommunications and Media Publishing.

Hunnicutt, B. K. 1996. *Kellogg's six-hour day*. Philadelphia: Temple University Press.

Jackson, M. 1998a. Employees squeezed by job pressures. *AP Online* [on-line]. Lexis-Nexis Academic Universe/General News Topics/Wire Service Stories. [cited 15 April 1998].

———. 1998b. Two-income couples demanding career flexibility, U.S. study finds. *Toronto Star*, 22 January, E7.

Jackson, R. L. 1997. Clinton expands unpaid leave for federal workers. *Los Angeles Times*, 13 April, A1.

Jones, J., and P. Ghazi. 1997a. Get a life now. *Daily Telegram*, 25 January, 1.

———. 1997b. *Getting a life: The downshifter's guide to happier, simpler living*. London: Hodder and Stoughton.

Joyner, T. 1998. Work vs. life: Businesses fail to help employees juggle careers, families. *Atlanta Journal and Constitution*, 15 July, C2.

Juggling the demands of dependent care. 1997. *Work–family Roundtable* 7 (4): entire issue.

Kate, N. T. 1998. Two careers, one marriage. *American Demographics* 20 (4): 28.

Kelley, D. 1998. Findings from the Families and Work Institute's latest study on the changing workplace. *CNN Early Edition* [on-line]. Lexis-Nexis Academic Universe/General News Topics/Transcripts. [cited 15 April 1998].

Kempner, M., and M. C. Quinn. 1996. After the games: The Olympic gold rush; it's business as usual downtown; some workers want to retain their flexible hours, dress code. *Atlanta Journal and Constitution*, 11 August, P7.

Koenig, J. 1998. For better or for worse, most mothers now are part of work force. *Orlando Sentinel*, 11 May, 5.

Korte, W. B., and R. Wynne. 1996. *Telework: Penetration, potential and practice in Europe*. Amsterdam: IOS Press.

Kropf, M. B. 1997. A research perspective on work–family issues. In *Integrating work and family: Challenges and choices for a changing world*, edited by S. Parasuraman and J. H. Greenhaus. Westport, Conn.: Quorum Books.

Laabs, J. J. 1996. Downshifters: Workers are scaling back. Are you ready? *Personnel Journal* 75 (3): 62–76.

Levine, J. A., and T. L. Pittinsky. 1997. *Working fathers: New strategies for balancing work and family*. Reading, Mass.: Addison-Wesley.

Lewin, T. 1998. Men assuming bigger share at home, survey shows. *New York Times*, 15 April, A18.

Mann, J. 1998. The benefits of balancing work and home. *Washington Post*, 15 April, B11.

Marin, R., and T. T. Gegax. 1997. Sell in, bliss out. *Newsweek*, 8 December, 72–74.

Marshall, N. L. 1993. *Having it all: Managing jobs and children*. Wellesley, Mass.: Wellesley College, Center for Research on Women.

Marshall, N. L., and R. C. Barnett. 1993. *Family-friendly workplaces, work–family interface and worker health*. Working paper series no. 259. Wellesley, Mass.: Wellesley College, Center for Research on Women.

Miller, D. A. 1981. The "sandwich generation": Adult children of the aging. *Social Work* 26: 419–423.

Miranda, E. J., and B. E. Murphy. 1993. *Work–family: Redefining the business case*. Report no. 1050. New York: The Conference Board.

Murphy, E. 1996. *Flexible work*. London: Director Books.

Myerson, A. R. 1998. Ideas & trends: Virtual migrants; need programmers? Surf abroad. *New York Times*, 18 January, sec. 4, p. 4.

Newman, K. 1998. Findings from the Families and Work Institute's latest study on the changing workplace. *ABC Good Morning America* [on-line]. Lexis-Nexis Academic Universe/General News Topics/Transcripts. [cited 15 April 1998].

O'Brien, V. 1998. *Success on our own terms: Tales of extraordinary, ordinary business women*. New York: Wiley.

Olmsted, B. 1995. Flexible work arrangements: From accommodation to strategy. *Employment Relations Today*, 22 June, 11.

———. 1997. Negotiating for change at work. In *Having it all/having enough: How to create a career/family balance that works for you*, edited by D. Lee, with C. M. Zellerbach, C. Essex, L. P. Fisher, and B. Olmsted. New York: AMACOM.

Olmsted, B., and S. Smith. 1994. *Creating a flexible workplace: How to select & manage alternative work options*. 2d ed. New York: American Management Association.

———. 1996. *The job sharing handbook*. Rev. ed. San Francisco: New Ways to Work.

———. 1997. *Managing in a flexible workplace*. New York: AMACOM.

Parasuraman, S., and J. H. Greenhaus. 1997. The changing world of work and family. In *Integrating work and family: Challenges and choices for a changing world*, edited by S. Parasuraman and J. H. Greenhaus. Westport, Conn.: Quorum Books.

Patureau, A. 1991. Down the up staircase: People who were once driven by material measures of success are easing out of the fast lane. *Atlanta Journal and Constitution*, 6 August, B1.

Perlow, L. A. 1997. *Finding time: How corporations, individuals, and families can benefit from new work practices*. Ithaca, N.Y.: ILR Press.

Persoff, A. M. 1945. *Sabbatical years with pay: A plan to create and maintain full employment*. Los Angeles: Charter Publishing.

Peterson, K. S. 1998. Working hours are longer but workplaces seem nicer. *USA Today*, 15 April, D1.

Piotet, F. 1988. *The changing face of work: Researching and debating the issues*. Dublin, Ireland: European Foundation for the Improvement of Living and Working Conditions.

Pleck, J. H. 1994. *Family-supportive employer policies and men: A perspective*. Working paper series no. 274. Wellesley, Mass.: Wellesley College, Center for Research on Women.

President approves 24 hours of unpaid leave for family obligations. 1997. *Sun* (Baltimore), 13 April, A2.

Pristin, T. 1996. New Jersey daily briefing; repealing clean air law. *New York Times*, 31 May, B1.

Riley, F., and D. W. McCloskey. 1997. Telecommuting as a response to helping people balance work and family. In *Integrating work and family: Challenges and choices for a changing world*, edited by S. Parasuraman and J. H. Greenhaus. Westport, Conn.: Quorum Books.

Rogak, L. A. 1994. *Time off from work: Using sabbaticals to enhance your life while keeping your career on track*. New York: Wiley.

Ronen, S. 1981. *Flexible working hours: An innovation in the quality of work life*. New York: McGraw-Hill.

Roulstone, A. 1998. *Enabling technology: Disabled people, work and new technology*. Buckingham, England: Open University Press.

Sadowsky, D. 1997. Teleworking slowly gains workplace acceptance. *Atlanta Business Chronicle*, 9 May, B3.

Saltzman, A. 1991. *Down-shifting: Reinventing success on a slower track*. New York: HarperCollins.

Scandura, T. A., and M. J. Lankau. 1997. Relationships of gender, family responsibility and flexible work hours to organizational commitment and job satisfaction. *Journal of Organizational Behavior* 18: 377–391.

Schepp, D., and B. Schepp. 1995. *The telecommuter's handbook: How to earn a living without going to the office*. 2d ed. New York: McGraw-Hill.

Schrage, M. 1995. Innovation/Michael Schrage: Quake lessons one year later: No gold stars. *Los Angeles Times*, 12 January, D1.

Schwartz, D. B. 1994. *An examination of the impact of family-friendly policies on the glass ceiling*. New York: Families and Work Institute.

Seebacher, N. 1998. Workplace issues: How to make telecommuting a working business arrangement; growing home office trend provides efficient, flexible options for companies, staff. *Detroit News*, 4 May, F8.

The shape of work to come: A major research survey and report on changing patterns of work in UK organisations. 1995. Tolworth, Surrrey: Reed Personnel Services; Cambridge: The Home Office Partnership.

Silverstein, S. 1994. Telecommuting boomlet has few follow-up calls. Labor: Interest was high after Northridge quake but a host of factors held back wide adoption of the practice. *Los Angeles Times*, 16 May, A1.

———. 1998. Nation/world: The economy; telecommuting growth is slow, study says. *Los Angeles Times*, 12 March, D3.

Sims, W., M. Joroff, and F. Becker. 1996. *Managing the reinvented workplace*. Houston, Tex.: International Facility Management Association; Norcross, Ga.: International Development Research Council.

Study: We work more, but don't want to. 1998. *St. Petersburg Times*, 26 April, G1.

Stumps, D. 1997. The 10 million best companies to work for in America. *Training* 34 (12): 42–44.

Sunoo, B. 1997. Millions may retire. *Workforce* 76 (12): 48–50.

Swart, J. C. 1978. *A flexible approach to working hours*. New York: AMACOM.

Swiss, D. J. 1998. Good worker or good parent: The conflict between policy and practice. In *Shared purpose: Working together to build strong families and high-performance companies*, edited by M. G. Mackavey and R. J. Levine. New York: AMACOM.

Telecommuters by the millions—11 million, to be exact. 1997. *Telecommuting Review* 14 (8): 14–16.

Thynne, J. 1997. The good life was the rat race all along. *Sunday Times*, 2 February, features section.

Welch, J. 1996. Call for flexibility to stem carers exodus. *People Management* 2 (18): 5.

What's ailing your workforce? 1997. *HR Focus* 74 (11): 7.

Who works from home? 1998. *Detroit News*, 4 May, F9.

Workforce 2000: Work and workers for the 21st century. 1987. Indianapolis: Hudson Institute.

Work/Life programs target all employees. 1997. *Employee Benefit Plan Review* 52 (3): 31.

Zajac, A. 1997. Telecommuting needs right kind of employee, employer; many are taking advantage of technology to work at home, but such arrangements are not for everyone. *Star Tribune*, 3 November, D3.

CHAPTER 2

Scheduling Options

This chapter reviews the literature on a range of flexible scheduling options: flextime, compressed workweek, job sharing, voluntary part-time work, leaves and sabbaticals, phased retirement, voluntary reduced worktime, and work sharing. It examines the characteristics of flexible workers and the characteristics of flexible jobs. The advantages and disadvantages of specific arrangements are outlined. The barriers to workplace flexibility are identified. Some institutional and environmental constraints include a reluctance to experiment, the perception that an organization's size precludes the ability to be flexible, cost, perceived difficulty of supervising employees, and concern over the disruption of project completion schedules.

One workplace trend that is outside the scope of this book is the use of a contingency workforce to supplement core employees. Employers use contingency workers to reduce workforce size or to meet fluctuating workloads. Contingency workers include temporary-agency hires, independent contractors, workers on temporary fixed-term contracts, and outsourcing. Background information, data, and a discussion of the issues relating to the use of contingent workers can be found in an issue of *HR Executive Review*, a quarterly publication of the Conference Board (Contingent Employment 1995). In addition, Michael

Burr's (1997) insightful article on the federal government's use of temporary employees explains the forces driving the increase in the rise of contingent workers in both the public and private sectors. Readers can also gain a better understanding of the multiple aspects of this complex workforce trend by consulting *Contingent Work: American Employment Relations in Transition*, a volume edited by Kathleen Barker and Kathleen Christensen (1998).

FLEXTIME

Flextime is a scheduling option that allows workers to select their starting and quitting times within limits established by management. There are generally core hours when all employees must be present. Although starting and quitting times vary, employees are required to work a standard number of hours within a given time period. Olmsted and Smith (1994) have identified several variations on the use of flextime, including fixed starting and quitting times that vary daily, variations in the length of day with required core hours, and variations in the length of day without mandatory core hours. In addition, some flextime programs allow workers to bank hours for the future. Several synonyms have been used for flextime. These include gliding time, gliding hours, sliding time, sliding hours, adaptable hours, variable hours, and individual flexibility (Swart 1978).

As noted in Chapter 1, flextime originated in West Germany and was rapidly adopted in West Germany, Switzerland, France, and Scandinavia in the 1970s. Interest in flextime lagged behind in the United States in the 1960s and 1970s. J. Carrol Swart (1978) established several reasons for this lack of interest: a focus on the four-day workweek as the alternative to the standard five-day workweek; legislation, such as the Fair Labor Standards Act, establishing the eight-hour workday and the forty-hour workweek as the norm; disinterest by American management; different attitudes toward work and leisure; union resistance; indifference by the federal government; and a lack of detailed information about flextime programs. Swart summarized that "in virtually all circumstances, flextime entered the American consciousness in bits and pieces" (p. 89).

While Swart (1978) claimed that the federal government was initially disinterested in flextime, it was a pioneer in the area of workplace flexibility, offering a range of flexible scheduling options as early as the 1970s. In a status report on federal workplace family-friendly initiatives, Vice President Gore (1997) boasted that the federal government was "well ahead of private sector employers" in this regard (p. ii). Various federal agencies put pilot alternative work schedules in place in the 1970s. The first experimental alternative work schedule program was implemented by the Bureau of Indian Affairs in 1972. Six years later the Federal Employees Flexible and Compressed Work Schedules Act, Public Law 95-390, established a three-year governmentwide experiment with alternative work schedules (McCampbell 1996). In 1982 this program was extended for another three years and in 1985 Public Law 99-190 provided permanent authority for flexible and compressed work schedules (National Park Service 1987; McCampbell 1996). Almost half of all federal workers use some form of flexible work schedule, with the most heavily used options being flextime or compressed workweeks (Gore 1997). Data compiled by the Families and Work Institute indicate that many state governments offer a range of flexible work arrangements to employees (State employees flex their options 1995). However, most arrangements are on an ad hoc basis, since few states have formal policies regarding flexible work arrangements.

While flextime was slow to take off in the United States, it is now the most common type of flexible work arrangement. Hewitt Associates, an international consulting firm, has tracked the use of flexible scheduling options in large U.S. companies. Of the 1,020 major U.S. employers surveyed by Hewitt Associates in 1997, 69 percent offered some type of flexible arrangement, and 73 percent of these flexible employers offered flextime, compared to 55 percent in 1992 and 39 percent in 1990 (Compressed work weeks pick up steam 1998). Sue Shellenbarger (1997), a columnist for the *Wall Street Journal*, confirmed that there has been a significant rise in the use of flexible work arrangements since the mid 1990s. Shellenbarger attributed this increase to a healthy economy and a competitive labor market. In one of her "Work & Family" columns she wrote, "The strong economy and tight labor market are accomplishing what 10 years of proselytizing could not" and that as competition for talented workers escalates, "the workplace is getting more flexible fast" (p. B1). In late 1998 *Time* magazine published a special report on the growth of nontraditional benefits, including flexible work plans. The author, Laura Koss-Feder (1998), wrote that many companies have learned that nontraditional benefits (including alternative work arrangements) are an effective recruiting and retention strategy and can be a greater incentive than money.

What are the advantages of flextime for employees? One obvious advantage is that flextime allows employees to work according to their biological clocks (Ronen 1981; Nollen 1982; Grensing-Pophal 1993; Olmsted and Smith 1994; Peak 1996). Early risers can begin their workday early in the morning when they feel most alert. At the same time, staggered starting times accommodate workers who feel most productive later in the day. Another benefit of flextime is that it can result in reduced commutes (Ronen 1981; Nollen 1982). Employees may be able to arrange their schedule so they can travel to work during off-peak hours.

Another advantage of flextime for employees is that it increases their amount of leisure and family time (Ronen 1981; Friedman 1991; Still a Flexible Friend? 1996). It gives individuals the opportunity to take care of errands, appointments, and other personal tasks. Employees who are continuing their education through courses and other opportunities can find flextime helpful (Ronen 1981). Flextime can be particularly useful for parents, especially parents of school-age children. David Ralston's (1989) rigorous study of flextime in two state government agencies found that the major benefits of flextime are that it allows better coordination of work and family obligations, and it results in increased work satisfaction. A Conference Board survey of work/family professionals found that most companies offer flexible work schedules to assist employees with school-age children (Education Initiatives 1997). Levine and Pittinsky (1997) found that a flexible schedule is the work/family benefit fathers are most likely to utilize. Flextime gives fathers (and all employees) some control over their work hours without having to reduce their earnings.

Flextime can also be a morale booster to employees. It gives employees autonomy in selecting their own work schedules and makes employees responsible for getting work done within their own work schedules. Flextime emphasizes efficiency and the completion of projects. Ronen (1981) concluded that by implementing flextime an organization "expresses trust in the employee and considers him a responsible agent" (p. 31). Research has indicated that employees who know flexibility is available (even if they do not use it) experience less stress than workers who are employed in organizations without flextime policies (Gottlieb, Kelloway, and Barham 1998). McGuire and Liro's (1986) study of flexible work schedules in three New York state government agencies found that employees using flextime reported significantly higher levels of job satisfaction than those employees with standard hours or staggered fixed hours. Flextime can also be beneficial to employees because it allows them to develop their skills through cross-training. It can also result in increased job knowledge, since one employee may cover for another (Ronen 1981).

Does flextime have any drawbacks for employees? Some unions have been concerned about flextime's impact on overtime, the length of the workday, and whether this option is voluntary (Olmsted and Smith 1994). Although companies benefit from paying less overtime as a result of flextime, this may be a disadvantage for those employees who were counting on overtime pay (Ronen 1981). Some employees may feel that flextime is inequitable since some job functions are not suitable for flextime. Flextime may be difficult to apply in assembly-line operations, especially those with multiple shifts (Swart 1978; Ronen 1981; Nollen 1982). It is not always possible to have individual workers arriving and leaving at different times where there is continuous process work and moving assembly lines.

How does flextime benefit employers? A myriad of advantages have been reported, including reduced tardiness and absenteeism, reduced turnover, improved recruiting, decreased overtime, improved employee morale, and better utilization of plants and equipment (Swart 1978; Ronen 1981; Nollen 1982; Levine 1987a, 1987b; Tober 1988; Lussier 1990a; Friedman 1991; Sommer and Malins 1991; Bankston 1996; Olmsted and Smith 1994, 1997; Klaus 1997; Martinez 1997; Gill 1998; Gottlieb, Kelloway, and Barham 1998). Another benefit is that flextime allows businesses to extend their hours of operation (Bankston 1996; Still a Flexible Friend? 1996; Gottlieb, Kelloway, and Barham 1998). This is increasingly important in a global economy where clients across many time zones expect service twenty-four hours a day. Flextime can also improve scheduling, since it allows firms to respond to workload peaks and demands (Gottlieb, Kelloway, and Barham 1998). Another advantage of flextime is that it can result in a better organization of work (Olmsted and Smith 1994). Meetings, telephone calls, and client visits can be scheduled during core hours, while work requiring concentration can be done before or after core periods when there are fewer distractions.

One long-term benefit of flextime is improved managerial practices (Nollen 1982; Olmsted and Smith 1994). It treats employees like adults, emphasizes planning, and promotes a team approach to problem solving (Swart 1978; Ronen 1981; Nollen 1982). Olmsted and Smith (1994) have noted that flextime requires a shift from a controlling to a facilitative management style. Many companies have also found that flextime is a low-cost employee benefit (Friedman 1991; Olmsted and Smith 1994). It can be an important nonmonetary motivator (Klein 1989; Grensing 1991, 1996). This is especially important when there is no money for bonuses. Flextime has been used by many downsized organizations as a strategy to improve the morale of remaining employees (Downsizing 1997). This low-cost option can pay off in increased productivity. Firms implementing flextime have reported average productivity increases ranging from 1 to 5 percent (Gill 1998).

While employers have reported many benefits of flextime, they have also identified problems. From an employer's perspective, flextime can be disadvantageous, since it can lead to inadequate staffing during some hours, it can be more difficult to schedule staff meetings, key people may not always be available, it can be more cumbersome to track hours worked, and there can be higher utility and overhead costs if facilities have to be open more hours (Swart 1978; Ronen 1981; Nollen 1982; Levine 1987b; Tober 1988; Sommer and Malins 1991; O'Brian 1994; Olmsted and Smith 1994). Some front-line supervisors express concern about their ability to supervise employees on a variety of schedules (Flexible Work Schedules 1990; Monsour 1994; Olmsted and Smith 1994). If communication problems existed previously in an organization, flextime may aggravate the situation (Ronen 1981). Consequently, it is essential that flextime workers communicate their schedules to coworkers as well as supervisors. Some employers have worried that employees will abuse flextime. This has not been a problem, however, since most employees don't want to lose this privilege (Ronen 1981). Another employer concern is that workers unable to participate in a flexible schedule will be resentful of those who can participate (Ronen 1981, Flexible Work Schedules 1990).

Other barriers to the adoption of flextime have been reported. Middle-management resistance has been a major obstacle (Mattis 1990; Deutschman 1991; Maier, Thompson, and Thomas 1991). If workers want to bank hours, some employers may be reluctant to agree to flextime, especially since U.S. federal law requires employers to pay certain categories of workers (nonexempt) overtime for work that exceeds forty hours per week (Nollen 1982; Christensen and Staines 1990). Some unions have opposed flextime because they fear that it will decrease the need for overtime (Christensen and Staines 1990).

Who uses flextime? When Franklin Becker and his associates (1993) at Cornell University's International Workplace Studies Program conducted an international benchmarking study of flexible work options in 1993, they found that executives and managers are more likely to have flexible schedules and the data suggested that larger firms are more likely than smaller firms to offer flextime to their employees. While Debra Schwartz's (1994) study of the impact of family-friendly policies on the glass ceiling also indicated that there is strong evidence that large companies are more likely than smaller companies to provide flexible work arrangements, she noted that small firms are more likely to provide "more personalized scheduling options" (p. 9).

In 1998 the Families and Work Institute released the findings of its first Business Work-Life Study, a national survey of 1,057 U.S. companies with 100 or more employees. While the study confirmed that larger companies are more likely to offer flextime and other family-friendly benefits, it also found that companies offering these benefits were more likely to have women or minorities in senior management (Brooks 1998; Walker 1998). Flexible work arrangements were also more prevalent in companies where women comprised the bulk of the workforce (Brooks 1998). The study also found that companies in certain industries were more likely to offer these perks. The industries where family-friendly benefits are most likely to be found are finance, insurance, and real estate (Walker 1998).

A 1996 Conference Board survey of more than fifty companies with established flexible work initiatives found that shift workers find flextime the most difficult option to utilize, with job sharing a close second (Shift Work 1996). The most extensive analysis of flexible work arrangements in Canada has been done by researchers affiliated with the Canadian Aging Research Network (CARNET). CARNET has conducted three studies relating to the workplace: the 1993 Work and Family Survey, the 1994 Work and Home Life Survey, and the 1995 Workplace Flexibility Study. The results of these surveys have been summarized in *Flexible Work Arrangements: Managing the Work–Family Boundary* (Gottlieb, Kelloway, and Barham 1998). Flextime emerged as the most prevalent type of flexible work arrangement. Women are overrepresented in every type of flexible arrangement with the exception of telecommuting. Flextime workers were likely to have less years of service than full-time employees working conventional hours.

How does a firm establish a flextime option? Pilot projects and trials are a good way for companies to experiment with flexibility. Flexibility is incremental, it happens in stages. In their practical handbook, *Managing in a Flexible Workplace*, Barney Olmsted and Suzanne Smith (1997) reiterate the eight-step process in implementing flexibility that was defined in their earlier book, *Creating a Flexible Workplace* (Olmsted and Smith 1994). The eight steps are gaining support for the program, assigning responsibility for the administration of the program, designing the program, developing resource materials for employees and supervisors, announcing the program, promoting the program, evaluating the program, and fine tuning the program. Olmsted and Smith (1997) outline the specific steps involved in implementing flextime. These include analyzing staffing and work flow, meeting with managers to get their feedback on scheduling options and procedural matters, designing guidelines for employees that cover issues such as eligibility and the enrollment process, meeting with employees to review these guidelines, reviewing and approving employee applications, and running a three- to six-month flextime trial.

When designing flextime, managers need to consider a number of issues. Olmsted and Smith (1997) have created a simple worksheet that identifies the decisions that managers need to make when they are developing a flextime program. Using this worksheet as a guide, managers need to decide the following: the company's operating hours, the company's workweek, what (if any) hours will be considered core, allowable starting and quitting times, eligibility, how much individual flexibility employees will have, the length of the workday and the workweek, whether there are labor laws or unions contracts requiring a daily lunch hour, policies about banking hours, how to ensure that coverage and work flow are maintained, an employee evaluation process, the length of a flextime pilot and the process for evaluating it, and the process for periodical reviews so a flextime program can be adjusted.

COMPRESSED WORKWEEK

A compressed workweek refers to a full-time work schedule that is completed in fewer than five days. There are several variations. An employee may work four ten-hour days or three twelve-hour days. Another popular form is a schedule where four nine-hour days are worked the first week and five nine-hour days are worked the following week. Olmsted and Smith (1997) have observed that a modification of the compressed workweek, summer hours, has become increasingly popular. Under summer hours, employees work extra hours in the week in exchange for shorter hours on Fridays.

The compressed workweek was first implemented in North America in the late 1960s and early 1970s (Venne 1993). It gained popularity in the early 1970s as a compromise to the thirty-two-hour workweek advocated by some labor unions (Compressed Work Weeks Pick Up Steam 1998). However, the use of the compressed workweek leveled off by the end of the 1970s (Venne 1993). The Hewitt Associates 1997 survey of 1,025 large firms found that 24 percent of the companies surveyed used compressed workweeks, compared with 12 percent in 1990 (Compressed Work Weeks Pick Up Steam 1998). More companies are offering compressed workweeks as a recruiting and retention tool (Compressed Work Weeks Pick Up Steam 1998). In addition, companies with twenty-four-hour operations are finding that compressed workweeks can be an attractive alternative for shiftworkers (Maiwald et al. 1997). Recent research that indicates that a four-day workweek may be healthier for workers compared with the traditional workweek may also give the compressed workweek a boost (How Does a 4-Day Work Week Sound? 1997). This research, conducted by the MRC Body Rhythms and Shiftwork Center at the University of Wales, found that the twelve-hour shift workers in the study reported fewer symptoms of heart disease, were more alert on the job, and tended to sleep better compared with the eight-hour, five-day-per-week workers in the study.

Why do some workers like this option? Some employees like to work longer hours in exchange for longer weekends (Olmsted and Smith 1994). A compressed workweek gives workers a larger block of leisure time (Nollen 1982; Vega and Gilbert 1997). While some workers use this block of time to spend with their family, others use it to work a second job. For other workers, a compressed workweek can mean reduced commuting time (Nollen 1982; Olmsted and Smith 1994; Vega and Gilbert 1997).

What drawbacks does this alternative have for workers? Some cited disadvantages from the employees' perspective include fatigue, lowered morale, and greater difficulty in arranging for child care (Nollen 1982; Levine 1987b; Olmsted and Smith 1994; Gottlieb, Kelloway, and Barham 1998). In particular, working parents and older workers may be fatigued by long shifts. In turn, this fatigue may contribute to reduced productivity and an increase in on-the-job accidents (Nollen 1982). Some labor unions have been resistant to the implementation of compressed workweeks, citing concerns about the long-term impact of fatigue on employee health as well as fear that this option will decrease overtime (Nollen 1982; Olmsted and Smith 1994).

How does this option benefit employers? There is evidence that this scheduling alternative results in modest improvements in absenteeism, tardiness, and turnover (Olmsted and Smith 1994, 1997). Some companies have reported increased productivity (Sunoo 1996). Compressed workweeks can also be an effective recruiting tool (Venne 1993; Olmsted and Smith 1994, 1997; Compressed Work Weeks Pick Up Steam 1998), and can help with staffing problems. For example, compressed workweeks have allowed some companies to attract workers to less desirable shifts, such as the graveyard shift, since it gives workers blocks of time off. In addition, it can be used as a strategy to extend hours of service (Venne 1993; Olmsted and Smith 1997; Martinez 1997). Other commonly cited advantages for employers are reduced costs due to the reduction in startups and shutdowns, more efficient use of facilities and equipment, decreased overtime, and reduced commuting times (Nollen 1982; Levine 1987b; Olmsted and Smith 1994, 1997). Commutes can also be less burdensome for workers on compressed schedules when there are natural disasters such as blizzards, hurricanes, and earthquakes (Olmsted and Smith 1997).

Compressed workweeks can also be problematic for managers. Some states require that overtime be paid for hours worked in excess of eight hours a day and supervision can be complicated (Nollen 1982; Olmsted and Smith 1994). Another concern is that productivity may decrease at the end of long shifts (Olmsted and Smith 1994). This reduced productivity is attributed to fatigue.

Rosemary Venne (1993) has conducted extensive research on the compressed workweek. Her doctoral dissertation, "Alternative Worktime Arrangements: The Compressed Workweek," studied the impact of a trial compressed workweek for two data sets: a group of Canadian prison guards and a group of Canadian clerical workers. The first data set consisted of prison guards who switched from an eight-hour workday to a twelve-hour-day compressed workweek. Absenteeism rates were compared for this group and the comparison group, a group of guards who did not switch to the compressed workweek. The guards on the compressed workweek had a higher rate of absenteeism than the guards on the eight-hour workday. However, Venne found that the difference was not statistically significant. The second data set involved clerical workers. The clerical workers on the compressed workweek schedule reported less fatigue, greater job satisfaction, greater satisfaction with their schedule/workstyle fit, and improved client service compared to the comparison group, the noncompressed workweek.

Venne's (1993) thesis provides a history of the compressed workweek. Her review of the literature is impressive. She summarized the findings of research studies on compressed workweeks that have been conducted from 1970 to the early 1990s. She pointed out that much of the literature consists of "case studies often measuring short-term results" (p. 44) and emphasized the need for longitudinal studies. Small sample size is another problem. Some studies were poorly designed, since they lacked a control group for comparison. In addition, many of the studies did not differentiate between variations, such as ten-hour or twelve-hour schedules.

Who uses compressed workweeks? Venne (1993) found that usage is much higher in Canada than the United States, and overall the usage rate is higher in North American than elsewhere. Compressed workweeks have been used by hospitals, police and fire departments, manufacturing companies, and other organizations having continuous operations (Venne 1997). Although manufacturers were the pioneers in implementing compressed workweeks, a 1989 survey conducted by the Canadian Conference Board found that almost an equal percentage of companies implementing compressed workweeks were in manufacturing as in nonmanufacturing (Venne 1993).

Olmsted and Smith (1997) have created a checklist for managers interested in implementing compressed workweeks. First, it is essential that managers review state and federal labor laws as well as any existing labor contracts that might prohibit compressed schedules. Managers also need to determine the scope of the program (Is it companywide? Who is eligible?), scheduling models (ten- or twelve-hour shifts or some variation), operating schedules (Will the company operate fewer or more days or will the operating schedule remain the same?), shift schedules (Will new shifts be necessary, and what workflow allocations will have to be made?), holidays, paid time off, and duration of the compressed schedule (Will it be year round or only during summer months?).

JOB SHARING

Under job sharing, two employees voluntarily share one full-time position, with prorated salary and benefits. Each employee works part time. Job sharing can take various forms (Mattis 1990; Olmsted and Smith 1994; Solomon 1994). People who share jobs, often termed "partners," can share all responsibilities. Some partners divide responsibilities, with each partner handling separate tasks. Other partners perform unrelated tasks and have no or little interaction with one another.

The term "job sharing" was first used in 1983 by Catalyst (Chapin 1992). In the United States the federal government pioneered the use of job sharing (Olmsted and Smith 1994). New Ways to Work, a nonprofit organization, designed the first project to encourage private-sector experimentation with job sharing (Olmsted and Smith 1996). This project, Job Sharing Project, was initiated in 1975 in the Bay Area of San Francisco. New Ways to Work was instrumental in encouraging the state of California to experiment with job sharing and permanent part-time options. Of the 519 large U.S. employers included in a 1997 Watson Wyatt Worldwide survey, 26 percent responded that they offered job sharing (Boles 1997). The growing popularity of job sharing is reflected in the increasing coverage of this topic in popular and mainstream magazines. For example, the October 1999 issue of *Parenting* magazine had advice on successful job sharing (How to Make a Job Share Work for You 1999). Outside the United States, however, job sharing is relatively rare (Ferber, O'Farrel, and Allen 1991).

Job sharing was first viewed primarily as an option for women with young children (Olmsted and Smith 1996). Gradually, employers have recognized that it can be an alternative for a larger group of employees. For example, a senior-level employee may share a job as a way of phasing into retirement, while an entry-level employee may share a position while completing his or her education (Olmsted and Smith 1994). Job sharing can have many advantages for workers (Chapin 1992). Job sharing lets partners balance work and home responsibilities. Job sharers report high levels of enthusiasm, productivity, and job satisfaction. They also experience less stress and burnout. In addition, job sharing can give partners the ability to learn from one another.

At the same time, job sharers have reported problems with this arrangement (Chapin 1992). Some job sharers feel that they are perceived to be less committed to their work. Some report difficulty getting promoted. Other job sharers feel employers expect more output than is realistic. Some may work more hours than they are paid to work. If job sharers duplicate each other's work, they are less productive. A survey conducted by the Conference Board found other drawbacks to job sharing: reduced salary, fewer benefits, and lessened opportunities for job advancement (Job-Sharing 1994).

Job sharing can be highly advantageous to employers. It allows organizations to recruit and retain employees who want flexibility (Ronen 1984; *Job Sharing for Federal Employees* 1990, Olmsted and Smith 1994). Job sharers can both work during peak periods. Partners can have schedules that match workflow. When a job sharer is absent, his or her partner can cover, providing continuity. Organizations also benefit because two people bring a wider set of skills (*Job Sharing for Federal Employees* 1990). Employers offering job sharing can also find cost savings due to reduced overtime, decreased absenteeism, and reduced turnover (Ronen 1984; *Job Sharing for Federal Employees* 1990; Grensing 1991). Training costs may also be lower (compared to other part-time or full-time work) if one partner trains the other partner (Pesek and McGee 1989; Watson 1995). Improved productivity has been another reported benefit (Ronen 1984; Grensing 1991; Olmsted and Smith 1996).

The biggest barrier to job sharing may be management resistance (Job-Sharing 1994). There is the perception that it increases the workload for managers, since they have to supervise two employees instead of one (Ronen 1984; Job-Sharing 1994). Employers also worry that costs will increase with job sharing, especially if both partners receive benefits (Ronen 1984; Lussier 1990b). Another disadvantage is that it increases the number of employees on the payroll (Ronen 1984; Olmsted and Smith 1997). This can be an obstacle to job sharing if managers are under a directive to reduce head count. Another perceived disadvantage is that it may be difficult to recruit job sharers (Ronen 1984). In addition, employees are sometimes concerned that neither member of a job-sharing team will assume responsibility for the completion of a task or project (Ronen 1984). Research conducted by the Conference Board found that problems develop when partners have different communication and work styles as well as different standards of quality (Sheley 1996).

Although many companies remain skeptical about the benefits of job sharing, this option is growing in popularity, especially among Fortune 500 companies (Rich 1997). The Conference Board found that the type of jobs most likely to be shared are clerical and administrative positions (Job-Sharing 1994). Accounting, banking, teaching, and law are among the professions increasing the use of job sharing (Price and Rouse 1992). A survey conducted by Watson Wyatt Worldwide found that job sharing is most widely used in the electronics, computer, and health care industries (Boles 1997).

The Job Sharing Handbook, first published in 1983 and revised in 1996 (Olmsted and Smith 1996) provides profiles of job sharers and leads interested job sharers through the process of finding a partner, proposing a job-sharing scheme, devising a schedule, and working out problems. Olmsted and Smith (1997) provide additional advice on establishing a job-sharing option in their indispensable manual *Managing in a Flexible Workplace*. Another good source of practical suggestions is the second edition of the award-winning book *Creating a Flexible Workplace: How to Select & Manage Alternative Work Options* (Olmsted and Smith 1994). Olmsted and Smith (1997) view the implementation of job sharing as a two-step process. First, an organization needs to remove current obstacles to job sharing. For example, if the head-count system is in place, a company needs to count each partner as a "half a head" or "move toward a system of full-time equivalency" (p. 121). If one partner is using job sharing to phase into retirement, an organization needs to make certain that job sharing doesn't negatively affect that employee's retirement income. The second step of the job-sharing process is to create new policy supporting job sharing. Among the issues that this policy needs to address are eligibility, the application process, compensation and benefits, the impact on employee status (including seniority status and opportunities for advancement), scheduling, pair formation, replacement of partners, and conditions for returning to full-time work.

PERMANENT PART-TIME WORK

Permanent or regular part-time work refers to a work schedule that is less than 40 hours per week. In contrast to temporary or seasonal part-time workers, these employees are on a company's regular payroll and may or may not receive benefits (Christensen 1990). Another term that has been used to describe this arrangement is "career part-time" (O'Hara 1994).

Part-time work is the most commonly used type of flexible scheduling option worldwide (Becker et al. 1993; Brewster 1997). According to a 1998 report released by the AFL-CIO, 21 million Americans (almost 18 percent of the U.S. workforce) are part-time workers (Pay, Insurance Disparity Decried in Part-Timer Study 1998; Stafford 1998). The Association of Part-Time Professionals, an association based in Falls Church, Virginia, reports a slightly higher number, claiming that there are more than 23 million part-time workers in the United States, nearly 20 percent of the workforce (Poole and Conwell 1997). A 1996 report published by Eurostat, indicates that 16 percent of all European Union (EU) workers are employed part time, with the level of part-time work in the EU ranging from a low of 5 percent in Greece to a high of 38 percent in The Netherlands (Employment: 16% of EU Workers Are Part-Time 1997). Casey, Metcalf, and Millward's (1997) study of nonstandard working-time patterns in Britain found substantial growth in the use of part-time workers. Their study used data from two large-scale British surveys: the Labour Force Survey and the Workplace Industrial Relations Survey. Data from these nationally representative surveys indicated that the use of employees employed on a part-time basis in Britain increased by 25 percent between 1984 and 1994. In 1994, 25 percent of employees worked part time.

Economists have noted that the growth of a part-time workforce is one of the major labor-market developments in the post–World War II period (Tilly 1996). There are several demographic and economic factors behind this development of part-time work (Olmsted and Smith 1994; Tilly 1996; Bolle 1997). More women have entered the workforce since the late 1970s, many with small children. The economy has changed from a production-based economy to a service-based economy, and part-time work is more prevalent in service industries. Many workers prefer to work less than a full-time schedule in order to balance work/family obligations, return to school, volunteer in their community, or pursue other interests. At the same time, companies have increased the use of part-time workers as a strategy to reduce labor costs.

In the 1950s and 1960s many employers viewed part-time workers as "peripheral, casual, and expendable" (O'Hara 1994, 29). Bruce O'Hara, one of Canada's strongest advocates for workplace flexibility, stresses that this notion of part-time employment, as well as the position of many labor unions on this issue, is based on outdated ideas about part-time workers. According to O'Hara the new part-time worker is often the following: working to provide basic family income (not pin money), a committed professional, a self-supporting adult with as much need for job security and benefits as other employees, highly productive, and a permanent member of the labor force. Unfortunately, negative stereotypes about part-time workers still prevail. A study of managerial attitudes toward part-time workers in the food-service industry found that many managers regard part-timers as less committed, less loyal, less reliable, less competent, and less hard working than their full-time counterparts (Inman and Enz 1995).

In 1998 Catalyst published *A New Approach to Flexibility: Managing the Work/Time Equation*, the first in-depth study of part-time employment among professionals. More than 2,000 people participated in this study through surveys, interviews, and focus groups. Participants included part-time professionals, their supervisors, their coworkers, their clients, and human resource professionals in four U.S. companies (a pharmaceutical company, a technology company, a law firm, and a consulting firm). Two of these firms had a long history of workplace flexibility, while two of the organizations had recently introduced flexibility. One important finding was that many part-time professionals regard their arrangement as permanent, not temporary. Many part-time professionals had no desire to return to full-time work because of child-care responsibilities or ongoing interests. Another common theme that emerged in focus groups and interviews was the perception that the workplace was changing and that the traditional eight-hour, five-day workweek was no longer the standard because of technological advances and the need to provide service to global clients and customers.

However, not all part-time workers work part time voluntarily. Chris Tilly (1996), author of *Half a Job: Bad and Good Part-Time Jobs in a Changing Labor Market*, noted that in 1993 approximately 6.1 million Americans worked part time voluntarily. In the United States the rate of involuntary part-time employment has increased over the past two decades even when the economy. has expanded. In addition, Tilly added that many Americans (as many as 3 million workers) are unable to find part-time jobs and are involuntary full-time workers. Tilly's book explores why companies have created part-time jobs even though a significant percentage of workers would prefer full-time positions. Reasons include demographic shifts, long-term growth in unemployment, and a widening differential between full-time and part-time employment. Tilly established that the median hourly wage for part-timers is 40 percent below that of full-time workers. However, these reasons account for a small part of the increase in part-time jobs. Tilly maintained that the major reasons are the move from a manufacturing to a service and trade economy, and the fact that businesses within virtually every industry have increased the rate of part-time employment.

Tilly distinguished between two types of part-time jobs: "secondary part-time jobs" (p. 48) and "retention part-time jobs" (p. 40). Tilly's distinction is important because "most literature on part-time employment has not recognized such differences between the part-time pool" (p. 49). Secondary part-time jobs fall into Tilly's category of "bad" (p. 48) part-time jobs. Workers in these jobs have lower skills and lower compensation than their full-time counterparts. Although secondary part-time jobs give employers scheduling flexibility and lower wage and benefit costs, the price is low productivity and high turnover. In comparison, retention part-time jobs are "good" (p. 40) part-time jobs. These employees have skills and compensation comparable or above their full-time counterparts. Their schedules have been negotiated as a strategy for employers to retain valuable employees or attract skilled employees. In the case of retention part-time jobs, productivity is high at the cost of decreased scheduling flexibility and increased benefit costs.

Tilly (1996) studied part-time workers using a sample of twenty-nine retail and insurance companies in two metropolitan areas: Boston and Pittsburgh. Based on these case studies, he drew broad generalizations about secondary part-time workers. Secondary part-time workers were characterized as having jobs involving less skill, responsibility, and training than their full-time counterparts, having lower fringe benefits, and having lower hourly wages. These workers were originally hired on a part-time basis, so a move to a full-time job represents a promotion. Tilly found that turnover is high among secondary part-time workers. He characterized retention part-time workers as tending to have greater skill and training than their coworkers, less responsibility (often because they are barred from manager or team leader positions), and the same fringe benefits and wages as coworkers. In most cases these workers were originally hired full time so the move to a full-time job represents a change in hours rather than a promotion. Low turnover was associated with retention part-time workers.

According to Tilly (1996), it is largely involuntary part-time employment that is growing and these jobs are secondary part-time jobs since employers recognize the economic benefits of secondary part-time workers. Many labor unions have opposed part-time employment as a threat to full-time jobs and compensation levels. Yet specific unions have different strategies. As Tilly explains, some oppose part-time jobs under all circumstances, some are trying to negotiate parity of benefits for part-timers, and some are trying to win the right to job share and gain protections for part-timers. Tilly identified the following problems with secondary part-time jobs: income inequality, lagging productivity, involuntary part-time and involuntary full-time status, and weakened union representation. Tilly argues that some policy intervention is necessary to curb the growth of "bad" part-time jobs. He believes unionization is the most effective strategy. Tilly concludes that more research needs to be focused on part-time work, since most scholarly literature overlooks part-time work even though almost one-fifth of the U.S. workforce works part time.

For those part-time employees working part time by choice, this arrangement can have several advantages (Part-Time, Work-at-Home Add Flexibility 1992; McCaffery 1996). Part-time schedules allow employees to maintain their careers while caring for children or elderly relatives. They also allow workers to pursue leisure activities, community service, or other interests. Some workers use part-time jobs to try out a new career or to learn new skills (Edwards 1998).

Experts besides Chris Tilly have cautioned, however, that part-time work is not always advantageous to workers. A research study conducted in Germany found that compensation is low, and job security and career opportunity may be lacking (Bosch 1995). This conclusion is mirrored in an analysis of part-time work published in the *International Labour Review* (Bolle 1997). Patrick Bolle, the author of this international overview of part-timers, found that the hourly wages were generally lower for part-time workers, they are often ineligible for benefits, and career advancement can be limited. Bolle went so far as to state that unless part-time work is voluntary, "it may leave them only marginally better off than if they were unemployed" (p. 557). The Catalyst (1998) study of part-time employment among professionals also indicated some problems from the perspective of the part-time worker. For example, many part-timers reported that their responsibilities were not reduced even though their work hours and compensation were. In addition, some part-timers in the Catalyst study reported fewer opportunities for "high-profile assignments" (p. 52). The AFL–CIO's 1998 report, "Part-Time Work, Full-Time Bills: The Problems of Part-Time Employment," highlighted salary and benefit discrepancies between full-time and part-time positions (Pay, Insurance Disparity Decried in Part-Timer Study 1998; Stafford 1998). According to the report, part-time workers earned lower hourly wages and were much less likely to have employer-provided health insurance, pensions, and paid vacations. The AFL–CIO document also reported that most part-time workers are not covered by several worker-protection laws, both at the federal and state levels.

Why have part-time arrangements become increasingly popular with employers? There are compelling business reasons for offering part-time employment. According to Olmsted and Smith (1994, 1997), companies use part-time workers in order to retain valued employees, as a recruitment tool, to provide more scheduling options, to reduce labor costs, to increase productivity and commitment, and as a strategy for retaining older workers. The last reason has become important as companies rush to resolve the year 2000 (Y2K) computer problem. Many companies brought back retirees with programming experience, especially those with knowledge of older computer languages, on a part-time basis to help with the Y2K problem (Dutton 1998). A research study conducted in Germany found that part-time employment is cost effective for employees, since companies can save some 2 to 4 percent of their labor costs as a result of increased productivity and reduced levels of sick leave (Government Launches Part-Time Work Initiative 1994). In a Conference Board study of part-time employment, a report based on the responses of 102 companies, the most commonly cited benefits of part-time employment were greater staffing flexibility, higher morale, reduced turnover, decreased costs, and higher productivity (Part-Time Employment 1996). Participants in Catalyst's (1998) study of part-time employment among professionals identified these compelling business reasons for offering part-time arrangements: retention of valuable employees, recruitment, and the need to provide expanded customer service, especially in a global economy. Participants also listed the following benefits: increased productivity, improved morale, improved work quality, and increased employee commitment to the firm.

While a strong business case can be made for the creation of permanent part-time positions, there are also many barriers to the implementation of this option. Union resistance has been a major deterrent, especially in the United States (Olmsted and Smith 1994; Poole and Conwell 1997). Unions have traditionally been suspicious about part-time work, fearful that part-time positions will undermine full-time employment. In contrast, trade unions in The Netherlands and Germany have begun to support part-time work (Lewis 1997). From the perspective of the employee, there may be financial barriers (Olmsted and Smith 1994). Not all workers can afford to work part time and the lack of full benefits may preclude some employees from accepting part-time work. Some older workers cannot work part time because their pensions are tied to the level of pay they received during their last years of employment. Catalyst's 1993 study of part-time options found that the major obstacles to implementing part-time arrangements were resistance by middle management, policy limitations (such as policies not making part-time options available to managers), corporate culture, and negative connotations about part-time workers. Many of these barriers remain, as documented by Catalyst's 1998 study on part-time work. Catalyst concluded that "persistent and formidable barriers limit the availability and use of part-time arrangements" (p. 9). The organization found a serious gap between theory and practice, noting, "In theory, flexibility is a viable and effective approach to managing work . . . yet in practice it has come to be perceived as an accommodation at best and a nuisance and liability at worst" (p. 38).

Who works part time? When comparing the growth of part-time work in industrialized countries, Colette Fagan and Jacqueline O'Reilly (1998) noted that "overall part-time work remains female dominated and disproportionately concentrated in low-paid, low-status jobs" (p. 18). Their edited volume, *Part-Time Prospects: An International Comparison of Part-Time Work in Europe, North America and the Pacific Rim*, brings together fourteen scholarly papers on the growth of part-time work in industrialized nations. Many of the chapters are comparative, looking at similarities and differences across countries. In the European Union most part-timers are women and part-time work is concentrated in the service industry (Employment: 16% of EU Workers Are Part-Time 1997). The use of part-time professionals in also growing. In the United Kingdom the sectors of the economy with the highest levels of professional part-time employees were consulting, education, health care, construction, and engineering (Managers and TUC Unite to Examine the Part-Time Worker 1996). Catalyst's 1993 study of part-time options for managers and professionals found that the fastest growing fields for part-time employment included engineering, mathematics, computer science, the natural sciences, health care, teaching, and law.

In the United States federal part-time workers work in a variety of positions at many grade levels (*Balancing Work and Family Demand Through Part-Time Employment and Job Sharing* 1995). As of September 1994 there were approximately 49,535 part-time permanent federal civilian employees in the executive branch (Postal Service employees are excluded in this figure). Among this group the profile of the typical part-time employee is as follows: 42.1 years old; has 9.7 years of service; 38.8 percent have a baccalaureate degree or higher; 70.6 percent are women; and 2.2 percent are supervisors or managers. In terms of occupational category, 86.4 percent are white-collar workers and 13.6 percent are blue-collar workers. The Federal Employees Part-Time Career Employment Act of 1978 encouraged a federal commitment to career part-time employment and job sharing. This legislation was strengthened on July 11, 1994, through a memorandum from President Clinton to the heads of executive departments and agencies. These part-time employees work between sixteen and thirty-two hours each week (or between thirty-two and sixty-four hours a pay period) on a prearranged schedule and are eligible for the same benefits as full-time employees.

Managing part-time workers requires special skills. Supervisors should make part-timers feel that they are in the mainstream, make sure that training is available to them, and ensure that part-time workers are eligible for promotion (Olmsted and Smith 1994). A common complaint voiced by participants in Catalyst's 1998 study of part-time employment was that there were no clear policies and guidelines about eligibility, the application process, benefits, compensation, and career advancement. The report stressed the need for managers to learn how to supervise employees using a range of flexible work arrangements, including part time. Organizations interested in establishing a regular part-time option program should use the worksheet found in Barney Olmsted and Suzanne Smith's (1997) indispensable manual *Managing in a Flexible Workplace*. The authors explain that setting up a part-time option is a two-step process. The first step is to remove current barriers in existing personnel policies and union contracts. The second step is to create new policy supporting the use of part-timers. Some of the issues that this policy must address are the voluntary nature of part-time employment, budget implications, eligibility, employment status, compensation, impact on retirement income, reductions in force (if policy states that part-timers must be laid off first, this discourages the use of this option), and changes in work schedule (including how part-timers can return to full-time employment).

LEAVES AND SABBATICALS

Olmsted and Smith (1994) define a leave as "an authorized period of time away from work without loss of employment rights" (p. 284). A leave may be paid or unpaid and is usually for an extended period of time. An employee may take a leave in order to recuperate from ill health; recover from job burnout; return to school; pursue volunteer interests; or care for a child, parent, or spouse. A sabbatical is generally a paid leave that is offered to employees at set intervals (Guiding Principles for Managing a Flexible Workplace 1997). Olmsted and Smith (1994) have documented some creative uses of other types of leaves. Hewlett-Packard was a pioneer, introducing its Flexible Time Off Program in the early 1980s, a program that gives employees five to thirteen days off a year (depending on their length of service) that can be used as vacation or sick time. Leave banks, policies that allow employees to pool their sick leave, have been used by the federal government since 1988. Some companies, such as IBM, offer extended unpaid leave programs. IBM established its Personal Leave of Absence Program in 1988, which allows absences of up to three years (with full benefits, service credit, and job security). Hallmark Cards allows voluntary leave during cyclical periods that are less busy. Continental Insurance allows employees to take ten days off per year without pay.

The word sabbatical means "every seventh year" and refers to a leave of absence granted every seventh year (Douglas 1995). The origin is biblical. Leviticus prescribes that the land should have a rest every seventh year. The idea of a sabbatical year is rooted in Leviticus 25:3–5, with the passage, "Six years you may sow your field, and six years you may prune your vineyard . . . but in the seventh year, the land shall have a Sabbath of complete rest, a Sabbath of the Lord" (Haffner 1997).

Helen Axel (1992) traced the history of sabbaticals in her groundbreaking Conference Board study on corporate sabbaticals. Although sabbaticals were first introduced in American universities in the late nineteenth century, they did not extend beyond academia until after World War II. Axel noted that a more thorough history of work sabbaticals could be found in Fred Best's 1981 book *Work Sharing: Issues,*

Policy Options and Prospects. Best found that sabbaticals were first introduced in the workplace as a strategy to preserve and/or create jobs. The term "worker sabbatical" was first used by Albert Morton Persoff in his proposal for a national strategy to reduce unemployment. In the early 1960s a thirteen-week sabbatical was negotiated for steel and aluminum workers in order to avoid massive layoffs. Axel points out that these so-called sabbaticals before the 1970s were not really sabbaticals but a strategy for work sharing. The first sabbaticals for employees in nonmanufacturing sectors were introduced in the 1970s. Some firms, such as Xerox, IBM, Control Data, and Wells Fargo Bank, offered paid leaves for community service. Xerox was a pioneer in this area, establishing its Social Service Leave Program in 1971. Several years later, Wells Fargo Bank modeled its Personal Growth Leave after Xerox's program. Other early (i.e., 1970s) proponents included Tandem Computers, Time Inc. Magazine Company, and McDonald's. Ray Kroc, the founder of McDonald's, established a Bonus Vacation Program as a strategy to prevent burnout. Growth in the offering of sabbaticals stalled in the 1980s as a result of layoffs, reorganizations, and early retirements. In the 1990s some companies (such as AT&T, Bell Atlantic, and IBM) began to offer extended unpaid leaves (with guaranteed continued employment) as a way to downsize.

Axel (1992) defined five categories of sabbaticals: traditional sabbaticals, leaves for personal growth, social-service leaves, extended personal leaves, and management-initiated voluntary leaves. Traditional corporate sabbaticals are modeled after the academic model. Companies offer paid leaves at recurring intervals to employees in good standing. At the end of the leave period employees generally return to their same positions. Leaves for personal growth provide time off so employees can pursue a personal interest. These sabbaticals may be paid or unpaid. Social-service leaves are generally paid and allow employees to take time off in order to perform community service. An extended personal leave is an unpaid leave that provides an employment break of two or more years with a return-to-work guarantee at the end of the leave. Companies usually offer a management-initiated voluntary leave when they need to temporarily reduce labor costs. The timing of these leaves is at the convenience of the employer.

How many corporations offer sabbaticals to employees? In 1985 trend spotter John Naisbitt (1985) estimated that 10 percent of U.S. corporations offered sabbaticals. Axel (1992) calculated that based on data from the Conference Board and other organizations, 14 to 24 percent of firms have sabbatical policies. Outside the United States, sabbaticals are common in Belgium, The Netherlands, and Australia (The Long and Short of Allowing Extended Leave 1997). Australia has an interesting history of worker sabbaticals. Extended paid leaves were originally introduced so European-born workers would have enough time to return home for a visit (Mendels 1992). Many high-tech firms have sabbatical policies. Sabbaticals are "becoming the norm in Silicon Valley" (Semas 1997, 122). Other professions that tend to offer sabbaticals include law, consulting firms, and journalism (Axel 1992). Axel noted that McDonald's sabbatical program is unique since it is one of the few outside high-tech or professional-services firms.

What are the advantages of offering leaves and sabbaticals? Leaves can be used as a tool to retain employees, as a strategy for dealing with burnout, to encourage employees to learn new skills, to help employees balance work and family, and to temporarily reduce labor costs (Olmsted and Smith 1994, 1997). Sabbaticals can also be a retention tool, prevent burnout, and give employees the opportunity to improve their skills. In addition, sabbaticals can boost morale, improve productivity, generate favorable publicity for a company, and represent a company's commitment to community service (Axel 1992). Lisa Rogak (1994), the author of a practical guide to planning a sabbatical, interviewed more than forty professionals who took a break from work. She found that people are interested in sabbaticals (which she defined as paid or unpaid time off, ranging from one month to one year) as a way to balance their professional and personal lives, as a way to examine other career options, and as a way to explore an avocation.

What are the obstacles to leave programs? Many managers worry about how work will be done when an employee is on leave (Olmsted and Smith 1994). Axel (1992) found several barriers, both from the perspective of the employee and the employer. Some coworkers expressed concern about having to take on additional work. Many employees were reluctant to take sabbaticals if the economy was uncertain or if the leave was unpaid. Some companies were critical of the concept, viewing sabbaticals as unnecessary, disruptive, and expensive perks. Although sabbaticals are increasingly popular in high-tech industries, Axel predicted only modest growth for paid sabbaticals and social-service leaves. Some companies, after weighing the pros and cons of sabbaticals, have rejected the idea of establishing a sabbatical program, or in the recent cases of Tandem Computers and Apple Computer, have phased out their sabbatical programs (Jackson 1998).

Other types of leaves from work, such as parental leaves, are more common outside the United States. In 1985 the International Labour Organisation (ILO) conducted a survey of maternity and family leaves in 118 countries (Ferber, O'Farrell, and Allen 1991). Only the United States lacked national legislation providing maternity rights and benefits. Marshall (1993) reported that more than 100 countries provide job-protected maternity leaves with some wage replacement. Ruhm and Teague (1997) have chronicled the history of family-leave legislation in Europe and North America. Germany was the first country to legislate maternity leave (doing so in 1883), followed by Sweden in 1891 and France in 1928. In the United States there was no national legislation mandating family leave until the passage of the Family and Medical Leave Act in February 1993 (Marks 1997; Ruhm and Teague 1997). The FMLA requires companies with fifty or more employees to give workers up to twelve weeks of unpaid leave in a twelve-month period to care for newborn or adopted children (Barnett 1997; Mann 1997). Employees who are covered under the legislation may also take unpaid leave to care for themselves or a seriously ill family member (Barnett 1997; Kruger 1998). However, in order to be eligible, an employee must have worked for the company at least a year and must have worked a minimum of 1,250 hours the preceding year (Family and Medical Leave 1994). There are two other important exceptions: companies with fewer than fifty workers within a seventy-five-mile radius and the highest-paid (top 10 percent earnings) employees in the firm, provided that their absence would result in significant hardship for the business (Family and Medical Leave 1994).

The FMLA covers only 50 percent of all employees in the United States and only allows employees to take up to three months of unpaid leave (Marshall 1993). The FMLA is different from European policies in two important ways: The leave is unpaid and the period of entitlement is much shorter (Ruhm and Teague 1997). Most industrialized countries offer some salary compensation to workers on leave and leave periods range from a minimum of fourteen weeks to more than five months (Marks 1997). In Europe paid family leaves average six months in duration (Mann 1997).

In the United States passage of federal legislation mandating family leave was highly controversial. A good legislative history of family-leave policy can be found in Steven Wisensale's (1997) article comparing the debates over family-leave policy during the Carter, Reagan, Bush, and Clinton administrations. A more detailed analysis of the partisan politics involved in the passage of the FMLA can be found in Michelle Marks's (1997) insightful case study of the FMLA. Both Wisensale and Marks conclude that the impact of the FMLA has been minimal, since most of the workers covered cannot afford to take unpaid leave. Since small businesses are exempt, the legislation only applies to 60 percent of the workforce.

Other researchers have documented the limitations of the FMLA. From a legal perspective, Eileen Drake (1997) considers the FMLA to be "only a partial solution to the challenge of blending family and work" (p. 123). She reiterates that only a small percentage of workers benefit from this legislation. Furthermore, she views the FMLA to be "flawed," since it "is at once too broad and too narrow" (p. 123). She considers its definition of "serious health condition" to be too broad, since it covers "medical conditions that in the past would not have fit the common understanding of what is a serious health condition" (p. 123). On the other hand, she views it as too narrow, since it limits coverage. For example, parents are covered but parents-in-law are excluded.

Other writers have pointed out the problems resulting from a vague definition of what constitutes a serious illness (Barnett 1997; Ginsberg 1997; Kruger 1998; Higgins 1999; Moskowitz and Rowell 1999; Paltell 1999). For example, a common cold or the flu qualifies if complications develop. Complications are defined as conditions that force an employee to miss three or more days of work and seek treatment (Higgins 1999). Recent court rulings, summarized in an issue of *HRMagazine*, may help confused employers interpret coverage (Paltell 1999). In addition, other useful articles, published upon the sixth anniversary of the act's passage, can help supervisors interpret the legal provisions of the FMLA (Flynn 1999; Zachary 1999). Some employers have also complained about the provision that allows employees to take leave in increments as small as an hour or less (Barnett 1997). Tracking these small increments of time can be a record-keeping headache for employers. A Conference Board survey ranked administrative record keeping as the greatest difficulty associated with FMLA implementation (Family and Medical Leave 1994).

What are the costs of FMLA implementation to employers? Among the costs cited in a Society for Human Resource Management survey were hiring of replacement workers, continuation of health insurance for workers on leave, loss of productivity, time spent communicating leave policies, costs related to tracking leave, and payment of overtime for workers not on leave (Flak over FMLA 1997).

However, a study conducted by the bipartisan Congressional Family Leave Commission found that the FMLA is not expensive to implement, nor has it resulted in problems for employers (Commission Finds Few Problems with FMLA 1996; Sunoo and Flynn 1996; Ginsberg 1997). The commission's findings, which are summarized in a report titled *A Workable Balance: Report to Congress on Family and Medical Leave Policies*, were based on two national surveys and three public hearings on the impact of FMLA implementation (Commission Finds Few Problems with FMLA 1996). The report concluded that "between 89 and 99 percent of covered work sites report no costs or small costs" and "between 86 and 96 percent report no noticeable effect on productivity, profitability, and growth" (Ginsberg 1997, p. H6). The commission's conclusions about the economic effects of the FMLA are interesting, because Ruhm and Teague's (1997) research on the economic impact of mandated family policies in Europe and Canada found that "moderate periods of parental leave" result in a "modest beneficial impact"

(p. 133). Ruhm and Teague used several variables to measure the effect of leave on economic performance in fifteen European countries, Canada, and the United Kingdom.

However, the Family Leave Commission found that few eligible employees use the provisions of the FMLA. In fact, only 2 to 4 percent of eligible workers take leave under the Family and Medical Leave Act (Sunoo and Flynn 1996). Unfortunately, the commission found that two-thirds of workers who reported that they needed family leave did not take leave under the FMLA because they could not afford the loss of wages (Armour 1998).

While the FMLA has been in effect for more than five years, both employees and employers are unsure about its provisions (Higgins 1999). A recent legal suit has highlighted this confusion. In 1999 a jury awarded Kevin Knussman, a Maryland state police paramedic, $375,000 in compensatory damages as a result of a discrimination case filed by the American Civil Liberties Union (ACLU) on Knussman's behalf (Valentine 1999). The ACLU maintained that Knussman was denied leave under the FMLA to care for his wife and newborn because he is male. His employer refused to grant him extended leave, arguing that he was not the primary caregiver.

Research has shown that few fathers take family leave under the FMLA. Pleck (1994) estimates that only 1 percent of fathers take formal leave because they cannot afford unpaid leave. However, Pleck's research indicates that about 75 percent of fathers take informal leave, averaging a little more than five days following the birth of a child. Levine and Pittinsky (1997) found that the FMLA has not had a dramatic impact on fathers' leave taking. Not only can fathers ill afford the loss of wages, but they worry about the impact of leave taking on their career and feel that the organizational culture does not support parental leave. Few fathers are eligible for paid paternity leave. Levine and Pittinsky (1997) estimate that only 1 percent of American fathers (in both public- and private-sector employment) are eligible for paid paternity leave. Corporate culture prevents both men and women from taking parental leave. Mindy Fried (1998) studied the impact of workplace culture on parental leave at a U.S. company that is recognized as being family friendly. Her findings are the basis of the book *Taking Time: Parental Leave Policy and Corporate Culture*. Fried found that parental leave is underutilized and that the "power of the overtime culture permeates life" (p. 185) at the company she studied as well as in most workplaces. Her findings are consistent with those of an earlier Conference Board survey that found that both men and women are reluctant to take family leave because they fear doing so will jeopardize their career advancement, and that leave taking is discouraged by the workplace culture (Family and Medical Leave 1994).

The FMLA will continue to be controversial because there have been proposals to expand the leave to small businesses (Commission Finds Few Problems with FMLA 1996; Jackson 1997; Kleiman 1997). In 1997 President Clinton signed a memorandum granting federal workers up to twenty-four hours of unpaid leave annually for family obligations (Jackson 1997; Clinton Steps Up Pressure for Family Leave 1997). On May 31, 1999, President Clinton sent a memorandum to the heads of executive departments and agencies, directing the director of the Office of Personnel Management to propose regulations to allow federal workers to use up to twelve weeks of accumulated sick leave to care for ill family members (Clinton 1999). This same memorandum ordered the creation of an Interagency Family-Friendly Workplace Working Group, to be charged with developing, promoting, and evaluating federal workplace initiatives.

It is possible that a solution to the problem of unpaid leave may be found at the state level. A few states are considering expanding temporary disability insurance programs to include family and medical leaves (Mann 1997). This strategy got a boost with President Clinton's May 31, 1999, memorandum on actions relating to the FMLA. President Clinton directed the secretary of labor to help states develop legislation enabling them to use the Unemployment Insurance System to support workers on family leave.

PHASED RETIREMENT

Phased retirement is a flexible work option that allows employees to reduce their work hours gradually over a defined time period (Olmsted 1987, 1990/1991; Christensen 1990; Olmsted and Smith 1994; Guiding Principles for Managing a Flexible Workplace 1997). Synonyms for phased retirement include gradual, gliding, flexible, and transitional retirement (Swank 1982; Claveria 1992). Workers may phase into retirement over several months or several years. The period of reduced hours can range from six months to ten years, and an employee phasing into retirement may reduce hours 5 to 50 percent and in some cases receive a prorated salary with continuation of full benefits (O'Hara and Williams 1990). A related option, partial retirement, allows older workers to work part time prior to full retirement (Olmsted 1990/1991). There is generally no set time limit with this arrangement, and in some cases workers combine their salary with partial retirement income (Olmsted and Smith 1994). Another related trend is the growth of "boomerangers" (Dym 1998). Boomerangers are retired workers who return to work for their former employer on an as-needed basis. The Monsanto Company has a formal program using boomerangers (who form the Retiree Resources Corps), and estimates that those retirees who bounce back to Monsanto cost 12 to 15 percent less than contingent workers (Dym 1998).

Both phased and partial retirement originated in the early 1970s in Europe, primarily in Great Britain, Germany, France, and Belgium (Olmsted and Smith 1994). In 1982 the National Council for Alternative Work Patterns conducted a study on the European experience with phased retirement. These findings are documented in Constance Swank's 1982 report, *Phased Retirement: The European Experience*. Swank examined thirteen European phased retirement programs in detail. In Europe employers, unions, and governments advocated the development of phased retirement options. During the late 1970s and early 1980s phased retirement options were implemented in the public and private sectors. All types of industries were represented and both blue- and white-collar workers were involved. A few programs excluded managers and senior staff. Participation was generally voluntary. Programs began anywhere between one and five years before retirement. Swank reported that, in general, employers were positive about phased retirement.

Management guru Peter Drucker advocated phased retirement in the late 1970s (Ronen 1984). In fact, he believed that it would be one of the crucial social issues of the 1980s. In the late 1970s and early 1980s a number of American public colleges and universities offered faculty early, partial, or phased retirement (Claveria 1992). Phased retirement gained popularity in the United States after mandatory retirement was abolished in 1987 (O'Hara and Williams 1990). One of the important trends identified by John P. Robinson and Geoffrey Godbey (1997) in *Time for Life*, their extensive study of how ordinary Americans' use of time has changed across the past three decades, is that more Americans are retiring or cutting back on work hours at earlier ages.

The state of California was a leader in promoting phased retirement. In 1974 the state developed a phased retirement program for public school teachers. This was extended to faculty members of the state's university system in 1980 and to state employees in 1984 (Olmsted and Smith 1994).

Except for California, few states have phased retirement programs. The notable exceptions are Iowa and Nevada (Claveria 1992). At the federal level the Environmental Protection Agency (EPA) has been a leader (Gardner 1997). The EPA established a senior program more than two decades ago. This program is now under the direction of the National Older Worker Career Center, a center that helps other federal agencies and large firms develop phased retirement programs and other options for older workers. Some private-sector companies have been leaders in the area: Aetna, Corning Glass, IBM, Levi Strauss,

Polaroid, Varian (a Silicon Valley electronics company), and the Travelers Companies (Ramirez 1989; Olmsted and Smith 1994, 1997; Cascio 1998; Dym 1998; Flexible Options for the Older Workforce 1998). A 1999 study conducted by Watson Wyatt Worldwide found that 16 percent of the 586 large companies surveyed offered phased retirement and 28 percent of the firms surveyed indicated that they may establish this option in the next three years (Burkins 1999).

Both private- and public-sector employees have become increasingly interested in phased retirement as a result of several demographic and economic factors. An excellent analysis of these factors can be found in Susan Claveria's 1992 report, *Phased Retirement for Public Employees*. The Legislative Reference Bureau produced this report at the request of the Hawaii legislature. The state of Hawaii was concerned about a mass retirement of older workers, given that one-third of the combined workforce of Hawaiian state and county government consists of workers aged fifty or older. Claveria found that Hawaii's predicament is not unique. Nationally, a large number of baby boomers will be reaching retirement age in the next twenty years. Employers with a large proportion of baby boomers will be impacted by the retirement of so many experienced workers at the same time. This is a particular problem for the public sector, since many state and local governments employ a large number of baby boomers. Mass retirement will also be a problem for unionized plants. A recent article in the *Wall Street Journal* quipped that more factories are worried about the year 2001 problem than the Y2K problem (Aeppel 1999). Higher education will also be strongly impacted by mass retirement. A recent survey indicates that almost one-third of full-time faculty in U.S. colleges and universities are age fifty-five or older (The Graying Professoriate 1999). Claveria warned that the problem would be widespread, given that the twenty-first century will be marked by an unprecedented growth in the elderly population. It is projected that more than 68 million Americans will be age sixty-five or older by the year 2050. Claveria's most startling statistic is that more Americans will be retiring between the years 2001 and 2019 than in any other period in history because of the sheer number of baby boomers. These first members of the baby boom generation will turn fifty-five in the year 2001, and the last members of this generation will turn fifty-five in the year 2019. In 1997 the U.S. Senate Special Committee on Aging held a forum on boomer retirement. Remarks presented at this forum were published in a document titled *Preparing for the Baby Boomers' Retirement: The Role of Employment* (U.S. Senate 1997). Many of the experts who testified warned that in the foreseeable future a chronic shortage of laborers rather than a shortage of jobs would mark the U.S. economy. In addition, research findings presented by a representative from the American Association of

Retired Persons (AARP) indicated that most older workers want to continue some paid work in retirement. Unfortunately, most of the pre-retirees AARP interviewed for this study did not feel that their employer offered this flexibility.

How does phased retirement benefit employees? Phased retirement allows workers to ease into retirement, lessening the shock of complete retirement. It also gives older workers more leisure time (Swank 1982; O'Hara and Williams 1990). Some older workers may use this time to pursue other interests, and a reduced schedule can be particularly helpful to workers with health problems (O'Hara and Williams 1990). A study conducted by Canada's National Forum on Health found that retirement could be a health risk to some employees (Health Risks of Retirement 1997). Consequently, the authors of this study supported phased retirement as a strategy to ease the transition from employment to retirement. Younger workers can also benefit from phased retirement, since it opens up new jobs for them as well as opportunities for career advancement and cross-training (O'Hara and Williams 1990; Olmsted and Smith 1997).

Does phased retirement have any drawbacks for employees? The two most cited disadvantages are economic (Claveria 1992). For some employees, phased retirement can result in insufficient income. In the United States and Canada participants generally receive a prorated salary. In contrast, European workers typically receive a wage subsidy to supplement their prorated salary. For other employees, phased retirement may negatively impact retirement benefits, such as pension income, health benefits, and other long-term benefits. O'Hara and Williams (1990) note that in order to be successful a formal phased retirement program must include pension protection and a full range of health benefits.

There are many business reasons to implement phased retirement. Some companies use phased retirement as a strategy to retain experienced workers (Claveria 1992; Olmsted and Smith 1997). This retention of older workers can be good publicity for a company, since it demonstrates that a firm has a long-term commitment to its workers (O'Hara and Williams 1990). Older workers on reduced work schedules can act as trainees and mentors (Swank 1982; Louchheim 1990; O'Hara and Williams 1990; Claveria 1992; Estess 1996; Olmsted and Smith 1997). Swank found that in the late 1970s and 1980s phased retirement gained support in Europe as a strategy to achieve voluntary workforce reductions. However, in the 1990s the reverse argument was being made for phased retirement. Economists warned that the aging of the population, combined with lowered global birth rates, would create a labor shortage for many countries. As a result, phased retirement gained support as a strategy to reduce labor shortages (Cliff 1991; Andrews 1992; Benson 1997).

What are the barriers to implementing phased retirement? Some firms have been reluctant to experiment with it for fear that it will result in additional record keeping and other administrative costs (Swank 1982; Claveria 1992). Like other flexible work options, it has met with resistance from lower and middle management (Swank 1982). Some companies fear noneligible coworkers will be resentful, especially if they have to pick up the slack of a colleague working a reduced schedule (Claveria 1992). Finally, there is not always support from the workforce. Claveria reported that a survey conducted by the American Society for Personnel Administration and Commerce Clearing House found that flexible retirement policies are not widespread and are not always enthusiastically endorsed by employees given several disincentives. These disincentives include penalties for earning more income than permitted by Social Security regulations.

How does an organization establish a phased retirement option? When designing a program for phased or partial retirement, managers need to address a number of critical issues. Olmsted and Smith (1997) have created a worksheet that identifies these key design issues. For example, managers need to understand the financial implications (such as the effect on Social Security, taxes, pensions, and health benefits) of phased or partial retirement and must be able to explain these implications to participating workers. Employers must determine eligibility, duration of enrollment, minimum and maximum time reductions, and schedules for reducing work time. A formal phased or partial retirement program should also address changes in work time and reversibility.

VOLUNTARY REDUCED WORK TIME

Voluntary reduced work time, sometimes referred to as V-Time, is an option where full-time employees voluntarily reduce their work hours and take a corresponding cut in pay (Olmsted and Smith 1994, 1997; Estess 1996). There is no loss of benefits. However, some benefits may be prorated. Unlike regular part-time employment, this arrangement is for a defined time period (generally a short period such as six to twelve months) and provides guarantees for a return to full-time work (Olmsted and Smith 1994, 1997). Reductions in work time and pay may range from 2 to 50 percent. Employees may choose to work a shorter workday, a shorter workweek, or may take blocks of time off.

Olmsted and Smith (1994) have traced the history of this work arrangement. The county of Santa Clara, California, introduced V-Time in 1976. San Mateo County (California) implemented V-Time in 1981. Both counties initially offered V-Time as a strategy to reduce county costs. In 1984 New York state made V-Time an option for civil-service employees. In the public sector New York state has been a leader in workplace flexibility. In addition to V-Time, employees may choose to reduce work time through job sharing and regular part-time employment. The first private-sector company to use V-Time was the Shaklee Corporation, which introduced it in 1983. However, Olmsted and Smith noted that there is very little private-sector experience with V-Time. Few companies have even experimented with V-Time.

What are the advantages of V-Time? Reduced work time can be an attractive option to some employees, especially working parents and those sandwich-generation employees caring for both children and elderly parents simultaneously. Betty Ann Biernat (1997) studied approximately 200 working (full-time employed) parents of children under age eighteen from two computer-related companies in the Minneapolis area. This research was the basis for her doctoral dissertation, "Employed Parents' Preference for Reduced Job Hours in Relation to Job and Family Characteristics." Almost 60 percent of parents indicated that they would prefer reduced job hours and would accept a reduced salary if career advancement, job security, and benefits were guaranteed. Respondents were asked to select one of four options for reducing work hours: shorter workdays, shorter workweeks, more paid vacation time, and expanded leaves. The most popular option was shorter workweeks. The majority of respondents preferred to reduce job hours one day or less per week or one month or less per year. Consequently, most respondents were interested in a relatively small amount of time off. Biernat's dissertation is important, because there have been a paucity of studies on parental preference for job hours.

A strong business case can be made for V-Time. V-Time can reduce turnover, improve retention, increase employee morale and commitment, and result in cost savings (Olmsted and Smith 1997). The smaller work time (and salary) reduction can be more attractive to employees than regular part-time jobs, making V-Time an effective recruiting tool. From a management perspective, V-Time can be easier to implement than other schemes, since it standardizes the use of reduced schedules.

Why has V-Time not been widely adopted? Olmsted and Smith (1994) found that managers may be resistant, concerned that V-Time will leave units with a large workload. They also found that unions are hesitant to embrace V-Time, fearing that full-time jobs will be lost. Biernat (1997) identified these barriers to reduced job hours: an employee's inability to afford reduced salary and benefits, the inability to distribute workload, concerns about job security, and fears that one could be viewed as being less committed.

Organizations interested in introducing V-Time may want to begin by surveying employees regarding their interest in reduced work time. The second edition of Olmsted and Smith's (1994) award-winning book

Creating a Flexible Workplace provides a sample employee survey on reduced work time. If an organization decides to move forward and design a V-Time option, there are a number of issues a V-Time program must address. These include scope of program, eligibility, range of reductions, how reductions can be taken, the enrollment process, duration of enrollment, assignment of responsibility for approving or denying V-Time requests, program termination for individual participants and the impact of V-Time on employee status and benefits (Olmsted and Smith 1994, 1997). Once again, Olmsted and Smith's (1997) indispensable manual, *Managing in a Flexible Workplace*, guides organizations through the implementation process.

WORK SHARING

Unlike V-Time, work sharing is an involuntary reduction of work hours. It is defined best as "an alternative to layoffs in which all or part of an organization's workforce temporarily reduces hours and salary in order to cut operating costs" (Olmsted and Smith 1994, 315). The theory is that by instituting shorter work hours work can be spread among more employees. Work sharing has been widely used in Europe. German unions, representing many industries, have negotiated for a reduction in the standard workweek since the mid-1980s (Hunt 1999). One of the most publicized case studies is Volkswagen, AG, Germany's largest automobile manufacturer. In 1994 Volkswagen instituted a four-day workweek, reducing work time to 28.8 hours a week in order to avoid cutting Volkswagen's workforce by almost one-third (Olmsted and Smith 1994; Flexibility Options Continue Growth 1996). Gerhard Bosch's (1990) study of the reduction of the workweek in the Federal Republic of Germany provides relevant background to work-sharing developments in a reunited Germany. Work sharing has become standard in the German automobile industry and the German government has encouraged other industries to adopt Volkswagen's work-sharing scheme (Mueller 1996). Jennifer Hunt (1999) examined the impact of work sharing in Germany by analyzing data on thirty manufacturing industries for a ten-year period from 1984 to 1994. She concluded that work sharing "allowed those who remained employed to enjoy lower hours at a higher hourly wage, but likely at the price of lower overall employment" (p. 145).

Jens Bastian (1994) reported that work-sharing proposals gained attention across Western Europe in the 1990s. Bastian noted that in the early 1990s much of Western Europe experienced high rates of unemployment; in fact, the highest rates since the 1930s. In his book *A Matter of Time*, Bastian compared working-time policies in Belgium, France, and Britain from 1979 to 1994 and examined work sharing as a strategy for ameliorating the unemployment problem. In 1998 the French workweek was shortened by law from thirty-nine to thirty-five hours, effective January 1, 2000 (Busted—For Working Hard 1999). In October 1999 thousands of French employers held a rally protesting the thirty-five-hour workweek, arguing that it was unrealistic and would undermine France's ability to compete globally (French Employers Protest Shortened Workweek 1999). Sweden provides another interesting case study of work-time reduction (Pettersson 1993). Unlike other countries in Europe, Sweden has not shortened working hours to reduce unemployment. Working hours have been reduced to protect the health of workers and to give workers more leisure time. A 1982 law establishes forty hours per week as the maximum working time and guarantees that workers have thirty-six hours of continuous free time.

Work sharing is slowly gaining interest in North America. Bruce O'Hara (1993), the founder of Work Well, an organization that promotes flexible work options, has proposed the implementation of a four-day, thirty-two-hour workweek in Canada. O'Hara found an advocate in the Canadian Autoworkers Union, one of Canada's largest unions. The union has bargained for overtime restrictions, phased retirement, and a shorter workweek. Harvey Schachter (1996) featured the idea of a shortened workweek for Canadians in an article in *Canadian Business*, a mainstream business publication.

Olmsted and Smith (1994) have traced the history of work sharing in the United States. During the recession of 1975 Hewlett-Packard and Pan American World Airways, Inc. reduced work time rather than laying off employees. High-tech companies in California's Silicon Valley have used work sharing during down times. Non-high-tech companies, including Charles Schwab (the discount broker), Motorola, and Chrysler, have also used it.

From an employee's perspective, work sharing is preferable to layoffs. However, there are other business reasons for instituting work sharing (Olmsted and Smith 1994, 1997). Work sharing allows firms to retain skilled employees. It can result in increased employee morale and commitment to an organization. In addition, it can be an effective strategy for dealing with economic downturns. When the economy improves, the company is in a better position than firms that instituted layoffs, since it has retained its experienced workforce. The one disadvantage of work sharing is that it is more expensive than some of the other reduced work options.

Because American experience with work sharing is so minimal, Olmsted and Smith's (1997) manual *Managing in a Flexible Workplace* is essential for any organization considering work sharing. It is one of the few sources of practical information on establishing a work-sharing program. The worksheet that is included in their chapter on work sharing can help a firm set up a formal work-sharing program.

SUMMARY

Flextime originated in West Germany in the 1960s and spread to the United States in the early 1970s. It is the most common type of flexible arrangement. Studies have consistently shown that flextime is the flexible work option most desired by employees. Many advantages have been associated with flextime, including reduced tardiness, decreased absenteeism, and improved recruitment and retention of employees. It allows companies to extend their hours of operation and to respond to peaks and demands. At the same time, several disadvantages have been identified. If it is not properly managed, it can lead to inadequate staffing during some hours. Some supervisors report that it is difficult to communicate with workers on different schedules and to track hours worked. Other supervisors express concern about their ability to supervise employees on a variety of schedules. Some requests for flextime cannot be accommodated, especially for those employees working on an assembly line. Labor unions are concerned about flextime's impact on overtime, the length of the workday, and whether the option is voluntary.

Like flextime, the compressed workweek originated in the late 1960s. The three most common variations are 4/10 (four ten-hour days); 3/12 (three twelve-hour days); and 9/80 (a week of four nine-hour days and one eight-hour day followed by a week of four nine-hour days). The compressed workweek is used most extensively in public agencies (especially police and fire departments) and in small manufacturing companies. Since some employees like to work longer days in exchange for longer weekends, the compressed workweek can be an effective recruitment tool. Some firms that have implemented this scheme have reported modest improvements in absenteeism, tardiness, and employee turnover. Another cited advantage is that it can help with staffing programs. It has helped some companies attract workers to undesirable shifts since it gives workers more concentrated time off. This option can also alleviate commuting problems. In some cases it has resulted in reduced labor and utility costs, since startups and shutdowns are reduced. Overall, facilities and equipment can be used more efficiently. However, a compressed workweek scheme may not be cost effective in states that require that overtime be paid for hours worked in excess of eight a day. There may also be union resistance, since unions have expressed concern about fatigue and encroachment of overtime pay. Some workers on compressed work schedules report problems with fatigue and child care. Consequently, this scheduling option can negatively impact production and morale. In addition, supervision can be more complicated.

In the United States the federal government has been committed to job sharing. Organizations implementing job sharing have cited many advantages. It allows firms to accomplish extra work without the expense of overtime. Job sharing can allow organizations to recruit and retain employees who want flexibility. It can result in scheduling flexibility, job enrichment, and cost savings. However, many companies question the viability of this arrangement. Some feel that hiring two part-time employees is less productive than hiring one full-time employee. Other firms worry that costs will be higher because of compensation, administration, and training. Some job sharers have also reported difficulty getting promoted and receiving full benefits. In addition, some job sharers work more hours than they are paid to because employers expect more output than is realistic. Job sharing also presents some important management challenges. For example, each job sharer should have a job description that accurately defines his or her responsibilities and each job sharer should be evaluated separately. Research has shown that certain characteristics are associated with successful job sharers. These include good communication skills; flexibility; compatible work styles; complementary skills, knowledge, and abilities; willingness to make job sharing work; and a high degree of commitment to the job.

The use of part-time workers has increased worldwide, even during times when the economy has expanded. Many companies have increasingly created part-time positions as a strategy to cut labor costs. Firms have also used this option to improve scheduling, especially during peak periods. In some cases part-time positions are used to retain and recruit employees. Many labor unions have been suspicious about the creation of part-time jobs and perceive part-timers as exploited workers. Part-time employment is not always advantageous to workers. Many times compensation is low, benefits are nonexistent, and there is a lack of job security and career opportunity. A significant proportion of part-time workers work part time voluntarily. This work option also requires special managerial skills. Part-time workers must be made to feel they are in the mainstream. The research conducted by Chris Tilly (1996) is critical to understanding this work scheme, since Tilly has made the important distinction between good and bad part-time jobs. Tilly has proposed unionization as the best strategy for curbing the growth of bad part-time jobs.

Although sabbaticals were first introduced in American universities in the late nineteenth century, these sanctioned leaves did not extend beyond academia until after World War II. In the early 1960s a sabbatical was negotiated for steel and aluminum workers in the United States in order to avoid layoffs. Following this experiment, sabbaticals were introduced outside of manufacturing. However, the growth of corporate sabbaticals stalled in the 1980s as a result of layoffs and reorganization. There has been some resurgence with the competition for high-technology workers. Firms offering sabbaticals have found that this benefit offers a recruiting and retention advantage. Sabbaticals can be a morale builder, can improve productivity, and can be used to prevent burnout. These leaves provide employees with the opportunity to improve their skills and to develop a personal interest. However, many firms have been reluctant to offer sabbaticals. Some companies claim they are expensive perks and view them as disruptive to the work environment. Some employees are reluctant to take a sabbatical if the economy is uncertain or if the leave is unpaid. Others are reluctant to have colleagues assume additional work.

An option related to corporate sabbaticals is family and parental leave. Most European countries have some form of parental leave. However, in the United States the Family and Medical Leave Act has only benefited a small percentage of workers. Many experts believe the act to be flawed for several reasons. The act's definition of serious health conditions is too broad. At the same time, the act is too narrow, since coverage is limited. For example, parents are covered while parents-in-law are excluded.

Phased retirement can be a way for individuals to retire gradually. These employees reduce their full-time employment over a specified time period. Partial retirement is a related option that allows older workers to work part time before full retirement. This allows employees to combine their salary with partial retirement income. Phased retirement originated in Europe in the 1970s. In the United States most of the experimentation with this option has been in the public sector. The state of California has been one of the pioneers in this area. However, there have been some initiatives in the private sector.

Voluntary reduced work time is the flexible scheduling option that has been least utilized. In contrast, there has been growing interest in work sharing. Employees prefer this option to layoffs. Employers find this option attractive since it reduces labor costs and allows firms to respond to economic downturns.

What are the barriers to these flexible scheduling options? First, there are organizational constraints. Companies continue to reward employees on the basis of the amount of visible time spent at work. Many firms continue to use time rather than results to assess performance. Some employees are reluctant to experiment with some of these options, fearing that participation will negatively impact their career development. Middle management is the biggest obstacle. Many managers fear that they will lose control if some of these options are implemented. There are also obstacles caused by misconceptions surrounding flexible scheduling. For example, some managers are afraid to allow flexible work arrangements for fear that everyone would want a flexible schedule. There is also a perception that some of these options are difficult to organize. There is also the notion that there is no need to change the status quo. Policies can also be a barrier to implementation. Since many firms lack formal written guidelines, approval of flexibility is often ad hoc, inconsistent, and dependent upon individual managers. In addition, reporting systems can be a deterrent to flexibility. For example, many companies use a head count system, which penalizes workers working part time or sharing positions. Flexible scheduling options may also face resistance by unions. Finally, labor laws are often a barrier to flexibility. In the United States some states require employers to pay overtime to workers who work more than eight hours a day. Many countries, especially those in Europe, have laws governing the length of workdays and the scheduling of hours.

REFERENCES

Aeppel, T. 1999. Plants face challenge as boomers retire. *Wall Street Journal*, 12 July A1.

Andrews, E. S. 1992. Expanding opportunities for older workers. *Journal of Labor Research* 13 (1): 55–65.

Armour, S. 1998. Unpaid leave costly proposition, few employees feel they can take the time off. *USA Today*, 9 February, 4B.

Axel, H. 1992. *Redefining corporate sabbaticals for the 1990s*. New York: The Conference Board.

Balancing work and family demand through part-time employment and job sharing. 1995. Washington, D.C.: Office of Personnel Management, Office of Labor Relations and Workforce Performance, Work and Family Program Center.

Bankston, K. 1996. Flextime. *Credit Union Management* 19 (5): 38–41.

Barker, K., and K. Christensen, eds. 1998. *Contingent work: American employment relations in transition*. Ithaca, N.Y.: ILR Press.

Barnett, A. A. 1997. Fixing dysfunctional family leave. *Business and Health* 15 (3): 22–25.

Bastian, J. 1994. *A matter of time: From work sharing to temporal flexibility in Belgium, France, and Britain*. Aldershot, England: Avebury.

Becker, F., A. J. Rappaport, K. L. Quinn, and W. R. Sims. 1993. *New working practices: Benchmarking flexible scheduling, staffing and work location in an international context*. Ithaca, N.Y.: Cornell University, International Workplace Studies Program.

Benson, M. 1997. Economics of aging rattles many nations. *The Star Ledger* (Newark, N.J.), 1 June, 12.

Best, F. 1981. *Work sharing: Issues, policy options and prospects.* Kalamazoo, Mich.: W. E. Upjohn Institute for Employment Research.

Biernat, B. A. 1997. Employed parents' preference for reduced job hours in relation to job and family characteristics. Ph.D. diss., University of Minnesota.

Boles, M. 1997. Flexible work arrangements go mainstream. *Workforce* 76 (8): 24.

Bolle, P. 1997. Part-time work: Solution or trap? *International Labour Review* 136: 557–579.

Bosch, G. 1990. From 40 to 35 hours: Reduction and flexibilisation of the working week in the Federal Republic of Germany. *International Labour Review* 129: 611–627.

———. 1995. *Flexibility and work organisation: Report of Expert Working Group.* Luxembourg: Office for Official Publications of the European Communities.

Brewster, C. 1997. Flexible working in Europe: A review of the evidence. *Management International Review* 37 (1): 85–103.

Brooks, N. R. 1998. Work and careers balancing act: New studies show dollar benefits of flexible work arrangements. *Los Angeles Times*, 9 August, D5.

Burkins, G. 1999. A special new report about life on the job—and trends taking shape there. *Wall Street Journal*, 5 October, A1.

Burr, M. 1997. Permanent temps. *Government Executive* 29 (3): 40–45.

Busted—for working hard. 1999. *Business Week*, 3 May, 64.

Cascio, W. F. 1998. *Managing human resources: Productivity, quality of work life, profits.* 5th ed. New York: McGraw-Hill.

Casey, B., H. Metcalf, and N. Millward. 1997. *Employers' Use of Flexible Labour.* London: Policy Studies Institute.

Catalyst. 1993. *Flexible work arrangements II: Succeeding with part-time options.* New York: Catalyst.

———. 1998. *A new approach to flexibility: Managing the work/time equation.* New York: Catalyst.

Chapin, V. J. 1992. *Work life and personal needs, the job-sharing option: A background paper.* Ottawa: Women's Bureau, Labour Canada.

Christensen, K. 1990. Here we go into the "high-flex" era. *Across the Board* 27 (7–8): 22–23.

Christensen, K. E., and G. L. Staines. 1990. Flextime: A viable solution to work/family conflict? *Journal of Family Issues* 11 (4): 455–476.

Claveria, S. K. 1992. *Phased retirement for public employees.* Honolulu: Legislative Reference Bureau.

Cliff, D. 1991. Negotiating a flexible retirement: Further paid work and the quality of life in early retirement. *Ageing and Society* 11: 319–340.

Clinton steps up pressure for family leave. 1997. *New York Times*, 13 April, sect. 1, p. 27.

Clinton, W. J. 1999. Memorandum on new tools to help parents balance work and family. *Weekly Compilation of Presidential Documents* 35: 978–979.

Commission finds few problems with FMLA: President Clinton proposes law's expansion. 1996. *Employee Benefit Plan Review* 51 (3): 36.

Compressed work weeks pick up steam. 1998. *St. Louis Post-Dispatch*, 24 September, C5.

Contingent Employment. 1995. *HR Executive Review* 3 (2): entire issue.

Deutschman, A. 1991. Pioneers of the new balance. *Fortune*, 20 May, 60–68.

Douglas, G. H. 1995. Sabbaticals in the age of productivity. *Chronicle of Higher Education*, 13 October, B3.

Downsizing. 1997. *Work–Family Roundtable* 7 (2): entire issue.

Drake, E. 1997. A legal perspective on work–family issues. In *Integrating work and family: Challenges and choices for a changing world*, edited by S. Parasuraman and J. H. Greenhaus. Westport, Conn.: Quorum Books.

Dutton, G. 1998. Retirees take an encore. *HR Focus* 75 (5): 1, 6.

Dym, B. 1998. Retire: No way. *Boston Globe*, 20 September, F1.

Education initiatives. 1997. *Work–Family Roundtable* 7 (1): entire issue.

Edwards, B. 1998. Part of the whole: Part-time job a good way to try out a new career. *Chicago Tribune*, 11 October, sect. C, p. 69.

Employment: 16% of EU workers are part-time. 1997. *European Report*, 20 September, sect. 2252.

Estess, P. S. 1996. *Work concepts for the future: Managing alternative work arrangements*. Menlo Park, Calif.: Crisp.

Fagan, C., and J. O'Reilly. 1998. Conceptualising part-time work: The value of an integrated comparative perspective. In *Part-time prospects: An international comparison of part-time work in Europe, North America and the Pacific Rim*, edited by J. O'Reilly and C. Fagan. London: Routledge.

Family and medical leave. 1994. *Work–Family Roundtable* 4 (4): entire issue.

Ferber, M. A., B. O'Farrell, and L. R. Allen, eds. 1991. *Work and family: Policies for a changing work force*. Washington, D.C.: National Academy Press.

Flak over FMLA. 1997. *HR Focus* 74 (6): 7.

Flexibility options continue growth. 1996. *European Industrial Relations Review*, May, 27–29.

Flexible options for the older workforce. 1998. *HR Focus* 75 (1): 5.

Flexible work schedules. 1990. *Supervision* 51 (6): 3–4.

Flynn, G. 1999. What to do after an FMLA leave. *Workforce* 78 (4): 104–107.

French employers protest shortened workweek. 1999. *New York Times*, 5 October, international business sect., p. 4.

Fried, M. 1998. *Taking time: Parental leave policy and corporate culture*. Philadelphia: Temple University Press.

Friedman, D. E. 1991. *Linking work–family issues to the bottom line*. New York: The Conference Board.

Gardner, M. 1997. Innovative programs aim to keep seniors as productive workers. *Christian Science Monitor*, 14 November, 10.

Gill, B. 1998. Flextime benefits employees and employers. *American Printer*, February, 70.

Ginsberg, S. 1997. To some employers, an expanded family leave act won't fly. *Washington Post*, 23 March, H6.

Gore, A. 1997. *Turning the key: Unlocking human potential in the family-friendly federal workplace: A status report on federal workplace family-friendly initiatives*. Washington, D.C.: GPO.

Gottlieb, B. H., E. K. Kelloway, and E. J. Barham. 1998. *Flexible work arrangements: Managing the work–family boundary*. Chichester, England: Wiley.

Government launches part-time work initiative. 1994. *European Industrial Relations Review*, August, 21–22.

The graying professoriate. 1999. *Chronicle of Higher Education*, 3 September, A18.

Grensing, L. 1991. *Motivating today's work force: When the carrot can't always be cash*. North Vancouver, British Columbia: Self-Counsel Press.

———. 1996. When the carrot can't be cash. *Security Management* 4 (12): 25–27.

Grensing-Pophal, L. 1993. Flextime lets night owls and early birds soar. *Office Systems* 10 (6): 66–67.

Guiding principles for managing a flexible workplace. 1997. *Getting Results . . . for the Hands-On Manager* (special report supplement), October, 1–2.

Haffner, D. W. 1997. A sabbatical's lessons. *SIECUS Report* 25 (3): 3.

Health risks of retirement. 1997. *Worklife Report* 10 (3): 2–3.

Higgins, A. 1999. Medical leave law has questions. *Gannet News Service* [online]. Dow Jones Interactive/Publications Library. [cited 13 April 1999].

How does a 4-day work week sound? May be healthier. 1997. *Executive Health's Good Health Report*, 1 January, 8.

How to make a job share work for you. 1999. *Parenting*, October, 63.

Hunt, J. 1999. Has work-sharing worked in Germany? *Quarterly Journal of Economics* 114: 117–148.

Inman, C., and C. Enz. 1995. Shattering the myths of the part-time worker. *Cornell Hotel and Restaurant Administration Quarterly* 36 (5): 70–73.

Jackson, M. 1998. Working life: Companies weigh pros and cons of sabbaticals. *The Record* (Northern New Jersey), 28 September, H8.

Jackson, R. L. 1997. Clinton expands unpaid leave for federal workers. *Los Angeles Times*, 13 April, 1.

Job sharing for federal employees. 1990. Washington, D.C.: Office of Personnel Management, Career Entry and Employee Development Group, Office of Staffing Policy and Operations.

Job-sharing: Widely offered, little used. 1994. *Training* 31 (11): 12.

Klaus, L. A. 1997. Work-life programs help reduce employee absenteeism. *Quality Progress*, 1 November, 13.

Kleiman, C. 1997. Leave act that may grow: Good news for workers at smaller firms. *Chicago Tribune*, 21 October, business sect., p. 4.

Klein, E. 1989. Beyond the paycheck. *D and B Reports* 37 (2): 36–39.

Koss-Feder, L. 1998. Perks that work: Flexible benefits are taking some interesting new twists, and turning a profit from employee loyalty. *Time*, 9 November, *Time* select business report section.

Kruger, P. 1998. Family leave: Debating the future. *Parenting*, February, 61.

Levine, H. Z. 1987a. Alternative work schedules: Do they meet workforce needs? Part 1. *Personnel* 64 (2): 57–62.

———. 1987b. Alternative work schedules: Do they meet workforce needs? Part 2. *Personnel* 64 (4): 66–71.

Levine, J. A., and T. L. Pittinsky. 1997. *Working fathers: New strategies for balancing work and family*. Reading, Mass.: Addison-Wesley.

Lewis, S. 1997. An international perspective on work–family issues. In *Integrating work and family: Challenges and choices for a changing world*, edited by S. Parasuraman and J. H. Greenhaus. Westport, Conn.: Quorum Books.

The long and short of allowing extended leave. 1997. *Management Today*, October, 10.

Louchheim, F. P. 1990. Executive retirement: Change trauma into retirement. *Personnel Journal* 69 (3): 26–32.

Lussier, R. N. 1990a. Should your organization use flextime? *Supervision* 51 (9): 14–16.

———. 1990b. Should your organization use job sharing? *Supervision* 51 (4): 9–11.

Maier, M., C. Thompson, and C. Thomas. 1991. Corporate responsiveness and resistance to work–family interdependence in the United States. *Equal Opportunities International* 10 (3/4): 25–32.

Maiwald, C. R., J. L. Pierce, J. W. Newstrom, and B. P. Sunoo. 1997. Workin' 8 p.m. to 8 a.m. and lovin' every minute of it. *Workforce* 76 (7): 30.

Managers and TUC unite to examine the part time worker. 1996. *Management Services* 40 (11): 4.

Mann, J. 1997. Taking family leave the next step. *Washington Post*, 30 May, E3.

Marks, M. R. 1997. Party politics and family policy: The case of the Family and Medical Leave Act. *Journal of Family Issues* 18 (1): 55–70.

Marshall, N. L. 1993. *Having it all: Managing jobs and children*. Wellesley, Mass.: Wellesley College, Center for Research on Women.

Martinez, M. N. 1997. Work-life programs reap business benefits. *HRMagazine* 42 (6): 110–114.

Mattis, M. C. 1990. New forms of flexible work arrangements for managers and professionals: Myths and realities. *Human Resource Planning* 13 (2): 133–146.

McCaffery, M. K. 1996. Part-timers pick up speed. *Management Review* 85 (11): 6.

McCampbell, A. S. 1996. Benefits achieved through alternative work schedules. *Human Resource Planning* 19 (3): 30–37.

McGuire, J. B., and J. R. Liro. 1986. Flexible work schedules, work attitudes, and perceptions of productivity. *Public Personnel Management* 15 (1): 65–73.

Mendels, P. 1992. Corporate sabbaticals take bite out of burnout, keep worker fresh. *Ottawa Citizen*, 9 May, business sect., p. J2.

Monsour, T. 1994. Friendly persuasion. *Working Mother*, February, 38–40.

Moskowitz, D. B., and N. Rowell. 1999. Struggling with FMLA's scope. *Business and Health* 17 (9): 45–46.

Mueller, B. 1996. The buzzword for carmakers is flexibility. *Worldbusiness* 2 (5): 12.

Naisbitt, J. 1985. Corporate sabbaticals take off. *San Diego Union-Tribune*, 19 November, p. C2.

National Park Service. 1987. *Alternative work schedules in the National Park Service: A handbook for supervisors*. Washington, D.C.: Branch of Labor and Employee Relations, Personnel Division.

Nollen, S. D. 1982. *Work schedules in practice: Managing time in a changing society*. New York: Van Nostrand Reinhold.

O'Brian, J. D. 1994. Flexible scheduling has many benefits and pitfalls. *Supervisory Management* 39 (9): 1–2.

O'Hara, B. 1993. *Working harder isn't working*. Vancouver, British Columbia: New Star Books.

———. 1994. *Put work in its place: How to redesign your job to fit your life*. 2d ed. Vancouver, British Columbia: New Star Books.

O'Hara, B., and G. Williams. 1990. *A manager's guide to phased retirement*. Victoria, British Columbia: Work Well Publications.

Olmsted, B. 1987. (Flex)time is money. *Management Review* 76 (11): 47–51.

———. 1990–1991. Flexible work arrangements: A sea of change for managers: Flexibility is the key for staffing and scheduling in the 1990s. *Employment Relations Today* 17 (4): 291–296.

Olmsted, B., and S. Smith. 1994. *Creating a flexible workplace: How to select & manage alternative work options*. 2d ed. New York: AMACOM.

———. 1996. *The job sharing handbook*. Rev. ed. San Francisco: New Ways to Work.

———. 1997. *Managing in a flexible workplace*. New York: American Management Association.

O'Reilly, J., and C. Fagan, eds. 1998. *Part-time prospects: An international comparison of part-time work in Europe, North America and the Pacific Rim*. London: Routledge.

Paltell, E. 1999. FMLA: After six years a bit more clarity. *HRMagazine* 44 (9): 144–150.

Part-time employment. 1996. *Work–Family Roundtable* 6 (1): entire issue.

Part-time, work-at-home add flexibility. 1992. *Employment Benefit Plan Review* 46 (9): 26–28.

Pay, insurance disparity decried in part-timer study. 1998. *Baltimore Sun*, 21 August, 3C.

Peak, M. H. 1996. Face-time follies. *Management Review* 85 (3): 1.

Pesek, J. G., and C. McGee. 1989. An analysis of job sharing, full-time and part-time work arrangements: One hospital's experience. *American Business Review* 7 (2): 34–40.

Pettersson, L. 1993. Sweden. In *Times are changing: Working time in 14 industrialised countries*, edited by G. Bosch, P. Dawkings, and F. Michon. Geneva: International Institute for Labour Studies.

Pleck, J. H. 1994. *Family-supportive employer policies and men: A perspective*. Working paper series no. 274. Wellesley, Mass.: Wellesley College, Center for Research on Women.

Poole, S. M., and V. Conwell. 1997. UPS vs. Teamsters: Some prefer to put in less than 40 hours. *Atlanta Journal and Constitution*, 6 August, Business sect., p. 3E.

Price, M. S., and S. L. Rouse. 1992. Attorney job-sharing: A workable alternative. *Colorado Lawyer* 21 (1): 53–56.

Ralston, D. A. 1989. The benefits of flextime: Real or imagined? *Journal of Organizational Behavior* 10: 369–373.

Ramirez, A. 1989. Making better use of older workers. *Fortune*, 30 January, 179.

Rich, J. R. 1997. Double your pleasure, double your fun—job sharing can work for all involved. *Boston Herald*, 12 October, Job sect., p. 87.

Robinson, J. P., and G. Godbey. 1997. *Time for life: The surprising ways Americans use their time.* University Park: Pennsylvania State University Press.

Rogak, L. A. 1994. *Time off from work: Using sabbaticals to enhance your life while keeping your career on track.* New York: Wiley.

Ronen, S. 1981. *Flexible working hours: An innovation in the quality of work life.* New York: McGraw-Hill.

———. 1984. *Alternative work schedules: Selecting . . . implementing . . . and evaluating.* Homewood, Ill.: Dow Jones Irwin.

Ruhm, C. J., and J. L. Teague. 1997. Parental leave policies in Europe and North America. In *Gender and family issues in the workplace,* edited by F. D. Blau and R. G. Ehrenberg. New York: Sage.

Schachter, H. 1996. Slaves of the new economy. *Canadian Business* 69 (4): 86–92.

Schwartz, D. B. 1994. *An examination of the impact of family-friendly policies on the glass ceiling.* New York: Families and Work Institute.

Semas, J. H. 1997. Taking off from the hi-tech grind. *HRMagazine* 42 (9): 122–129.

Sheley, E. 1996. Job sharing offers unique challenges. *HRMagazine* 41 (1): 46–49.

Shellenbarger, S. 1997. Sought-after workers now have the clout to demand flexibility. *Wall Street Journal,* 17 September, B1.

Shift work. 1996. *Work–Family Roundtable* 6 (3): entire issue.

Solomon, C. M. 1994. Job sharing: One job, double headache? *Personnel Journal* 73 (9): 88–96.

Sommer, K. L., and D. Y. Malins. 1991. Flexible work solutions. *Small Business Reports* 16 (8): 29–40.

Stafford, D. 1998. Labor report: Part-time workers are missing out. *Sacramento Bee,* 6 September, D3.

State employees flex their options. 1995. *Training and Development,* October, 11–12.

Still a flexible friend? A survey of flextime arrangements. 1996. *IRS Employment Review,* March, 5–16.

Sunoo, B. P. 1996. How to manage compressed workweeks. *Personnel Journal* 75 (1): 110.

Sunoo, B. P., and G. Flynn. 1996. FMLA found to be neither expensive nor overused. *Personnel Journal* 75 (3): 19.

Swank, C. 1982. *Phased retirement: The European experience.* Washington, D.C.: National Council for Alternative Work Patterns.

Swart, J. C. 1978. *A flexible approach to working hours.* New York: AMACOM.

Tilly, C. 1996. *Half a job: Bad and good part-time jobs in a changing labor market.* Philadelphia: Temple University Press.

Tober, P. A. 1988. The emerging flexible workplace. *Compensation and Benefits Review* 20 (1): 70–74.

U.S. Senate. 1997. *Preparing for the baby boomers' retirement: The role of employment: Forum before the Special Committee on Aging.* Washington, D.C.: GPO.

Valentine, P. W. 1999. Paramedic wins suit over parental leave. *Washington Post,* 3 February, B3.

Vega, A., and M. J. Gilbert. 1997. Longer days, shorter weeks: Compressed work weeks in policing. *Public Personnel Management* 26: 391–402.

Venne, R. A. 1993. Alternative worktime arrangements: The compressed workweek. Ph.D. diss., University of Toronto.

————. 1997. The impact of compressed workweek on absenteeism. *Relations Industrielles* 52: 382–400.

Walker, T. 1998. Female-laden firms best for work–family workplace: A survey examines which firms provide such things as child-care assistance and flextime. *Orange County Register*, 15 July, C1.

Watson, B. S. 1995. Share and share alike. *Management Review* 84 (10): 50–52.

Wisensale, S. K. 1997. The White House and Congress on child care and family leave policy: From Carter to Clinton. *Policy Studies Journal* 25 (1): 75–86.

Zachary, M. K. 1999. Labor law for supervisors: FMLA poses many issues for companies. *Supervision* 60 (7): 23–26.

CHAPTER 3

Telecommuting

Jack Nilles (1998), the scientist who is regarded as the father of telecommuting, coined the term in the early 1970s. Nilles defines telecommuting as "periodic work out of the principal office, one or more days per week either at home, a client's site, or in a telework center" (p. 1). Although the term "telework" is often used in Europe instead of telecommuting, Nilles does not regard them as interchangeable. He views teleworking as a strategy for "moving the work to the workers instead of moving the workers to work," and defines teleworking as "any form of substitution of information technologies (such as telecommunications and computers) for work-related travel" (p. 1). Nilles (1994, 1998) regards telecommuting as a form of teleworking.

NO UNIFORM DEFINITION

However, there is no generally accepted definition of telecommuting or teleworking. Various synonyms have been used for telecommuting and telework. Frank Schiff used the term "flexiplace" as early as 1971 (Telework—Attitudes of the Social Partners 1986). Futurist Alvin Toffler (1980) wrote about the electronic cottage in *The Third Wave*. Other terms used to describe this new way of working include electronic home-work, flexplace, remote work, dispersed working, telesubstitution, independent work location, home-based work, alternative officing, distributed work, the virtual office, geographically independent work, distance work, distance staffing, off-site work, home working, and telecottage (Telework—Attitudes of the Social Partners 1986; Christensen 1990; Gray, Hodson, and Gordon 1993; Olmsted and Smith 1994; Richter 1996; Thompson 1996; Guiding Principles for Managing a Flexible Workplace 1997). Telecommuters have also been called flexiworkers, teleguerillas, home-based nomads, and electronic moon-lighters (Nilles 1998; Qvortrup 1998). June Langhoff (1999), a veteran telecommuter and leading authority on remote work, views telecommuting as "a major sociological trend" that has created "the anyplace, anytime workspace" (p. 17). Langhoff's definition reflects the recent trend toward the notion that work can be performed any-where (Qvortrup 1998).

Some definitions of teleworking and telecommuting exclude a sig-nificant proportion of people who work out of their homes, such as home-based businesses, consultants, and freelance workers (Qvortrup 1998). Richter (1996) makes the distinction between "working at home" and "working from home" (p. 4837). Lars Qvortrup (1998) defines telework as electronically mediated work across distance and includes individuals working for companies as well as the self-employed. Alice Bredin's (1996) definition of the virtual office is broad enough to in-clude those that "operate with just a phone and a pad of paper" (p. 3). Bredin's virtual office workers include road warriors, salespeople working on the road with portable computers, cellular phones, and other technologies. The lack of a uniform definition of telework or telecommute is problematic, since it makes it difficult to count the number of remote workers (Huws, Korte, and Robinson 1990). Lars Qvortrup (1998) developed an excellent analogy for this problem of defining teleworkers. He noted that "counting teleworkers is like mea-suring a rubber band" since "the result depends on how far you stretch your definition" (p. 21). Since there is no universally accepted defini-tion of telecommuting or teleworking, these terms are used inter-changeably in this chapter. Although there is no consistency about defining remote workers, there is a general consensus that telecom-muters can be full-time or part-time workers.

THE HISTORY OF TELECOMMUTING

Korte and Wynne (1996) have characterized the history of telecom-muting as being "more evolutionary than revolutionary" (p. 5). This evolution is traced by Jackson and Van der Wielen (1998a) in the introductory chapter of *Teleworking: International Perspectives: From Telecommuting to the Virtual Organisation*. They provide a decade-by-decade summary of telecommuting. In the 1970s telecommuting was perceived as a strategy to save energy and reduce commuting time. According to Jackson and Van der Wielen, in the 1980s telecommuting was viewed as an option to help workers balance work and home and to recruit employees in areas where there were shortages. Finally, in the 1990s the authors argue that telecommuting was perceived as an arrangement that could make work time and work space more productive. Another account of the first two decades of telecommuting can be found in Huws, Korte, and Robinson's (1990) comprehensive study of telecommuting in fourteen European countries.

The first writings on telecommuting emerged in the 1970s. One of the most important was *The Telecomunications–Transportation Tradeoff: Options for Tomorrow* (Nilles et al. 1976). This book introduced the idea that information technologies could substitute for the journey to work. Many of the early writings on telecommuting were overly optimistic. Some writings from this period predicted that most Americans would be working remotely by the year 1990 (Korte and Wynne 1996). Huws, Korte, and Robinson noted that the 1980s publications were more balanced, presenting both negative and positive views of telecommuting. More important, they noted that the 1980s saw the development of research studies on telecommuting, substantive articles in management and computing periodicals, manuals for managers, and policy overviews and conference proceedings by government agencies. Both the 1980s and 1990s were marked by visionary writings about the impact of telecommuting. Four futurists in particular (Alvin Toffler, Roger Naisbitt, Nicholas Negroponte, and William Knoke) projected that telecommuting will eliminate the need for face-to-face interactions and will make cities obsolete (Gaspar and Glaeser 1996). McCloskey and Igbaria (1998) conducted a comprehensive review of the literature on telecommuting. While they found several hundred articles on the topic in practitioner-oriented periodicals and many practical manuals, they found only thirty-two published empirical research studies.

A brief history of telecommuting in the United States can be found in Jack Nilles's (1998) most recent book, *Managing Telework: Strategies for Managing the Virtual Workforce*. The oil crisis of the early 1970s induced interest in telecommuting in the United States. During this period, Jack Nilles was an engineer who worked on projects for the National Aeronautics and Space Administration (NASA). Nilles was frustrated by the gridlock he encountered every morning on his commute to work in southern California. He envisioned telecommuting as a strategy to reduce commuting time and in turn save energy. In the early 1970s Nilles led an interdisciplinary research team that received funding from the National Science Foundation to study telecommuting. The demonstration project that his team conducted during 1973–1974 provided evidence that telecommuting could be an effective strategy for reducing energy consumption. In the 1980s Nilles helped the state of California develop large-scale telecommuting pilots. During this same period, Nilles persuaded a group of Fortune 100 companies to participate in a telecommuting pilot headed by the University of Southern California's Center for Futures Research. These telecommuting pilots in the public and private sectors were successful. In all of the tests, however, Nilles found that the major barriers to telecommuting were management resistance and inadequate training for managers of telecommuting. These demonstration projects provided the impetus for the governor of California to require state agencies to consider telecommuting as an option for state employees, effective 1990. In the early 1990s the state of California established neighborhood telework centers throughout the state.

While the state of California has been a leader in experimenting with telecommuting, other states have also experimented with remote work. June Langhoff's (1999) inventory of states with telecommuting projects includes not only California, but also Arizona, Colorado, Connecticut, Florida, Georgia, Hawaii, Massachusetts, Minnesota, New Jersey, Oregon, Utah, Virginia, Washington, and Wisconsin. The federal government has also been a leader in the development of telecommuting initiatives. In 1989 former president George Bush publicly endorsed telecommuting as a strategy to retain and recruit employees, reduce office space, and reduce traffic congestion, pollution, and energy consumption (Speeth 1992). The General Services Administration and other federal agencies have experimented with telecommuting as part of the Federal Flexible Workplace Project, a project which encompasses a range of flexible options (U.S. House 1992). Telecommuters working for federal agencies work at home as well as in interagency satellite work centers. The General Services Administration operates these telecommuting centers around Washington, D.C., Los Angeles, Atlanta, Chicago, Philadelphia, and other cities (Gore 1997). Sims, Joroff, and Becker (1996) describe these centers as "like—but not like—a central office" (p. 89). A typical center has workstations, conference rooms, networked personal computers, telephones, fax machines, copiers, and a kitchenette. Most of the federal employees who use them live nearby. Employees from several federal agencies use them. Langhoff (1999) found telecommuting programs in place at many federal agencies, including the Air Force, the commerce department, the General Services Administration, the Environmental Protection Agency, the department of the interior, the labor department, the National Aeronautics and Space Administration, the Navy, the Smithsonian Institution, the transportation department, and the state department. In 1997 Vice President Gore reported that about 10,000 federal workers were working from home, at telecommuting centers, or at other remote locations. The goal of the federal government is to have 60,000 federal telecommuters (3 percent of the federal workforce) telecommuting by the end of 2002 (Gore 1997; Langhoff 1999). The federal government estimates that this would result in a net savings of $150 million per year (Langhoff 1999).

Interest in teleworking is growing rapidly in Canada. The Canadian Telework Association's Web site provides valuable information on the status of telecommuting in Canada, including survey data (*Canadian Telework Scene* 1999). A 1998 study involving several thousand Canadians found that half of Canadian workers (55 percent) want to telework now. In 1993, 600,000 Canadians telecommuted. In 1997 the number of telecommuters grew to 1 million. By 2001 the number of teleworkers is projected to grow to 1.5 million. Teleworking may experience phenomenal growth given several conditions favorable to telecommuting. First, Canada has a high per capita ratio of information workers. Personal-computer ownership is high and Internet access costs are low. Since Canada is geographically vast, working at a distance would be an attractive alternative to traveling to work.

It is more difficult to track the history of commuting in Europe. Korte and Wynne (1996) observed that researching European teleworking is particularly problematic, since information is dispersed across many publications from different countries. In addition, they found that much of the literature was general and difficult to compare. The lack of a uniform definition contributes to this problem. Lars Qvortrup (1998) noted that in the 1970s and 1980s European teleworking was often associated with low-paid, unskilled office work done on a contractual or freelance basis. Nilles (1998) recalled that some small-scale teleworking projects were carried out in Europe in the late 1970s and early 1980s. For the most part, teleworking was not implemented in Europe until the 1980s, and in the mid-1980s European teleworkers were most likely to be data processors or salespersons (Korte and Wynne 1996). In the spring and summer of 1996 the *European Industrial Relations Review* published a three-part series titled "Teleworking in Europe." These articles provide a good status report on teleworking practice in fifteen European countries.

Celia Stanworth (1996) has chronicled the history of teleworking in the United Kingdom. Teleworking was largely ignored until the late 1980s. The exceptions were the pioneers, a small number of firms (such as the FI Group, Rank Xerox, and ICL) who were using teleworkers. The first groups of British teleworkers were technical specialists and professionals, mostly in the area of information technology. Teleworking then spread to other sections of the economy, such as finance and local government. However, Stanworth concluded that although teleworking is still relatively rare in the United Kingdom, "there are signs that it is becoming an option which is being used by a wider range of employers, both in services and in manufacturing" (p. 11). In late 1994 and early 1995 Andrew Bibby (1995) investigated teleworking practice in Britain and Ireland. His visited a number of community-based telecottages and teleworking offices. In addition, he interviewed individual teleworkers throughout the United Kingdom and Ireland. This research was the basis for his book *Teleworking: Thirteen Journeys to the Future of Work*, a highly readable and interesting account of what is actually happening in practice with regard to remote work.

In the mid-1980s, 16,000 households in Germany, France, Italy, and the United Kingdom were surveyed regarding their attitudes toward telework. About 4,000 people were interviewed in each country. Questions were restricted to home-based telework for fear that respondents would be unfamiliar with concepts such as satellite work centers. The results of this survey are reported in two separate books: *Telework: Towards the Elusive Office* (Huws, Korte, and Robinson 1990) and *Telework: Penetration, Potential and Practice in Europe* (Korte and Wynne 1996). Interest in telework varied widely between these countries. Interest in telework was 8.5 percent in Germany, 11 percent in Italy, 14 percent in France, and 23 percent in the United Kingdom. Lack of interest in telework was highest in Germany (53 percent of the sample had no interest in telework) and lowest in Italy (where 28 percent had no interest). However, interest in telework grew significantly in Europe between the mid-1980s and the mid-1990s. In mid-1994 more than 5,000 people were interviewed in Germany, France, Italy, and the United Kingdom regarding their interest in telework. In addition, approximately 2,500 managers were interviewed regarding their interest in telework. The results of these surveys can be found in *Telework: Penetration, Potential and Practice in Europe*. Korte and Wynne compared this 1994 survey data to the survey data from the mid-1980s. In 1994 interest in telework approached 40 percent in France, Italy, and the United Kingdom. German interest in telework still lagged behind, but by a smaller margin. Interest in telework was 40 percent in France, 36 percent in Italy and the United Kingdom, and 31 percent in Germany.

In the mid-1980s Empirica interviewed 4,000 managers in Germany, France, Italy, and the United Kingdom regarding their attitudes and willingness to experiment with teleworking. These survey results can also be found in *Telework: Towards the Elusive Office* (Huws, Korte, and Robinson 1990) and *Telework: Penetration, Potential and Practice in Europe* (Korte and Wynn 1996). These managers represented a cross-section of manufacturers and service industries in both the public and private sectors. These interviews indicated that the greater the size of a company, the greater the interest in telework. The only exception was among Italian managers. Also, the larger the company, the greater the variety of tasks considered appropriate for telework. The 1994 surveys on European teleworking indicated that the interest in telework far outweighed the willingness of managers to experiment with teleworking. Obstacles to teleworking were not technological but related to the perception that teleworking was difficult to manage (Korte and Wynne 1996).

In the early 1990s European telework got a boost with the Telework Developments and Trend (TELDET) project. This project, funded by the European Commission, began in 1994 and was completed in June 1995. *Telework: Penetration, Potential and Practice in Europe* (Korte and Wynne 1996), was a result of this project. The project had three goals: surveying the penetration, potential, and practice of telework in Europe; providing European case studies on teleworking; and analyzing the conditions for the development of European teleworking. Almost sixty case studies of teleworking were analyzed. The majority of these case studies came from the private sector and began in the mid 1980s and early 1990s. One exception was the teleworking scheme implemented by ICL Enterprise Systems, a British computer company, in 1969. The types of tasks involved in these case studies included data entry, translating, typing, computer-assisted design, consulting, sales, marketing, and legal work. In the majority of these case studies teleworkers worked on average three days at home per week. Teleworkers were spaced out between metropolitan, urban, suburban, and rural areas. These case studies represented a diversity of projects. Some of the most interesting case studies were conducted in Scandinavia, particularly in Finland and Denmark. Some projects, such as the project for telework in the Archipelago of Southwest Finland, used telework to promote development. Another interesting initiative was the project developed by Ireland's Ability Enterprises Ltd. to give disabled workers an opportunity to telework.

The telecottage movement originated in Scandinavia in the mid-1980s and is an established movement in Europe (Reid 1993; Huws 1995). A telecottage is slightly different from a telecenter. *Follow-Up to the White Paper* (Huws 1995), a European Commmunity publication, provides a detailed definition and history of teleworking from telecottages. The concept of the telecottage is attributed to Hennig Albrechtsen, a linguist and former U.N. interpreter (Reid 1993). Albrechtsen retired to Vemdalen, a remote village in northern Sweden, and was concerned by the lack of employment opportunities. He established what is considered the first telecottage in Vemdalen. In Britain the first telecottage was established in 1989. More than 100

British telecottages are associated with the Telecottage Association. Most telecottages are established by local individuals or groups with a range of social and economic missions. These include generating local employment, encouraging the development of new businesses, providing information-technology training, and providing information-technology services for local businesses. Some telecottages act as employment agencies, negotiating contracts between local or distant employers and local people doing the work. Others act as brokers, putting teleworkers in contact with potential employers but not negotiating the individual contract. Some telecottages focus on training. Telecottages may also provide a workspace so people who are already employed can work locally instead of commuting.

In contrast, a telecenter is defined as a neighborhood telework center equipped with childcare facilities. Telecenters were viewed as a positive development since they could provide social interaction and child care for workers. However, as *Follow-Up to the White Paper* (Huws 1995) notes, there have been several well-publicized failures in Sweden, France, Denmark, and the United Kingdom. Early experiments with telecenters and telecottages often involved workers with low-level skills such as data entry and typing and word processing. However, some experts believe that there are now many highly skilled professionals in Europe who would be willing to move to rural areas and work out of these telecottages or telecenters.

In 1996 Brunel University (England) sponsored a workshop titled "New International Perspectives on Telework." This interdisciplinary workshop brought together researchers in management, sociology, economics, anthropology, philosophy, and transportation studies. The book *Teleworking: International Perspectives: From Telecommuting to the Virtual Organisation* (Jackson and Van der Wielen 1998b) grew out of this workshop. The first part of this book traces the evolution of teleworking. As more scholarly publications on telecommuting emerge, the history of this movement should be better chronicled.

FACTORS DRIVING THE GROWTH OF TELECOMMUTING

The energy crisis of the 1970s and the need to save fuel drove the early development of telecommuting. Even after the oil crisis abated, telecommuting was perceived as a strategy for reducing traffic congestion, air pollution, and commuting time. In 1990 the Clean Air Act was amended to include a provision requiring companies with 100 or more employees to reduce the number of workers commuting by car (Richter 1996). Telecommuting was a means to achieve this reduction. In addition, several regions of the United States were identified for air pollution cleanup: Baltimore, Boston, Chicago, Houston, Los Angeles, New York, Philadelphia, San Diego, and California's Ventura County (Schepp and Schepp 1995). Some states also passed clean-air amendments (Eldib and Minoli 1995). Many companies experimented with telecommuting in an effort to avoid penalties associated with non-compliance with these regulations. European interest in telecommuting has also been driven by congestion in major cities (Moorcroft and Bennett 1995).

Technology has enabled and driven the telecommuting movement (Hollister 1995). Personal computers have become widely available and affordable as well as portable computers, cellular phones, voicemail, and fax machines. Improvement in the telecommunications infrastructure has resulted in the development of high-speed data links between the home and office. The growth of an information-based economy has created a large number of jobs suitable for telecommuting.

Workers have become interested in telecommuting for a variety of reasons. Eldib and Minoli (1995) have identified several employee-driven factors: a desire to become more productive, a need to better balance work/family obligations, a desire to reduce commuting time, a need for a more flexible schedule, and a desire to be one's own boss. Richter (1996) observed that telecommuting fits well with the mindset of many baby boomers who want autonomy, are entrepreneurial, and are less concerned with career advancement. Many experts believe that interest in telecommuting will increase because young workers moving into the workforce are much more comfortable with computers and grasp the potential of this way of working (Moorcroft and Bennett 1995; De Lisser 1999). This hypothesis was supported by a European research study that found interest in teleworking was significantly higher among workers under the age of forty (Moorcroft and Bennett 1995).

Many employer-driven factors are driving the growth of telecommuting. Telecommuting is being used as a tool to recruit and retain highly skilled workers, especially information-technology workers. Jack Nilles works as a consultant to organizations implementing telecommuting. In a 1999 interview he reported that the primary reason his clients developed telecommuting initiatives was to improve the recruitment and retention of workers (Dash 1999). The ability to telecommute can be a powerful retention tool. In another interview, Nilles estimated that "employees who telecommute are 30 percent to 40 percent more likely to stay with a company than those who do not" (Koch 1998, A18). By reducing turnover, companies are also able to reduce recruitment and training costs. A 1998 survey commissioned by the Colorado Telework Coalition (a coalition of more than 200 Colorado businesses, government agencies, and business organizations)

found that Colorado companies were unable to attract high-tech workers because the number of workers demanding flexibility was greater
than the number of Colorado firms permitting telecommuting (Closing the Telework Gap Critical if Colorado Is to Retain Lead in Competition for High-Tech Workers 1998).

Telecommuting also gives companies the ability to hire the best can-
didate for a job, regardless of where the company or employee is located. This can be a real advantage for small companies that might
otherwise have difficulty recruiting talented workers. Hollister (1995)
contends that this recruiting edge can result in higher success rates for
small startup businesses. Telecommuting can also help small firms
enlist the help of experienced professionals on a contractual basis
(Davey 1998). Companies have also used telecommuting as a strategy
to utilize new groups of workers, such as the disabled. Control Data
Corporation (which is now Ceridian) was one of the first companies
to investigate telecommuting. It began a telecommuting project for
disabled workers in 1978 (Berner 1994; Schepp and Schepp 1995). It
eventually developed a similar program for nondisabled employees.
It can help U.S. firms comply with the American with Disabilities Act,
legislation that requires companies to accommodate disabled employees (McCloskey and Igbaria 1998). In Europe teleworking has been
used as a strategy for creating jobs for specific targeted groups, such
as women with children (Korte and Wynne 1996).

Firms have also adopted telecommuting as a strategy to cut costs.
Telecommuting has been implemented in an effort to reduce real estate, overhead, and relocation costs (Schepp and Schepp 1995; Korte
and Wynne 1996; Richter 1996; Shillingford 1997; Mahlon 1998; Nilles
1998). The ability to reduce office space can be a real incentive to companies located in high-rent cities, especially major European cities
(Moorcroft and Bennett 1995). Brenda Thompson (1996) estimates that
cost savings from reduced overhead, reduced real estate and office
space, and increased employee productivity may average between
$6,000 and $12,000 per telecommuter. AT&T, a telecommuting pioneer,
calculated that if an employee telecommutes full time it saves the company $8,000 annually on overhead. Part-time telecommuters save
AT&T $3,000 a year (Koch 1998).

The move toward virtual workers is reshaping corporate architecture. SAP America Inc.'s new headquarters in the Philadelphia area (a
software firm) provide an interesting case study (Blakinger 1999). Since
nearly 50 percent of the company's 1,100 Philadelphia-area employees are virtual, the new headquarters building was designed to reflect
this change. Rather than having an assigned workspace for each employee, there are plenty of seats in the coffee bar and auditorium

(equipped with plug-ins for portable computers) that can be used for remote workers when they stop in at the main office.

Companies have also embraced telecommuting as a strategy to increase productivity (Eldib and Minoli 1995; Shillingford 1997; Nilles 1998). Pilot telecommuting projects have shown increases ranging from 10 to 40 percent (Schepp and Schepp 1995). Some tasks can be performed more efficiently away from the office. These include data entry, form processing, and professional work requiring long periods of time without distractions (Olmsted and Smith 1994; Warner 1997). Some downsized companies have introduced telecommuting as a strategy to increase productivity and improve moral (Schepp and Schepp 1995).

Telecommuting has also been used as a strategy for economic growth, especially in some European communities (Moorcroft and Bennett 1995; Korte and Wynne 1996). There is the belief that it can provide jobs and develops the skill base in rural areas. In the United States some progressive city planners have envisioned telecommuting as a strategy for urban economic development, especially if telecommuting centers were located in low-income residential neighborhoods to provide new job opportunities for the urban poor (Goldman and Goldman 1998).

Telecommuting allows companies to continue to operate under adverse situations, ranging from storms and earthquakes to special events such as the Olympics (Olmsted and Smith 1994). In San Francisco many employers established telecommuting programs following the 1989 earthquake (Richter 1996). Within hours of the 1994 Los Angeles earthquake Pacific Bell (which has a long-established telecommuting program for its own employees) offered free installation and loaner equipment so people impacted by the earthquake could work at home (Berner 1994). The company also played an important role in promoting telecommuting. The federal government also responded quickly to the disaster by establishing teleworking centers in Northridge (Sato and Spinks 1998).

Finally, telecommuting has been driven by changes in corporate culture. Richter (1996) views telecommuting as part of the movement toward flatter, nonhierarchical organizations. It can eliminate layers of middle management. In addition, it reflects the trend toward managing by results rather than by sight.

THE NUMBER OF TELECOMMUTERS

It is impossible to be exact about the number of remote workers, since definitions of telecommuting and teleworking vary. In 1990 the International Labour Organisation released a study on telework. The

ILO study found that telework was most prevalent in the United States, followed by the United Kingdom and France (*Homeworking in the European Union* 1995). Gray, Hodson, and Gordon (1993) estimated that in 1993 there were 5.89 million teleworkers in the United States (4.8 percent of the U.S. workforce) and 1.27 million teleworkers in the United Kingdom (4.6 percent of the U.K. workforce). A 1996 article on European teleworking, published in the *European Industrial Relations Review*, estimated that teleworking is most widespread in Sweden, Norway, and Finland, and moderate in Germany, The Netherlands, and the United Kingdom (Teleworking in Europe: Part One 1996). Portugal and Greece had the lowest numbers of estimated teleworkers. The European Commission is promoting telecommuting. One of its stated goals is to have 10 million teleworking jobs by the year 2000 (Qvortrup 1998). In the United States it is estimated that there were 6 million telecommuters in 1996 and 8 million in 1997 (Lucent Leads Trend in High-Tech Home Building 1998). June Langhoff (1999) calculated that as of early 1999, 11 percent of the U.S. population telecommuted. Others calculate that 15 to 20 percent of the U.S. workforce now telecommutes a minimum of two days a week (Lucent Leads Trends in High-Tech Home Building 1998). The International Telework Association and Council estimated that more than 19.6 million Americans telecommuted in 1999 (Employers Save $10,000 per Telecommuter in Reduced Absenteeism and Retention Costs 1999). In late fall 1999 the number of telecommuters in the United Kingdom was estimated to be between 1.5 and 2 million (Future Work Means Flexible Work 1999). LINK Resources, a consulting firm that has tracked telecommuting trends since the mid-1980s, estimated that in the United States telecommuting grows at the rate of 20 percent per year (Romei 1996). Jack Nilles projects that as many as 50 million Americans will be home-based telecommuters or telecommuting from a telework center by the year 2030 (Goldman and Goldman 1998).

The United States has the largest number of telecommuters. However, Jack Nilles (1998) believes that the member countries of the Organization for Economic Cooperation and Development (OECD) have a tremendous potential for telecommuting. OECD nations include not only the countries of Western Europe, but Australia, Canada, and Japan. In fact, Nilles projects that the number of telecommuters in OECD countries will exceed the number of U.S. telecommuters around the year 2008. Nilles believes that the potential for telecommuting is also very high in Indonesia, the Philippines, South Korea, Taiwan, and India. He predicts that there may be more than 30 million teleworkers in the Asia Pacific region by the year 2030 and there is a potential for 50 million future teleworkers in India. Although an insufficient infrastructure and educational lags undermine teleworking potential in Latin

America and the Caribbean, Nilles predicts that a significant percentage of the Brazilian workforce could telecommute in the future. Nilles does not believe that the number of teleworkers in Africa and the Middle East will reach 1997 U.S. levels until beyond 2017.

Recent estimates of the number of Japanese teleworkers are small. A 1997 survey indicated that approximately 680,000 white-collar Japanese workers (only 4 percent of white-collar workers) telecommute one or more days a week (Sato and Spinks 1998). Research conducted by Franklin Becker and his associates (1993) unveiled interesting cultural explanations for why there are more telecommuters in the United States than in other countries. Telecommuting is more prevalent in the United Sates because homes are generally larger and they are often empty during the day. In addition, there is no stigma associated with not being seen leaving for work.

PROFILES OF TELECOMMUTERS

In 1993 Joanne Pratt published the most exhaustive study to date on the demographic, occupational, and personal characteristics of telecommuters. This report, *Myths and Realities of Working at Home: Characteristics of Homebased Business Owners and Telecommuters*, used data from the National Longitudinal Survey cohorts, collected by the U.S. Bureau of Labor Statistics. Pratt found that telecommuters were demographically similar to nontelecommuters and that the work patterns for both groups were similar. Telecommuters do not telecommute as a child-care solution. Telecommuters were more likely to receive promotions than nontelecommuters and most telecommuters felt more positive about their work than nontelecommuters did. Contrary to popular myth, telecommuters were not resented by their nonteleworking colleagues. Overwhelmingly, telecommuters were managers and professionals working in sales and clerical jobs. There was a concentration in the professional-services industry. On average, telecommuters earned more than nontelecommuters did. One of Pratt's most interesting findings was that telecommuters were less likely to smoke, drink, or use drugs than nontelecommuters.

Cyber Dialogue has conducted a more recent study on the demographics of U.S. telecommuters (*Telecommute Magazine* Launched 1998). This study found that almost half (48 percent) of telecommuters are full-time workers, 39 percent have children at home, 40 percent are between the ages of thirty and forty-nine, and more than half (59 percent) are married or have a live-in partner. In terms of geographic distribution, California's Silicon Valley has the largest number of telecommuters (Smart Valley Closes Its Doors 1998). This is not surprising, since Silicon Valley founded the Smart Valley project in 1993 to promote Internet access, electronic commerce, telecommuting, and other technology initiatives. Although the Smart Valley project ended in late 1998, telecommuting is well established in this region of the country, as well as in the state of California. In the United States six of the top ten telecommuting cities are located in California (Himmelberg 1997).

Historically, telecommuting has been related to company size. Debra and Brad Schepp (1995), authors of *The Telecommuter's Handbook*, noted that telecommuting used to be limited to either very large companies (those employing more than 1,000 workers) or very small companies (those with fewer than 100 employees). However, using data collected by the LINK Resources consulting firm they concluded that the greatest growth in telecommuting is occurring in mid-size companies; that is, those firms employing between 100 and 1,000 workers. The Schepps also identified another important trend. Traditionally, telecommuting has been associated with high-tech firms. The Schepps found that more companies across the board are adopting telecommuting. Eldib and Minoli (1995) found that formal telecommuting programs are most likely to be adopted by large organizations. Most of these formal programs began as small pilot projects.

JOBS SUITABLE FOR TELECOMMUTING

In a speech delivered at the International Conference on Homework (a symposium held in Toronto in 1992), Kathleen Christensen, a leading researcher on workplace flexibility, identified three groups within teleworking (Korte and Wynne 1996). These included independent contractors (freelance workers, consultants, and temporary workers), home-based clerical workers (many of whom were performing outsourced work), and higher-paid professionals and managers. Christensen noted that although the clerical workers were the largest group, the professional group received the most publicity and was the prevailing image of teleworkers.

Several researchers have tried to identify jobs or functions suitable for telecommuting. Eldib and Minoli (1995) identified these job holders as the most likely candidates for telecommuting: corporate executives, lawyers, accountants, financial managers and analysts, procurement managers, engineers, technicians, software developers, market researchers, customer-service representatives, telemarketers, and order-entry clerks. Neil Hollister (1995) has identified segments of industries well suited to telecommuting and mobile networking: the information industries (companies whose work is directly related to the gathering, generating, and processing of information), information-technology companies, accounting firms, journalism, advertising agencies, telecommunications companies, real estate agencies, government and education, and utilities. Jack Nilles (1998) has created a rough list of teleworkable jobs, ranging from architect to school administrator. His list of suitable teleworkable jobs for city of Los Angeles employees exceeds 400 job classifications.

Many experts stress that it is important to look at job requirements before determining whether a job is suitable for teleworking. Dinnocenzo (1999) believes that jobs suitable for telecommuting have these characteristics: They require minimal face-to-face interaction; involve tasks that can be completed via phone, fax, or email; and have output that can be monitored and measured. Richter (1996) also identified characteristics of jobs suited to telecommuting. She believes they include routine information processing, heavy computer use, a project-specific orientation, a minimal need for extensive support or work space, and a significant degree of autonomy. She notes that teleworking is best suited to tasks "from opposite ends of the work spectrum": routine data entry and complex and creative professional work (p. 4840).

TRAITS OF SUCCESSFUL TELECOMMUTERS

Not all employees are suited to telecommuting. Most experts agree that new employees are not the best prospects for telecommuting, since it is important for employees working away from the principal office to have a good knowledge of their job (Thompson 1996). It is also important for telecommuters to be savvy with technology so they can be technologically self-sufficient (O'Connell 1996). There are several other personal traits associated with successful remote workers. Gil Gordon, a renowned telecommuting consultant, was interviewed for an article that appeared in a 1999 issue of the popular magazine *Good Housekeeping* (Hoffman 1999). The coverage of this trend in a magazine like *Good Housekeeping* indicates that telecommuting has moved into the mainstream. When asked about telecommuter traits, Gordon responded that if you want to telecommute, "you need many of the same traits as entrepreneurs," including "self-discipline, self-motivation, and the ability to work alone" (p. 99).

Alice Bredin (1996), author of *The Virtual Office Survival Handbook*, identified five skills essential for the successful virtual worker. These include time management, the ability to handle challenges, the ability to handle distractions, the ability to manage business support relationships, and the ability to balance work with nonwork obligations. Her handbook includes a self-survey that individuals can use to gauge their potential to work remotely. Debra Dinnocenzo's (1999) *101 Tips for Telecommuters* lists some other attributes of successful telecommuters, such as the ability to work with minimal supervision, exemplary organizational skills, and the ability to solve problems independently. Sandra O'Connell's (1996) list of personal traits for successful telecommuting also included adaptability, the ability to compromise, a familiarity with organizational procedures, and a results orientation. Korte and Wynne's (1996) report on European teleworking found that the majority of European organizations used similar criteria to select teleworkers. These criteria included self-motivation, the ability to work with minimal supervision, strong organizational skills, reliability, productivity, flexibility, good knowledge of job, and trustworthiness.

What about the successful attributes of telemanagers? Most research has focused on the telecommuter or the organization, not the manager. Lauren Speeth's (1992) doctoral dissertation provides valuable insight into the factors that make telecommuting programs successful. She interviewed thirty managers of telecommuters in an effort to identify traits of successful telemanagers. All the telemanagers in her study had supervised telecommuters for at least six months. All had allowed at least one-fourth of their staff to telecommute at least one day per week. Speeth found that telemanagers were experienced (on average, they had more than eight years of supervisory experience), effective, well educated, and had high levels of personal achievement. She concluded that level of experience, effectiveness, and training contributed to the success of the telecommuting programs she studied. Speeth learned that experienced, effective managers ran more successful telecommuting programs. Trust in employees was the most important factor contributing to the success of a telecommuting program. The next most important factor was voluntary participation, followed by the support and enthusiasm of management and staff, especially upper-management support.

TYPES OF TELECOMMUTING

There are several forms of telecommuting. One of the primary types is home-based telecommuting. Employees work at home a designated number of days per week. They return to the office for meetings and other group activities. According to Jack Nilles (1998), most U.S. telecommuters are home based. Although home-based telecommuters can work remotely on a full-time or part-time basis, most work away from the principal office only part of the time. The average U.S. telecommuter works from home two days a week (Berner 1994).

Telecommuters can also work in telework centers. Other terms for this concept include satellite offices, telecommuting centers, telecottages, telecenters, neighborhood work centers, and telebusiness centers (Becker et al. 1993; Huws 1995; Nilles 1998). These centers are often located near employee's homes. They may also be located in airports, in downtown areas, or in other company facilities located near clients. These centers provide a limited range of services and support systems.

Detailed data on North American and Japanese telework centers can be found in *Telework Centers: An Evaluation of the North American and Japanese Experience*, a report produced by Franklin Becker and his associates (1993) at Cornell University's International Workplace Studies Program. The purpose of this report was to identify as many telework centers as possible in the United States, Canada, and Japan and to examine cost, space, and technology implications of telework centers. Becker and his colleagues also identified factors critical to the success of telework centers, as well as obstacles to the development of these centers. These researchers identified five objectives and goals for telework centers: reducing traffic congestion, reducing commuting time, reducing employee stress, promoting the use of new technologies, and promoting rural development.

The authors were able to create profiles of North American and Japanese centers. In North America the average distance from the principal office location was sixty-three miles, compared to nineteen miles in Japan. The typical telework center was 2,000 square feet. Most centers had open rather than private or semiprivate offices. Some centers provided conference rooms, copy and fax areas, and break rooms. Japanese telework centers had amenities such as exercise equipment and were more spacious than traditional Japanese offices. The standard technology in most centers included phones, e-mail, voicemail, computers, modems, printers, fax, and copy machines. Japanese centers tended to have more sophisticated technology. Most telework centers have a full-time administrator and most of the users are professionals with a high degree of autonomy. Costs were subsidized and not generally transferred to users, since many centers were pilot projects funded by government grants or private-sector donations.

Becker and associates (1993) found that users were very positive about using telework centers. Both employees and their managers agreed that telework centers enhanced workers' productivity. In North America telework centers saved about seventy-six minutes per day each way in commuting time. This figure was twenty-five minutes for Japanese workers. Most telework center users returned to the central office two to three times a week.

More detailed information on telework centers can be found in Jack Nilles's 1998 book *Managing Telework: Strategies for Managing the Virtual Workforce*. Nilles divides potential teleworkers into two categories: home-based and telework-center teleworkers. Potential telework-center workers have these characteristics: They have a preference for working in a center rather than telecommuting from home, perform tasks better suited for satellite teleworking than home-based telecommuting, have equipment and/or facilities requirements, work for firms operating (or willing to experiment with) telework centers, and live a short distance from a telework center. Some home-based telecommuters are also good candidates for part-time telework-center telecommuters. Nilles found that most U.S. telework centers have 100 or fewer employees. Small neighborhood telework centers have an average of twenty teleworkers. One variation of the telework center that is gaining popularity according to Nilles is the multiclient telework center. Under this arrangement one organization rents or leases space to other organizations or individual teleworkers. The firm operating the center is responsible for the administrative details. This approach is increasingly being used by the federal government.

Telework centers have had limited success. Why haven't telework centers grown dramatically in number? Becker and colleagues (1993) found that it might be hard for companies to justify these centers, since this arrangement represents additional costs not offset by savings in real estate or administrative costs. Also, if employees drive a significant distance to these centers there is not a significant savings in fuel and energy. Becker and associates also identified a fascinating cultural barrier to the success of this concept. While North American workers appreciated the lack of distractions (including interruptions by coworkers) at these centers, Japanese workers found telework centers to be socially isolating. These Cornell researchers concluded that few companies "have the combination of management skills and practices, training programs, and technological sophistication to exploit the potential advantages of telework centers" (p. xvi).

Another form of telecommuting is teleworking on remote sites controlled by the employer. Under this scheme, groups of workers are physically concentrated on the same site, located at a distance from the employer. More information on this variation of remote work can be found in *Follow-Up to the White Paper* (Huws 1995). This type of teleworking often involves low-skilled workers with depressed wages (such as data-entry workers in developing countries and offshore information processing). These sites are often in inaccessible areas such as converted warehouses or on the outskirts of a town. This European Community report found that many of these workers feel that there is little chance of promotion, and some have reported health problems because of repetitive work. However, other experiments have been successful. In 1990 Lloyds Bank, the large British bank, opened the first of several remote processing centers. Since then other functions have been decentralized to regional centers. In 1989 the Swedish Customs and Excise Authority, headquartered in Stockholm, established a teleworking pilot involving a remote site. At this remote rural site workers checked customs declarations and other forms for accuracy. The experiment was successful, resulting in higher productivity and lower turnover.

Mobile teleworkers, or road warriors, comprise another category of teleworkers. These employees work anywhere, anytime. They use portable technologies to keep in touch with their employees and their customers. In 1994 LINK Resources estimated that there were 7 million mobile teleworkers in the United States, and the number was projected to increase to 25 million by the year 2000 (Huws 1995). Huws conducted a survey of mobile teleworkers in 1989. The results are reported in *Follow-Up to the White Paper*. Her research indicated that the typical home-based teleworker was a woman in her mid to late thirties with young children, working part time. In contrast, mobile teleworkers were likely to be male, younger, and often worked more than sixty hours per week.

There are several interesting case studies of companies that have implemented a mobile workforce (Sims, Joroff, and Becker 1996). American Express replaced the field-office concept with this virtual-office concept. It made its virtual-office program mandatory for all sales representatives and closed down district offices. Great Plains Software has one of the oldest and most successful virtual work programs. It began its virtual-office program in the late 1980s. Verifone is a global company that implemented a virtual-workplace strategy in all of its offices worldwide. Each employee is issued a laptop (with modem and fax capability) and a cellular phone. All corporate manuals, reports, budgets, forms, and other material are available on-line twenty-four hours a day.

Mobile teleworkers have been less studied than other types of remote workers. An important contribution is a book chapter authored by Bruce Rollier and Yihwa Irene Liou (1998) on the mobile workforce. They identified the advantages of a mobile workforce, including increased productivity, improved customer service, the ability to adapt to change more quickly, and savings in real estate and other overhead. Rollier and Liou also provide advice on implementing a successful mobile workforce program.

Another variant of telecommuting is the non-territorial office. This is one of the strategies researchers Sims, Joroff, and Becker (1996) refer to as part of the reinvented workplace. Their study of non-territorial offices is included in their report *Managing the Reinvented Workplace*. This report looks at the experiences of more than twenty-five companies that have been innovative in implementing alternative work options. The purpose of the book is to provide best practices to organizations that are interested in workplace flexibility. An entire chapter focuses on the non-territorial office. This term, coined by MIT researcher Thomas Allen, means "any space allocation program that does not assign desks or workstations to specific individuals" (p. 39). Variations of this concept include "just-in-time" (Andersen Consulting's term), "hoteling" (the term coined by Ernst and Young), "hot desking" (a term coined by the U.S. Navy), and "red carpet" (Hewlett-Packard's term) (p. 39).

What is the rationale behind this strategy? Research conducted by Becker and associates (1993) at Cornell University's International Workplace Studies Program indicated that the average occupancy rate for traditional offices (those with personally assigned workstations) ranged from 30 to 50 percent. This average applies to offices in North America, Europe, and Japan. However, occupancy levels are even lower for jobs requiring a great deal of customer interaction (such as sales) or in organizations that have implemented telecommuting or cross-functional teams. As a result, companies are spending lots of money on space that is not being used efficiently. The Cornell research center conducted a series of studies of non-territorial offices in the United States, the United Kingdom, Europe, and Japan over a five-year period in the 1990s. These researchers found that non-territorial offices helped companies reduce costs while maintaining or improving employee performance and quality of work life.

Managing the Reinvented Workplace (Sims, Joroff, and Becker 1996) presents interesting case studies of non-territorial offices. This strategy has been adopted by IBM (in the United States and the United Kingdom), Andersen Consulting, Arthur Andersen, Aetna, General Electric, Amdahl Computers, and Ernst and Young. Ernst and Young implemented the first computerized hoteling system in an office in Chicago's Sears Tower in 1992. Its database maintains a profile for each consultant, including materials that a consultant needs.

TELECOMMUTING COSTS

How much does telecommuting costs employers? Start-up costs for telecommuting are low. JCPenney found that the costs for a telecommuter were less than half that of an equivalent office installation (Langhoff 1996). AT&T found that it costs approximately $6,000 to set up a home office per employee and this expense was recouped in one year by savings in real estate costs (Sims, Joroff, and Becker 1996). Hewlett-Packard spends $4,000 to $6,000 per telecommuter (Langhoff 1999). June Langhoff calculates that telecommuting two days per week results in annual savings of approximately $7,500 per employee. Her calculations (based on an annual salary of $40,000) assumed a productivity increase of 15 percent, an absenteeism reduction of 10 percent, a 40-percent reduction in parking, and another 40-percent reduction in office space. This approximates Jack Nilles (1994, 1998) projection that net benefits (benefits minus costs) average $8,000 or more annually per telecommuter. Nilles rule of thumb is that an organization should use 5 percent of telecommuters' salaries to cover the costs of establishing a telecommuting program. This includes computer, software, training, and evaluation costs. A 1996 Society for Human Resources management study concluded that part-time telecommuters (those who work at home one or two days a week) save a company $6,000 to $12,000 annually due to reduced overhead, lower turnover, and increased productivity (Fisher 1998; Kirschner 1998). Data released by the International Telework Association and Council in October 1999 indicated that telecommuting can save employers $10,000 per telecommuter in reduced absenteeism and job retention costs (Employers Save $10,000 per Teleworker in Reduced Absenteeism and Retention Costs 1999). This study, sponsored by AT&T, was the first research study to quantify the financial impact of telecommuting in terms of employee absenteeism and retention.

The most comprehensive analysis of the direct and indirect costs relating to the implementation of telecommuting can be found in Nilles's (1998) book *Managing Telework*. Nilles identified twelve categories of direct costs. While some are obvious, such as telecommunications costs and computer costs, others are less evident. For example, many organizations fail to consider additional training costs, costs associated with the moving of equipment from the central office to homes or satellite offices, and liability costs relating to the need to cover work-related accidents at employees' homes. Nilles also identified two categories of potential direct costs: increased building energy consumption and increased local traffic congestion.

THE BENEFITS OF TELECOMMUTING

How does telecommuting benefit employees? Respondents to a Conference Board survey cited improved employee morale as the chief benefit of telecommuting (Technology's Effect on Work/Life Balance 1998). Telecommuting gives employees more control over how they get their work done and can help them balance work and family responsibilities. This improved quality of life was also confirmed by data from the California Telecommuting Pilot Project, a pilot conducted from 1988 to 1990. Detailed data on this multiagency project involving both full-time and part-time state agencies can be found in Simani Price's (1991) report on the pilot project. The number of telecommuters and control-group members fluctuated during the pilot project. At one time during the project there were 329 telecommuters and 231 control-group members. Most of the participants were managers and professionals. However, some secretaries and clerical workers were included. Both telecommuters and control-group members were asked to assess their effectiveness over the two-year period. Their supervisors were also asked to assess their effectiveness. Telecommuting was associated with lower stress levels and increased feelings of control over one's life. Telecommuters also reported higher levels of effectiveness, measured by accomplishing more of their required daily tasks than control group-members accomplished. Debra and Brad Schepp (1995) argue that telecommuting is good for families. Parents can be available in the case of emergencies, to attend school functions, and to deal with eldercare responsibilities. The Schepps add that telecommuting exposes children to the world of work. Jack Nilles (1998) has identified one benefit that is often overlooked. He believes that telecommuting allows workers to get more involved with their communities since it reduces their travel time. Another tangible benefit is reduced work-related expenses. It has been estimated that a full-time telecommuter saves approximately $4,600 annually as a result of reduced travel, a reduced clothing and dry cleaning budget, and fewer lunches eaten out (Hoffman 1999).

Respondents to the Conference Board survey on telecommuting cited other benefits of telecommuting: improved productivity, reduced turnover, recruitment advantage, and reduced absenteeism (Technology's Effect on Work/Life Balance 1998). Other organizations have reported similar benefits. Mountain Bell, AT&T, and Bell Atlantic (all companies with large telecommuting programs) have reported productivity increases in the range of 30 percent, accompanied by decreases in absenteeism (Sims, Joroff, and Becker 1996). AT&T also reduced facilities costs. The option to telecommute can also save relocation costs. These costs can be staggering. It is estimated that relocation costs about $80,000 per employee (Langhoff 1999). Telecommuting can be an effective retention tool. Several surveys of telecommuters have shown that more than one-third of telecommuters would leave if their organization no longer permitted telecommuting. Telecommuting can also be an effective recruitment tool. In addition, it broadens the labor pool, since companies can attract a wider range of employees, including disabled workers (Langhoff 1999). Another benefit is improved customer service (Simmons 1996; Johnson 1998). Scott Johnson's (1998) scholarly article on teleworking in customer-service jobs addresses the benefits of delivering service remotely. Jobs with considerable customer interactions can be well suited for teleworking. Scott found that many firms that have allowed employees in sales, service, and support positions to work away from the central office (including AT&T, IBM, Aetna, Arthur Andersen, Ernst and Young, and Pacific Bell) have reported significant increases in customer contact and improved relationships with customers.

Telecommuting can also help companies comply with legislative requirements, such as air-quality standards requiring a reduction in employee commuting time (Piskurich 1996; Dinnocenzo 1999). Telecommuting also helps an organization respond to disasters. Teleworking allowed work to continue after the 1994 Los Angeles earthquake, the Oklahoma City bombing in 1995, and the severe blizzards and storms during the winters of 1996 and 1998 (Langhoff 1999).

DRAWBACKS OF TELECOMMUTING

Teleworking can have drawbacks for employees. One of the major concerns is that remote workers will feel lonely and isolated, especially those workers who like the social aspects of the workplace (Tessier and Lapointe 1994; Cooper 1996; Piskurich 1996; Richter 1996; Simmons 1996; Langhoff 1999). Franklin Becker and Carolyn Tennessen (1995) studied mobile workers in the United Kingdom to determine the social impact of mobile work. The research site was Digital Equipment Corporation's flexible program in Newmarket, England. The company closed a large traditional office and required employees to become mobile workers. The 100 mobile workers worked from a telecenter, other corporate offices in the United Kingdom, customers' offices, their cars, and hotels. Becker and Tennessen found that technology was not a complete substitute for face-to-face interaction. Mobile workers appreciated face-to-face contacts during office meetings. One interesting finding was that the mobile environment was not especially conducive to the integration of new employees. New employees had a hard time getting to know coworkers.

Not all individuals are suited for remote work. LINK Resources found that 20 percent of home-based telecommuters wanted to return to the central office or reduce their telecommuting time in a national survey of people who work at a distance (Schepp and Schepp 1995). Family members, household chores, television, or the refrigerator can distract some telecommuters. Others have a tendency to put in too many hours since the line between work and home blurs. Some telecommuters worry that they will be bypassed when it comes to promotions. However, it is not clear if telecommuting can hinder a career.

A 1997 survey of telecommuters found that only 3 percent of telecommuters were negatively impacted in terms of career advancement (Langhoff 1999).

Follow-Up to the White Paper (Huws 1995) documented several problems relating to telework. This report found that some studies have indicated that full-time home-based teleworkers suffer from social isolation and stress. Some receive lower pay and have less job security than on-site workers. They may also suffer health problems if the work is repetitive. Teleworking on remote sites controlled by the employer was often problematic. Wages are generally depressed and sites are often located in inaccessible areas. These workers may have little chance of promotion and also experience health problems because of the repetitive nature of the work.

In a study of European telework (Huws, Korte, and Robinson 1990), teleworkers cited four major disadvantages: the lack of office services; the lack of benefits, perks, and pension plans; the lack of clear boundaries between work and home; and level of pay. In this same study, telemanagers cited these drawbacks: increased training costs, lack of equipment, technical problems, and organizational difficulties. Managers have consistently expressed concern over the difficulty of managing remote workers and fear that key staff will not always be available as a result of remote work. Other European publications on teleworking have addressed pay and equity issues. Moorcroft and Bennett (1995) expressed concern that teleworkers do not receive equal pay, equal training, and equal career-advancement opportunities. As a result, labor unions have become interested in guaranteeing equal pay, training, and opportunities for teleworkers. In the United Kingdom teleworking has largely been used to cut costs (Stanworth 1996). Some teleworkers have essentially been forced to become self-employed, with no guaranteed income, paid sick days, paid vacation, pensions, or other benefits.

There are other drawbacks to telecommuting. Hollister (1995) noted productivity losses resulting from the lack of immediate access to co-workers, as well as from time spent coming to the office for meetings and other reasons. In addition, he noted the difficulty of coordinating work groups and teams. Olmsted and Smith (1994) identified other problems. For example, telecommuting requires new managerial skills. Rather than monitoring employees, supervisors have to evaluate output. However, according to these authors, managers often have reservations about telecommuting. Some supervisors worry that remote employees will feel less loyalty to the organization. Others are concerned about security issues, worrying about telecommuters having unrestricted access to company data. There is also an apprehension on the part of labor unions. Olmsted and Smith note that labor unions argue that it is difficult to enforce labor standards designed to protect workers when these workers aren't in sight.

BARRIERS TO TELECOMMUTING

Managerial resistance is one of the biggest barriers to telecommuting (Wilson 1991). Piskurich (1996) found that some managers are reluctant to embrace telecommuting because they fear losing control over their employees. Piskurich also found that they worry their job will be eliminated. In addition, they believe communication will suffer and some employees will not be productive. Middle-management resistance is a major hurdle. In 1994 the Conference Board studied more than 100 companies with telecommuting programs. The most startling finding was that less than 1 percent of workers took advantage of telecommuting because of "middle-management hostility" (Olen 1996, 55).

Cynthia Prok Ruppel's 1995 dissertation, "Correlates of the Adoption and Implementation of Programmer/Analyst Telework: An Organizational Perspective," examines why telecommuting has not been more widely adopted and implemented. She identifies factors related to the adoption and implementation of telecommuting. Her study focused on telecommuting among programmers and analysts. Ruppel found that some variables were related to the adoption of telecommuting but not to the implementation of it, and vice versa. Some of the variables significantly related to the implementation of telecommuting included training managers about the benefits of telework, key management support, the existence of a champion for teleworkers, and the existence of a career ladder for teleworkers.

Eldib and Minoli (1995) identified two major barriers to the growth of telecommuting: managerial resistance and resistance by unions. Labor unions in Europe have been particularly opposed to teleworking. European trade unions have voiced these concerns: teleworking is really a strategy for cutting costs, teleworkers will be isolated and more difficult to unionize, and uncertainty over who is responsible for teleworkers' health, safety, insurance, and equipment cost and maintenance (*Homeworking in the European Union* 1995). Government regulations and policies can also be obstacles. In some communities zoning regulations prohibit working at home (Goldman and Goldman 1998). In addition, tax laws that do not allow home-office deductions discourage telecommuting. Finally, employees themselves can hinder the development of telecommuting. A 1995 survey found that many workers want to telecommute but were afraid to for fear that it would negatively impact their careers (Langhoff 1999).

PRACTICAL ASPECTS OF TELECOMMUTING

There is a practical side to telecommuting that has to be anticipated and planned for in order to achieve some measure of success. Efficient telecommuting depends upon management of a number of human factors in tandem with the technical aspects of working from a remote site. The very real problems of handling distractions, coping with isolation, and avoiding overwork and burnout must be expected and treated with the same attention as the selection of appropriate office equipment, software, and mastery of technical skills.

June Langhoff (1999), in *The Telecommuter's Advisor*, describes and offers guidance on a wide range of situations likely to be faced by telecommuters. Workers must negotiate a variety of hurdles in the productivity arena (organizing work, dealing with distractions, communicating with the office, safeguarding work performed at home, and getting technical support and service). In addition, telecommuters have to be concerned with the proper setup of a remote office (issues of design, safety, selection of phones, work stations, fax, managing e-mail and messages) as well as intangibles such as dealing with isolation and staying visible so as not to lose out on perks and promotions. Langhoff pays particular attention to the practical aspects of selecting equipment (for example, advantages and disadvantages of different fax technologies, how to choose the appropriate telephone and associated services, and what type of modem to choose).

Similarly, Debra Dinnocenzo (1999), in *101 Tips for Telecommuters*, recognizes many of the problems telecommuters are likely to experience. She provides suggestions for techniques that can be used in areas such as time management, managing expenses, negotiating family expectations and agreements, maintaining contact with coworkers, dealing with resentment from coworkers, choosing appropriate technologies, and getting the necessary technical support. As these problems have varying dimensions, Dinnocenzo's approach is to help the reader sort through the situations that seem to be relevant and to tailor an individual solution.

Technology obviously plays a critical role in the life of most telecommuters. Although it is not the intent of this chapter to discuss pros and cons of particular technologies or to advocate purchasing one brand of equipment over another, there are general issues related to technology that bear investigation. One of the most helpful ways to think about technology is provided by Jack Nilles (1998) in his book *Managing Telework: Strategies for Managing the Virtual Workforce*. Nilles has eight "General Rules of Technology" that form a solid base for making decisions about appropriate technologies. He believes:

1. A technology that costs twice as much as you can afford to pay today will be down to your price threshold if you wait two years.

2. By buying the best technology available for a certain job you increase the odds that it will still be useable in three years.

3. Almost anyone can telecommute for at least part of the time without investing in technology beyond the absolute fundamentals.

4. To decide whether a particular technology is worth spending money on, figure out if the cost of the technology is less than the value of the increased competitive advantage.

5. Telecommuting often decreases the start-up costs of adopting a new technology because much of the work of learning the technology occurs at home in a more productive environment.

6. The start-up technology costs for telecommuting can be quite low if duplication of technology is minimized.

7. Any organization deficient in the area of digital communication networks will have to get up to speed quickly just to stay in business, and thus telecommuting will become even more practical in the near future.

8. Software used by telecommuters should be completely compatible with software used by the home office.

The most important technical decisions faced by telecommuters and companies they work for are related to network capabilities and data transmission. Most internal and external communication within organizations depends upon efficient use of the Internet as well as intranets. The pace of change in this area is staggering, but taking advantage of new technology as it becomes generally available is crucial to economic survival. Nilles (1998) states quite simply that "if you don't have a web address, you don't exist" and "the ability to interact on the internet will be an absolute requirement for commerce in the 21st century" (p. 80).

The bottom line is that one's viability as a telecommuter is directly linked to good Internet access. Anyone who needs access (from outside the office) to his or her internal "work-related" e-mail (as opposed to personal e-mail), electronic resources located on a company or organization's internal network (an intranet), or Web sites necessary for work-related purposes needs a dependable Internet service provider (ISP). Internet service providers are as varied as the services they provide, but there are some key points to consider.

In some cases a company or organization provides its own Internet access. Companies often have their own Internet servers that connect directly to an ISP chosen by the company, or at times connect directly to the Internet backbone. As an example, take the case of a professor working for a university. Universities are usually part of the Internet backbone and generally provide access to the Internet from "remote" sites. That is, the university allows students and employees to connect via modem to servers on campus. The professor in this example can use the servers on campus to gain access to the Web for general browsing. The professor may also have permission to connect directly to an internal server that will allow him or her to get access to internal information and resources as well as browse the Web. The professor will be able to work from home on documents stored centrally on a departmental network, use forms stored on a central server meant only for people within his or her department, and monitor information students may be adding to a class Web site. The professor in this example is using both the Internet and an intranet. Other examples of companies providing their own Internet access and remote intranet access are common, as are examples of companies contracting directly with an ISP on behalf of telecommuting employees. To be efficient in working from a remote location, telecommuters need a data connection of equal speed to the connection provided at the regular work site. The primary task is to make sure the equipment used from the remote site is capable of taking advantage of the best data transmission speed offered by the provider and that software-compatibility issues have been addressed.

In cases where a telecommuter needs to find his or her own ISP, the prime considerations will be

1. data transmission speed the provider is offering.
2. whether the provider is capable of meeting the demand for service at peak times or if getting a busy signal will be likely.
3. cost of service as compared to competing suppliers.
4. track record in terms of the provider's reliability.
5. ancillary services the supplier is offering such as e-mail or space for Web sites.
6. the provider's ability to provide technical support.

Of course, the issues of adequate equipment at the remote site and software compatibility apply here as well. To a certain extent, technological preferences in terms of an Internet service provider also come into play. The decision of whether to access the Internet via the cable television network, as opposed to satellite, fiber-optic cable, or high-speed phone lines relate to issues of speed, reliability, availability, and cost as well as more intangible personal preferences.

At this point it is appropriate to heed the advice of Tom Reynolds and David Brusseau (1998) authors of *Cyberlane Commuter*, who remind us quite bluntly that "technology that cannot be trusted is ineffective" (p. 125). The amount of technical support needed by telecommuters is extensive and capable of blindsiding employers as well as workers themselves. As Bob Suttling and Dave Wood (1997) explain, "Staff on the move and those who work from home have the same difficulties with technology as those based in the office. The impact of these difficulties can be far greater for those who work away from the office. Simple technology problems in the office can often be resolved by talking to a colleague. For the flexible worker, simple problems can become a major crisis when there is no one to provide local help and guidance" (p. 62). When equipment fails, telecommuters may be unable to work at all. The sense in many corporations is that telecommuters may also experience much higher levels of frustration with technology problems than office-based employees (Dryden 1997).

Organizations are dealing with technical support issues by educating help-desk staff to make them more responsive and sensitive to the needs of remote workers. By making help-desk improvements, organizations hope to avoid the expense of creating a separate infrastructure designed just for telecommuters. Another tactic used to increase the effectiveness of help desks is to standardize the equipment used by telecommuters. Without standardization, "it takes a unique staff to sufficiently isolate multi-vendor problems" (Greene 1997, 27). Many companies, among them Pacific Bell, have decided not to support employee-owned equipment at all. Support is only provided for standard company-issued hardware and software. Pacific Bell's approach has been to preload laptops with security software, preconfigure the modems to avoid common set-up problems, and to make it easy to swap out equipment in need of repair (Greene 1997).

A recent trend in provision of technical support to remote workers is outsourcing of help-desk activities. Companies often outsource help desks simply because they do not have the people internally to handle support. In addition, it is becoming increasingly difficult for many corporations to keep up with advances in technology requiring "frequent and costly reinvestment in modem pools, remote access servers, and other network infrastructure. . . . The result is a turning away from the do-it-yourself approach to outsourcing remote access and other applications" (Berendt 1998, 33). Many corporations believe that they need to focus more on their core business. A utility-company executive explained his corporation's decision to outsource its information-technology business, including all help-desk functions, by saying, "We're not in the technology business; we're in the kilowatt business" (Wallace 1999, 34).

To be competitive, many companies feel they can't be spending ever-increasing amounts of time fixing laptop computers or dealing with network management. Berendt (1998) believes that corporations are making three central demands: performance, better security, and simplicity. As software applications become increasingly sophisticated, demands upon corporations escalate to support these applications. Similarly, as the number of telecommuters increases within a corporation, concerns over security increase. "The desire by corporations to simplify working processes is a major opening for single solution providers. . . . Development of help desk services will be vital to complete solution providers" (p. 35).

In the case of telecommuters operating without a company-sponsored help desk, support issues assume a much higher profile. Debra Dinnocenzo (1999) counsels teleworkers to be proactive in planning for support. She recommends that telecommuters examine their work critically to determine "1) whose help is vital; 2) where you do and do not have backup options for critical functions; 3) any gaps in your current support system; and 4) an action plan to close the gap" (p. 142). She recommends that workers articulate their support needs to providers before purchasing equipment or services. Dinnocenzo also suggests that telecommuters "make a long list of 'what if' questions regarding possible equipment failures and potential disasters for your productivity. Consider what resources you have currently or would need to have available as back-up options for your critical equipment and functions. Prioritize the list of additional options, alternatives, resources or tangible pieces of equipment you would need to have available" (p. 178).

SECURITY ISSUES RELATED TO TELECOMMUTING

Organizations have a host of issues to deal with in setting up and managing a telecommuting program. However, given the critical role the Internet plays in most telecommuting scenarios, security concerns often top the list. As Nilles (1998) states, in today's economic climate "it is not possible to totally exclude outside access to the [company] data while operating in a teleworking environment, as most companies must. Teleworkers could be restricted to using only non-sensitive data while they are teleworking but that would ultimately restrict the amount of teleworking—and its benefits—available to employees" (p. 83). Organizations must develop plans to keep their networks and data secure before rolling out telecommuting programs. Corporate security basically involves keeping sensitive information out of the hands of people who are not authorized to see it, and/or making the information useless to unauthorized individuals if they do see it.

Pacific Bell has developed a list of questions that organizations should consider when structuring a telecommuting security policy. They recommend looking first at existing internal policies (for example, does the company have a remote-access security policy or a policy for "appropriate" personal use of company equipment), before addressing security as it applies to telecommuters. Following this, among their suggestions are examining existing authentication procedures to see if remote workers can still be identified, determining if access privileges can be maintained remotely, seeing if an appropriate audit trail exists for review by security personnel, determining whether physical security at remote sites is appropriate and whether confidential data can be disposed of properly, thoroughly reviewing the existing security administration for weaknesses, and developing a telecommuter education program so workers receive training in security issues. (*Pacific Bell Telecommuting Guide* 1998).

Secure access to data on the part of remote users is the objective of a telecommuting security policy and Nilles (1998) summarizes the approaches often taken to protect access to this data:

1) having the telecommunications server either not directly connected to the mainframe or local area network, or examining all incoming data streams for the authorized signatures (that is, the server is a firewall); 2) using "smart cards" that display a password or token that changes every 30 seconds or so, in synchronization with a password identifier in the computer being called (the teleworker pulls out her smart card, dials up the company machine, and enters the password appearing on the card at the moment); 3) using a call back system—assuming all the password routines are completed correctly, the central computer dials the teleworker's home or other prearranged phone number; 4) requiring a positive identification of the caller, such as a retinal scan, fingerprint, or hand shape detector; 5) sensitive information can be encrypted, only the authorized teleworker or others who know the key can decipher it. (p. 84)

Many companies decide they need several layers of protection and use both hardware devices and software firewalls (York 1999).

Once security issues have been dealt with to an organization's satisfaction, managers find they must define the scope of a telecommuting program and resolve issues related to worker expectations as well as management expectations. Jeff Meade (1993), in *Home Sweet Office*, lists several areas where policies and planning are needed. Among the most critical are: (1) guidelines for who is eligible to participate in a telecommuting program, including any limits on the length of the agreement; (2) guidelines for managers in choosing individual participants for a program; and (3) training for managers so they learn to judge performance by productivity, not visibility, and have clear evaluation procedures for telecommuters. Olmstead and Smith (1997) add to this list with recommendations to (1) examine legal and tax considerations (problems with neighborhood zoning laws affecting home offices, insurance questions, etc.), (2) review compensation and benefits, (3) set clear scheduling expectations, and (4) design an application process for employees interested in telecommuting.

The experience of Alltel Information Services illuminates several of these recommendations (Deeprose 1999). Through its planning efforts Alltel was prepared for many human resource issues and designed a pilot telecommuting program with well-considered policies. The company identified job functions that were good candidates for moving to telecommuter positions (programmers, instructional designers, etc.) and set eligibility requirements for telecommuters (applicants had to receive recent evaluations where they demonstrated they "met job requirements" or better and had to receive their manager's approval for a telecommuting assignment. Alltel provided training for potential telecommuters as well as their managers so that both employees and managers had a better idea of how to deal with the changes that telecommuting introduces to work conditions and relationships.

Other guidelines Alltel developed dealt with areas such as scheduling, supplies, performance, equipment, and dependent care. The company felt it was important for telecommuters to have regularly scheduled hours during which they would be accessible. Alltel provides office supplies and all telecommuting equipment (and specifies that no other software be loaded on company-provided workstations), but has employees supply their own office furniture. The company expects telecommuters to make arrangements for care of dependents (children under ten as well as elderly or disabled adults), and does not want employees providing primary care during at-home work hours. Alltel has been specific about how telecommuting employees will be evaluated. Employees are assigned well-defined tasks and are measured on results.

SELECTING EMPLOYEES

A telecommuting program must be implemented carefully to avoid claims of illegal discrimination in the selection process. Brenda Thompson (1996) has these suggestions:

1) establish selection criteria that are work-related; 2) include the selection criteria in a written telecommuting policy; 3) make it clear to employees in both oral and written communication that telecommuting is a job assignment, not a benefit of employment; 4) provide each employee with a copy of the telecommuting policy and require each of them to sign a statement acknowledging receipt of the policy; 5) consider requiring that employees who wish to telecommute submit a written request to do so on a form supplied by the company; 6) instruct managers—via manager training sessions and written

guidelines for managers—to select telecommuters for work-related reasons only and to carefully document the selection process for each telecommuting applicant. If an employee is not permitted to telecommute because of a poor job performance history, that decision should be supported by prior documentation of the performance problems in the employee's file; 7) if an employee's telecommuting request is denied, be sure to advise the employee of the reason(s) why; 8) if possible, offer a range of flexible work options so that employees not eligible to telecommute have other flexible work alternatives available. (p. 13)

Olmsted and Smith (1994) offer these points for managers to take into account when evaluating the "potential of the employee to work off-site" (p. 81):

1. Does the employee have the self-motivation and self-discipline as well as the necessary job skill and experience to work off-site?
2. If there were any problems in a recent performance evaluation, how would telework affect these areas?
3. Has the employee been with the organization long enough to be familiar with its culture, policies, and procedures?
4. How aware is the employee of his or her own work style and its attendant strengths and weaknesses? Is telecommuting likely to increase job satisfaction?
5. Does the employee's job require time for creative thinking?
6. Will the employee be able to function without much social interaction with colleagues?
7. Does the employee have good communication skills and the ability to sustain regular interaction with colleagues from a remote site?
8. Does the employee have a strong desire for the telecommuting arrangement to work?

In addition to evaluating employee traits, Olmsted and Smith (1997) remind managers to review the actual job characteristics to determine whether the tasks can be done efficiently from a remote site, to determine whether the employee actually has a suitable "off-site" environment to work in, to make sure the employee has child care and/or dependent adult care arranged for, and to make a preliminary assessment of the kind of equipment and software that will be needed in the remote office. Olmstead and Smith also recommend that employees prepare a work plan if they wish to telecommute. They believe that employees should suggest ways to measure output and assess the quality of work produced at home.

Employers may also want to think about asking for a specific time commitment to a flexible work arrangement when negotiating with employees over telecommuting. Some employers ask for an initial commitment to the program of six months or a year. After this period the assumption is that both parties will review their experiences with the telecommuting agreement and reaffirm the agreement or renegotiate it. This ensures that both the company and the employee value each other's investments in telecommuting and also provides for reversibility of arrangements if they are not suitable (Olmsted and Smith 1994).

TRAINING

Experts in telecommuting consider training for telecommuting employees and their managers to be critical to a program's success. Nilles (1998) points out that "employees and managers alike may be intimidated by the concept, non-teleworking colleagues have misapprehensions about the nature of teleworking, families need to understand the changing roles of home teleworkers, and the work patterns of the teleworkers themselves tend to change. It is extremely important to provide pre-implementation and during implementation training (and assessment) for all of those who are directly affected by teleworking" (p. 190). Nilles advocates surveying potential teleworkers to get an initial reading of the kinds and amount of training they need in various areas.

Olmsted and Smith (1994) summarize the areas in which most telecommuters will need training. These include time management, setting objectives and measuring performance, office setup, security issues and security protocols, technical skills (such as use of voicemail, how to use a help desk), and procedures or record keeping required by the employer (how to keep track of time worked, how often to check in with a central office, etc.). Employees may also need help with the general psychology of working at home: how to cope with feelings of isolation, how to resist temptations (watching television, snacking, etc.), and other issues.

On the manager side, topics appropriate for training sessions might include how to screen employees to determine who can successfully work off-site, how to manage at a distance by monitoring results as opposed to activity levels, how to increase efficiency through revamping work schedules, and how to deal with hostility from employees not selected for telecommuting (Olmsted and Smith 1994). Managers working with telecommuters often have to learn to adjust their style of managing. This can be difficult and made worse if managers are resistant to discussing their attitudes toward remote supervision. Managers may also need additional training on communicating effectively with remote workers. Managers often find they must be more explicit about their expectations and what it is they are assuming teleworkers will be able to accomplish. Nilles (1998) believes that training in communication skills must focus on task definition and performance expectations.

Stephen Simmons (1996), in his book *Flexible Working: A Strategic Guide to Successful Implementation and Operation*, has a slightly different approach to thinking about training needs. He sorts topics into three areas of competency and labels them "task competencies, operational competencies, and personal competencies," then forms a matrix with the individuals involved (directors, managers, flexible workers) and defines the individual competence levels required (light to heavy). So for every competency area a trainer would have some idea of who needs training and to what degree. Under "tasks" Simmons would place topics ranging from word processing to automated design, depending upon the type of work being done. "Operational" competencies would include the ability to use a fax machine, how to use e-mail, the ability to use videoconferencing software, and so forth. "Personal" competencies include topics such as time management, presentation and communication skills, and coping with a solitary work environment.

SUPERVISING TELEWORKERS AND EVALUATING PROGRAMS

Robert Ramsey (1997) lists some of the approaches managers can take to supervise telecommuters. He suggests techniques such as communicating priorities and timetables in writing, establishing benchmarks by which to gauge progress, communicating with remote workers on a regular basis (via phone, fax, or e-mail), watching for early warning signs of problems (missed deadlines, difficulty contacting an employee, etc.), giving remote workers regular feedback, and conducting periodic reviews to evaluate the degree of success for each telecommuter's work situation. Ramsey also advises managers to facilitate networking between telecommuting employees (they will be able to help each other) and to involve telecommuters with planning and strategy sessions for the company so they remain part of a larger team. He recommends that managers apply the same standards for performance whether an employee works in an office or telecommutes. Ramsey advocates tactics that help managers keep the "big picture" in mind as well. It is important for managers to have a sense of how telecommuting fits into the overall strategy for a company. Thus, managers must keep upper management informed with regard to how telecommuting arrangements are working out and must monitor costs and productivity so that the company can compare outcomes of traditional and nontraditional work arrangements. Finally, if a telecommuting program is not working as anticipated, or particular employees are not doing well, managers must know when to make adjustments or hard decisions about allowing employees to continue to telecommute.

George Piskurich (1998), author of *An Organizational Guide to Telecommuting*, describes an evaluation process for telecommuting that informs decisions ranging from the employee level to the company level. Companies can use a monitoring process that involves surveying telecommuters, their supervisors, and others who may have valuable input (could include customers, nontelecommuting employees, or upper management). Telecommuting at the employee level would be assessed using questions about the kinds of problems a telecommuter might be experiencing, whether the equipment in the home office is adequate, if the employee can demonstrate increased productivity, and whether job satisfaction is greater. Supervisors might be asked for evidence that objectives are being met, whether communication is working well with remote workers, whether there are performance problems, and if a sense of teamwork is sustainable.

Organizations with telecommuting programs normally start out with goals they expect to achieve through implementation of such a program. These goals may range from retaining talented employees to reducing costs. It is important for companies to develop objective measures for documenting their progress toward achieving these goals. Piskurich (1998) warns that it is extremely important for companies to measure corporate goals set forth in the vision statement for a telecommuting program, not simply things it can gather data about. He also cautions that any cost–benefit analysis must be objective and that solid data should be generated for both expenses and cost savings. The kinds of issues an organization should be investigating are training costs, office set-up expenses, telecommunications expenses, productivity increases, sick-day usage, employee turnover data, and energy consumption.

HEALTH AND SAFETY ISSUES

As Thompson states (1996), "The federal Occupational Safety and Health Act (OSHA)—not to mention numerous state OSHA statutes—imposes safety and health standards in the workplace. These standards apply to every work site, whether it be a central office, a remote work center, or a telecommuter's home" (p. 21). Companies clearly cannot monitor an employee's home for potential OSHA violations, but in the interests of minimizing their liability employers can take steps to minimize the occurrence of violations. Some employers conduct inspections of home offices. Thompson (1996) points out the drawbacks to inspections (intrusive, violation of employee privacy) and suggests that if inspections are held the parameters of inspections (timing, frequency, scope) should be spelled out in a written telecommuting policy and in a written telecommuting agreement between the employee and employer. She also recommends that inspectors receive specific training in proper conduct of home-office inspections.

Some employers make it the responsibility of employees to maintain a safe working environment at home. In this case the employer and employee again have a written agreement regarding expectations, and company expectations are also spelled out in a formal telecommuting policy. Employees are usually asked to affirm that the home office meets certain health and safety standards and that they promise to maintain those standards in the future. At a minimum, home offices should have smoke detectors, fire extinguishers, and be ergonomically correct.

Thompson (1996) summarizes the points surrounding liability for injuries in the home office. The bottom line is that clear policies and written agreements should be in place at the outset to avoid extreme difficulties later on. In general, companies that have worker's compensation insurance coverage for employees want the rules that apply to their regular offices to also apply in home offices. Thus, for telecommuters, the first question is what constitutes the work site? Ideally this should be a space set apart from the remainder of the house so that an injury in the office can be distinguished from an injury in the laundry room. Worker's compensation generally covers only injuries that occur at the work site, so the ability to define a site is critical. Second, what are the work hours? Worker's compensation normally covers only those injuries that occur during working hours. Finally, what is the policy for reporting injuries? Prompt reporting of work-related injuries is the expected norm in offices, and home offices should be no different. Employers should also evaluate their insurance policies to see if injuries to third parties that occur at remote work sites are covered. If a telecommuter is likely to have clients or customers present in a home office, additional liability insurance may be warranted.

LABOR LAWS AND TAX ISSUES

Although telecommuting has moved the workplace from centralized offices to home offices, employers are still expected to comply with the "same old labor and employment laws" (Norris 1997, 4). Managerial and professional telecommuters are exempt from the Fair

Labor Standards Act (which requires most employers to pay overtime rates for employees when they work more than forty hours in a week). However, nonexempt telecommuters can present problems for employers. If the number of hours worked is underreported the company could face substantial fines, as it would be in violation of the Fair Labor Standards Act.

Maureen Minehan (1996) counsels employers to carefully keep track of hours worked by off-site nonexempt employees. Good record keeping will help companies avoid problems created by both underreporting and overreporting of hours worked. Telecommuting policies should be explicit about the rules for record keeping and should address any flexibility in the actual schedule for hours worked. The rules should also be in place before any teleworking begins. As an informal check on hours being reported, Minehan advises employers to get a good idea of how long it should take an employee to accomplish certain tasks. Requiring employees to log in and log out of a network when they are telecommuting can also be used to roughly confirm the hours being reported. In the area of reporting hours worked, though, there is no substitute for the value of trust. Nilles (1998) does not recommend teleworking unless employers trust their employees to do their jobs, especially when the employees are out of sight.

For most telecommuters, there is no tax break gained from working at home. Deductions for home offices have been disappearing and tightening up throughout the 1990s. A home office must be used regularly and exclusively for business and must also meet one of three conditions: be used as a principal place of business (one or two days a week does not qualify), be a place to meet or deal with customers and clients, or be in connection with the business if the space is a separate structure from the home. Alice Bredin (1996) points out that "you still cannot take any deductions unless your telecommuting is for the convenience of your employer, not merely because it is appropriate and helpful. If you are audited you will have to present a note to the IRS stating that you are telecommuting at the request of your employer" (p. 116). Furthermore, if the employer is reimbursing the employee for expenses, then those expenses cannot be deducted by the employee. If an employer is contributing a monthly sum to cover expenses, the money must be reported by the employee as income (There's No Mercy from Uncle Sam 1997).

One additional issue that should be addressed is the possibility some companies see for saving money by converting telecommuters from employee to independent-contractor status. Gil Gordon (1997) summarizes the thinking on this topic. "Telecommuters sometime collude with this possibility by saying they would be very happy to be paid strictly on an hourly basis and forgo their benefits, especially if they have a spouse whose employment provides medical coverage.... This is a huge HR and legal minefield. Although there continues to be confusion about the employee versus independent contractor distinction, it is clear that the IRS and the courts do not look kindly on employers who interpret this confusion in their own favor" (p. 29). The IRS has made it clear that a change in where an employee works, particularly if the work and supervision remain unchanged, does not justify the independent-contractor label.

One final area that merits discussion is the special issues to consider if a telecommuting program is being implemented in an environment with unionized workers. Labor unions have expressed concerns regarding telecommuting and other flexible work arrangements. Some opposition is linked to the difficulty of enforcing labor standards that have been designed to protect workers when workers are based at home, and other opposition stems from the "potential for changing an employee's status from regular to independent-contractor as a condition of working from the home" (Olmsted and Smith 1994, 72). In other words, many unions are concerned that telecommuting offers a new way for employers to take advantage of employees. Other problem areas are discussed by Bredin (1996). These include the union stance that "employees should be compensated more for telecommuting since they are more productive as telecommuters" (p. 114) and also union concerns about the fact that not all employees are eligible for telecommuting (often an issue during an initial pilot program or demonstration phase of a telecommuting program). Thompson (1996) suggests heading off potential management–union problems by involving the union at the beginning of the planning process to avoid delays later, and paying attention to union concerns such as fairness in the selection process and compliance with wage and hour laws.

REFERENCES

Becker, F., A. J. Rappaport, K. L. Quinn, and W. R. Sims. 1993. *Telework centers: An evaluation of the North American and Japanese experience*. Ithaca, N.Y.: Cornell University, International Workplace Studies Program.

Becker, F., and C. M. Tennessen. 1995. *The hotel as office*. Ithaca, N.Y.: Cornell University, International Workplace Studies Program.

Berendt, A. 1998. The virtual enterprise gets real. *Telecommunications*, April, 32–36.

Berner, J. 1994. *The joy of working from home: Making a life while making a living*. San Francisco: Berrett-Koehler.

Bibby, A. 1995. *Teleworking: Thirteen journeys to the future of work*. London: Calouste Gulbenkian Foundation.

Blakinger, M. 1999. New headquarters punctuates its setting. *Philadelphia Inquirer*, 12 March, C1–C2.

Bredin, A. 1996. *The virtual office survival handbook.* New York: Wiley.

Canadian Telework Scene. 1999. <http://www.ivc.ca/part12.html.> [cited 10 November 1999].

Christensen, K. 1990. Here we go into the "high-flex" era. *Across the Board* 27 (7–8): 22–23.

Closing the telework gap critical if Colorado is to retain lead in competition for high-tech workers. 1998. *PR Newswire* [on-line]. Dow Jones Interactive/Publications Library. [cited 22 November 1998].

Cooper, R. C. 1996. Telecommuting: The good, the bad and the particulars. *Supervision* 57 (2): 10–12.

Dash, J. 1999. Telecommuting continues to rise. *Computerworld* 33 (42): 43.

Davey, S. R. 1998. Virtual staffing. *Occupational Health & Safety,* 1 August, 28.

De Lisser, E. 1999. Update on small business: Firms laden with virtual environments appeal to workers. *Wall Street Journal,* 5 October, B2.

Deeprose, D. 1999. When implementing telecommuting leave nothing to chance. *HR Focus* 76 (10): 13–15.

Dinnocenzo, D. A. 1999. *101 tips for telecommuters: Successfully manage your work, team, technology and family.* San Francisco: Berrett-Koehler.

Dryden, P. 1997. The vital lifeline. *Computerworld* 31 (5): 20.

Eldib, O., and D. Minoli. 1995. *Telecommuting.* Boston: Artech House.

Employers save $10,000 per teleworker in reduced absenteeism and retention costs. Teleworkers increase to 10 percent of U.S. adults. *International Telework Association & Council* [on-line]. <http://www.telecommute.org/.> [cited 10 November 1999].

Fisher, A. 1998. How do I persuade my boss to let me work at home? *Fortune,* 9 November, 264.

Future work means flexible work. 1999. *Management Services* 43 (9): 5.

Gaspar, J., and E. L. Glaeser. 1996. *Information technology and the future of cities.* Cambridge, Mass.: National Bureau of Economic Research.

Goldman, L. M., and B. A. Goldman. 1998. Planning for telework. In *Teleworking: International perspectives: From telecommuting to the virtual organisation,* edited by P. J. Jackson and J. M. Van der Wielen. London: Routledge.

Gordon, G. E. 1997. HR implications of officeless office work. *Employment Relations Today,* Summer, 23–32.

Gore, A. 1997. *Turning the key: Unlocking human potential in the family-friendly federal workplace: A status report on federal workplace family-friendly inititiatives.* Washington, D.C.: GPO.

Gray, M., N. Hodson, and G. Gordon. 1993. *Teleworking explained.* Chichester, England: Wiley.

Greene, T. 1997. Telecommuting is more than hardware and software. *Network World* 14 (27): 27.

Guiding principles for managing a flexible workplace. 1997. *Getting Results ... for the Hands-On Manager* (special report supplement), October, 1–2.

Himmelberg, M. 1997. NCR adapts to rules of the road on its telecommuting highway. *Orange County Register,* 10 November, D14.

Hoffman, E. 1999. Make money, work barefoot. *Good Housekeeping,* May, 99–102.

Hollister, N. 1995. *The mobile office: Towards the virtual corporation.* London: Financial Times Telecommunications and Media Publishing.

Homeworking in the European Union. 1995. Luxembourg: Office for Official Publications of the European Communities.

Huws, U. 1995. *Follow-Up to the White Paper*. Luxembourg: Office for Official Publications of the European Communities.

Huws, U., W. B. Korte, and S. Robinson. 1990. *Telework: Towards the elusive office*. Chichester, England: Wiley.

Jackson, P. J., and J. M. Van der Wielen. 1998a. Introduction: Actors, approaches and agendas: From telecommuting to the virtual organisation. In *Teleworking: International perspectives: From telecommuting to the virtual organisation*, edited by P. J. Jackson and J. M. Van der Wielen. London: Routledge.

————. 1998b. *Teleworking: International perspectives: From telecommuting to the virtual organisation*. London: Routledge.

Johnson, S. A. 1998. Teleworking service management: Issues for an integrated framework. In *Teleworking: International perspectives: From telecommuting to the virtual organisation*, edited by P. J. Jackson and J. M. Van der Wielen. London: Routledge.

Kirschner, S. 1998. Flextime, telecommuting ease jams. *St. Louis Post-Dispatch*, 28 May, B7.

Koch, K. 1998. More employers offer telecommuting to give workers flexibility. *Portland Oregonian*, 3 September, A18.

Korte, W. B., and R. Wynne. 1996. *Telework: Penetration, potential and practice in Europe*. Amsterdam: IOS Press.

Langhoff, J. 1996. *Telecom made easy: Money-saving, profit-building solutions for home businesses, telecommuters and small organizations*. 2d ed. Newport, R.I.: Aegis.

————. 1999. *The Telecommuter's Advisor*. 2d ed. Newport, R.I.: Aegis.

Lucent leads trend in high-tech home building; signs on new communities with contracts valued at more than $22 M. 1998. *Business Wire* [on-line]. Dow Jones Interactive, Publications Library. [cited 22 November 1998].

Mahlon, A. 1998. The alternative workplace: Changing where and how people work. *Harvard Business Review* 76 (3): 121–130.

McCloskey, D. W., and M. Igbaria. 1998. A review of the empirical research on telecommuting and directions for future research. In *The virtual workplace*, edited by M. Igbaria and M. Tan. Hershey, Pa.: Idea Group.

Meade, J. 1993. *Home sweet office: The ultimate out-of-office experience: Working your company job from home*. Princeton, N.J.: Peterson's.

Minehan, M. 1996. Consider all possibilities for telecommuters. *HRMagazine* 41 (11): 160.

Moorcroft, S., and V. Bennett. 1995. *European guide to teleworking: A framework for action*. Dublin: European Foundation for the Improvement of Living and Working Conditions.

Nilles, J. M. 1994. *Making telecommuting happen: A guide for telemanagers and telecommuters*. New York: Van Nostrand Reinhold.

————. 1998. *Managing telework: Strategies for managing the virtual workforce*. New York: Wiley.

Nilles, J. M., F. R. Carlson, P. Gray, and G. Hanneman. 1976. *The telecommunications–transportation tradeoff: Options for tomorrow*. New York: Wiley.

Norris, J. 1997. Labor law and telecommuting. *Getting Results for the Hands-On Manager* 42 (5): 4.

O'Connell, S. E. 1996. The virtual workplace moves at warp speed. *HRMagazine* 41 (3): 50–53.

Olen, H. 1996. Getting a handle on flextime. *Working Mother*, February, 55–56.

Olmsted, B., and S. Smith. 1994. *Creating a flexible workplace: How to select & manage alternative work options.* 2d ed. New York: AMACOM.

———. 1997. *Managing in a flexible workplace.* New York: AMACOM.

Pacific Bell Telecommuting Guide. 1998. San Francisco: Pacific Bell.

Piskurich, G. 1996. Making telecommuting work. *Training & Development* 50 (2): 20–27.

———. 1998. *An organizational guide to telecommuting: Setting up and running a successful telecommuter program.* Alexandria, Va.: American Society for Training and Development.

Pratt, J. H. 1993. *Myths and realities of working at home: Characteristics of homebased business owners and telecommuters.* Dallas: Joanne H. Pratt Associates.

Price, S. M. 1991. *California's telecommuting pilot project.* Lexington, Ky.: Council of State Governments.

Qvortrup, L. 1998. From teleworking to networking: Definitions and trends. In *Teleworking: International perspectives: From telecommuting to the virtual organisation,* edited by P. J. Jackson and J. M. Van der Wielen. London: Routledge.

Ramsey, R. D. 1997. How to supervise home workers. *Supervision* 58 (4): 9–12.

Reid, A. 1993. *Teleworking: A guide to good practice.* Manchester, England: Blackwell.

Reynolds, T., and D. Brusseau. 1998. *Cyberlane commuter.* Chula Vista, Calif.: Black Forest Press.

Richter, J. 1996. Teleworking. In *International Encyclopedia of Business and Management,* edited by M. Warner. London: International Thomson Business Press.

Rollier, B., and Y. I. Liou. 1998. The mobile workforce: Strategic opportunity, competitive necessity. In *The virtual workplace,* edited by M. Igbaria and M. Tan. Hershey, Pa.: Idea Group.

Romei, L. K. 1996. Your home office: A multiplicity of choices. *Managing Office Technology* 41 (1): 25–27.

Ruppel, C. P. 1995. Correlates of the adoption and implementation of programmer/analyst telework: An organizational perspective. Ph.D. diss., Kent State University.

Sato, K., and W. A. Spinks. 1998. Telework and crisis management in Japan. In *Teleworking: International perspectives: From telecommuting to the virtual organisation,* edited by P. J. Jackson and J. M. Van der Wielen. London: Routledge.

Schepp, D., and B. Schepp. 1995. *The telecommuter's handbook: How to earn a living without going to the office.* 2d ed. New York: McGraw-Hill.

Shillingford, J. 1997. Teleworking: Hard day at the semi. *Financial Times* (London), 10 September, 13.

Simmons, S. 1996. *Flexible working: A strategic guide to successful implementation and operation.* London: Kogan Page.

Sims, W., M. Joroff, and F. Becker. 1996. *Managing the reinvented workplace.* Houston, Tex.: International Facility Management Association; Norcross, Ga.: International Development Research Council.

Smart Valley closes its doors; information infrastructure thriving in Silicon Valley. 1998. *Business Wire.* [on-line]. Dow Jones Interactive, Publications Library. [cited 22 November 1998].

Speeth, L. M. 1992. The attributes of successful managers of telecommuters and successful telecommuting programs. Ph.D. diss., Golden Gate University.

Stanworth, C. 1996. *Working at home: A study of homeworking and teleworking.* London: Institute of Employment Rights.

Suttling, B., and D. Wood. 1997. Managing the virtual team. *Telecommunications* 31 (12): 61–64.

Technology's effect on work/life balance. 1998. *Work–Family Roundtable* 8 (2): entire issue.

Telecommute Magazine launched. 1998. *PR Newswire* [on-line]. Dow Jones Interactive, Publications Library. [cited 20 November 1998].

Telework—attitudes of the social partners, the labour force and potential for decentralized electronic work in Europe. 1986. In *New forms of work and activity,* edited by R. Dahrendorf, E. Kohler, and F. Piotet. Dublin: European Foundation for the Improvement of Living and Working Conditions.

Teleworking in Europe: Part One. 1996. *European Industrial Relations Review,* May, 17–20.

Teleworking in Europe: Part Two. 1996. *European Industrial Relations Review,* June, 18–21.

Teleworking in Europe: Part Three. 1996. *European Industrial Relations Review,* August, 18–23.

Tessier, A., and F. Lapointe. 1994. *Telework at home: Evaluation of a pilot project at Employment and Immigration Canada.* Laval, Quebec: Centre for Information Technology Innovation, Technological Innovation and New Forms of Work Organization.

There's no mercy from Uncle Sam. 1997. *Managing Office Technology* 42 (2): 20.

Thompson, B. B. 1996. *Telecommuting pluses and pitfalls.* Brentwood, Tenn.: M. Lee Smith.

Toffler, A. 1980. *The third wave.* New York: Morrow.

U.S. House. 1992. Committee on Energy and Commerce. *Telecommuting: Hearing before the Subcommittee on Telecommunications and Finance of the Committee on Energy and Commerce on H.R. 5082.* 102nd Cong., 2d sess., 29 July.

Wallace, B. 1999. Utility farms out IT. *Information Week,* 6 September, 34.

Warner, M. 1997. Working at home—the right way to be a star in your bunny slippers. *Fortune,* 3 March, 165–166.

Wilson, A. 1991. *Teleworking: Flexibility for a few.* Sussex, England: Institute of Manpower Studies.

A workstyle revolution. 1999. *Management Services* 43 (9): 4.

York, T. 1999. Telecommuting trials. *Infoworld* 21 (22): 87–88.

CHAPTER 4

Companies

This chapter will focus on companies that are leaders in providing flexible work environments. One of the issues that will be addressed is how an organization progresses from relatively traditional attitudes toward work and workers to more enlightened and family-friendly attitudes. Predictors of flexible organizations will be examined and descriptions of leading companies in various industry sectors will follow.

Ellen Galinsky is interested in the changing structure and culture of the workplace and has written extensively on the topic of how companies evolve. A number of factors can be identified that relate to reasons organizations perceive a need to change. Among these factors are the realization that corporate caretaking and family-friendly policies are actually good for business. Employers realize that quality-of-life issues at work matter if an organization hopes to retain top workers, recruit new workers, and foster a productive work environment. Galinsky, Dana Friedman, and Carol Hernandez (1991) identified a pattern to the evolution of company attitudes toward work and family issues and can point to stages in a company's progression.

In the first stage of a company's evolution, "The company realizes that some employees have family-related problems, although they're generally seen in terms of women's issues. A company identifies a problem and then selects what it sees as an appropriate solution" (Butruille 1990, 50). In other words, the company takes a programmatic approach and develops stand-alone programs that it believes will solve specific problems. Typical programs might include day care or flexible scheduling.

In the second stage of development, "The company moves into an integrated approach. At this point of the evolution, executives at the highest levels of the company begin to become involved in the issues because they see work–family balance as a bottom-line business issue (Solomon 1991, 59). In taking an integrated approach, companies go beyond superficial solutions and look for links to other issues. The relationship between work life and private life becomes clearer as factors emerge that affect morale and work productivity. Friedman and Galinsky (1992) can identify a number of topics that stage-two companies have addressed. These include eldercare and flexible work schedules (typically part-time arrangements, extended flextime, longer and more flexible leave policies, sick days that can be used for family members, and provisions for working at home). It should be noted that when companies explore flexible work arrangements at this stage they are attempting to help employees deal with stress and better manage the intersection of their professional and personal lives. Companies are not exploring flexible schedule options solely for the convenience of company business (Solomon 1991). In addition, companies often train managers to be more sensitive to work and family issues as they affect employees. Companies may also collaborate with the larger community to work on issues by providing start-up funds for partnerships in areas such as day care or eldercare (Butruille 1990).

The third stage of a company's evolution occurs when a company realizes that programs are not enough and begins to actually change the corporate culture. Companies at this stage acknowledge the importance of quality-of-life issues and may address such issues in a corporate vision statement. Such companies actively promote policies that are supportive of families and ensure that supervisors support company policies (Solomon 1991). Managers may even be evaluated on their ability to handle the work-life conflicts of employees (Lobel 1996).

Sharon Lobel (1996) believes that work-life benefits and policies are more important to employees than ever before, but organizations are moving less quickly to introduce and expand such programs than one might think. A significant reason for the lag is that human resource managers have difficulty demonstrating that such initiatives add value to the organization. Lobel discusses four obstacles that human resource managers are faced with. The first is that it is difficult for managers to describe less tangible but highly significant work-life supports. It is one thing to establish that a child-care referral program benefited employees, and quite another to attempt to show that a supportive culture was good for the company bottom line. How does a company objectively describe the term "supportive culture"?

The second problem is the difficulty of putting a price tag on interventions. A flexible organizational culture is the most important feature of a family-friendly company, but attaching an actual cost or financial benefit to the process of creating a flexible organizational culture is extremely difficult. How much does it cost or what value is added when a company attempts to teach managers to respond with sensitivity to employee needs while keeping business objectives in mind?

A third problem is that of tracking the beneficiaries of programs and policies. Many organizations do not monitor participation in programs, especially if some of the arrangements are informal. Employees may also expect a certain amount of privacy or anonymity with use of certain programs or referrals. Companies may not realize that the pool of beneficiaries may extend beyond the organization itself to include other family members or members of the community.

The final problem is that human resource managers may find it difficult to measure the effects of programs. Although a company can generate data to track the amount it invests in training, benefits, and salary for a given employee, it probably cannot isolate the effects of any specific work-life interventions at the employee level.

Lobel (1996) suggests four methods human resource managers can use to demonstrate the value added by work-life supports. The first method is a "human-cost" approach that highlights the reduced labor costs associated with specific programs. This is the most popular way of demonstrating the value of work-life investments. Absenteeism and turnover rates are commonly tracked, with some companies analyzing data to project cost savings. The second method is a "human-investment" approach that emphasizes the long-term organizational benefits to meeting employee work-life needs. With this model employees are viewed as "assets," and measures of success might include improved job performance, few disciplinary problems, low turnover, and so forth. The third method is a "stakeholder" approach. Managers using this technique can demonstrate the impact of various programs and policies on different groups of shareholders. Groups might include employees, shareholders, customers, suppliers, or communities. Desired impacts may vary from group to group; increased stock prices might be an indicator for the shareholder group, while high job satisfaction and productivity increases might be an indicator for the employee group. The final method is a "strategy" approach that demonstrates how work-life supports are linked to higher organizational goals such as the provision of superior customer service. Collecting these types of data is a long-term process. A company using this approach might attempt to demonstrate how flexible scheduling has helped the company anticipate and plan for meeting customer demands.

In spite of the difficulties that face organizations as they evolve into more flexible workplaces, the pace of change has been impressive. Lists of "good" and "best" places to work have become common. *Working Mother* has published an annual list of the 100 best family-friendly companies for the past fourteen years. The most recent issue (100 Best Companies 1999) looks at company performance in six areas: leave policies for new parents, flexibility, child-care programs, work-life issues, advancement of women, and compensation. Publications such as *BusinessWeek* and *Fortune* have also come out with special reports on similar themes. *Fortune's* report, "The 100 Best Companies to Work for in America" (1998) showcases many of the efforts companies are making to attract and retain talented workers and demonstrates that flexibility is "not something you have to beg for" (p. 70). Similarly, *BusinessWeek* (Work and Family 1996) documented the move toward increased flexibility as a competitive advantage for companies in looking at best practices from ten leading companies.

While flexible companies are an extremely varied group, there are some predictors of flexibility that are beginning to emerge. In her research on the impact of family-friendly policies on the advancement of women in organizations, Debra Schwartz (1994) found that programs such as flexible work arrangements, leave benefits, and dependant-care benefits are most likely to be offered by large companies. However, it is also the case that small companies may be able to provide employees with more personalized scheduling options. Schwartz's research indicates that companies offering family-friendly programs are part of economically healthy industries, rely on skilled workers, are operating in a tight labor market, and have a high percentage of women in their workforce.

In looking at access to family-friendly work arrangements, Schwartz (1994) found some interesting differences. Her research indicated that "in general, managers and professionals, those who earn more, and those with more education, have the greatest access to family-friendly policies" (p. 9). She did not find any indication that geographic region was related to access. Schwartz also states that "studies consistently show that greater time flexibility, rather than specific dependant-care benefits, is the family-friendly policy most desired by employed parents" (p. 17).

An area of concern to Schwartz (1994) is the degree to which certain programs are used (or actually not used). Her research suggests that the use of leaves and flexible work arrangements is relatively low and attributes this to the widespread existence of concern about career damage. This is in spite of the fact that preliminary research indicates the actual impact of use of such leaves is less than might be expected. More research is clearly needed. Schwartz also demonstrates that "supervisors are the key mediators affecting a range of outcomes in the workplace—employee satisfaction and loyalty, level of work–family conflict, perceived tradeoffs between work and personal life, and the impact of family-friendly policies. The research also indicates that supervisor supportiveness can be increased" (p. 26).

Schwartz (1994) states that "despite the increasing pace of change in U.S. companies . . . traditional beliefs about the nature of work persist. These include the notions that commitment to career and one's company are demonstrated by time spent in the office ('face time'), that presence and hours are the best indicator of productivity, that 'real' professional work can only be accomplished on a full-time basis, and that those who are serious about advancing will make themselves available to the office at all times" (p. 27). The company profiles that follow demonstrate that these traditional beliefs are changing.

AUTOMOBILE MANUFACTURERS

BMW

The German car manufacturer has implemented a number of flexible scheduling options. One of the more interesting examples is a working-time account. Employees work shorter or longer hours when required, building up a credit or debit of up to 200 hours in an "account." Credits can be cashed in for longer holidays and debits are usually repaid as production requirements increase. This typically meshes well with automobile production schedules: Overtime is needed when new models go into production and decreases as a model is phased out. Other options include four-day workweeks, four-day workweeks with an additional thirty-five minutes per day (yielding an extra-long weekend every five weeks), and part-time work with variability in the number of hours employees contract to work each week (for more information, see Crisis in the Motor Industry 1998).

DaimlerChrysler

The company sponsors an on-line job posting site that lists available job-sharing positions and employees seeking job-share partners. The company also makes a $4,000 deposit to every salaried nonunion employee in a "Work/Family Account" that can be used to pay for child care, adoption fees, education, eldercare, or retirement. The automaker also guarantees up to one year time off for new mothers and a phase-back period for new mothers, and offers a range of additional flexible work schedules (flextime, compressed workweeks, telecommuting, and part-time work) and a modest number of work-life programs (for more information, see 100 Best Companies 1999).

Ford Motor Company

Ford is a leader in the area of work-life benefits. The company offers flextime, compressed work weeks, telecommuting, part-time work, and job sharing. Subsidized child care and child-care and eldercare referral are offered. The company offers new mothers up to one year of guaranteed leave time. They also offer a phase-back period for new mothers (for more information, see 100 Best Companies 1999; Caudron 1998).

BANKING AND FINANCIAL SERVICE

First Tennessee

This is a midsize regional bank that has received a great deal of attention for its progressive work/family programs, which it initiated in 1992. Initial measures were aimed at increasing employee retention (customers complained about the high turnover rate). The lack of flexibility was clearly an issue. The company has integrated consideration of family issues with job design, work processes, and organizational structure. Workers set their own schedules and the company has a variety of options (flextime, flexweeks, job sharing, telecommuting, and part-time work). Over 90 percent of the employees are using some type of flexible scheduling.

The company has demonstrated that its policies have a positive impact. Branch offices where employees rated supervisors as supportive of work/family balance retained employees twice as long and kept 7 percent more retail customers. Higher retention rates alone contributed to a 55-percent profit gain in two years (for more information, see Gillian 1997; Hein 1996; Martinez 1997; 100 Best Companies 1999; Verespej 1999b; Work and Family 1996).

Merrill Lynch

This financial-services firm has implemented a highly structured telecommuting program. Employees must formally apply for telecommuting, undergo training, and participate in regular follow-ups involving focus groups and surveys. The company runs a telecommuting lab for prospective telecommuters. After extensive screening, employees are expected to spend two weeks working in a simulated home office. During this period employees communicate with managers, customers, and colleagues by phone and e-mail alone. If workers find they do not like the experience, they are free to drop out of the program and return to a traditional work environment. Merrill Lynch has found that these steps help clarify expectations of the program for employees as well as managers. The company also requires employees with dependents to provide documentation of arrangements for care before working from home. Other flexible work options are flextime, compressed workweeks, and job sharing (for more information, see Apgar 1998; Cottle 1999; 100 Best Companies 1999; Work and Family 1996).

National Westminster Bank

This U.K. bank introduced flexibility in scheduling as a means to retain highly trained female staff and as a way to meet customer demand for later hours and weekend service. Examples include job sharing, part-time work, flextime, telecommuting, and contracts for work during the school year only. The bank also offers "career breaks." The person on the break is expected to work at least two weeks per year, and the break can last for up to five years (for more information, see Hogg and Harker 1992).

Royal Bank of Canada

In 1990 the Royal Bank began rolling out family/work programs in areas such as leave policies and benefits, dependent care, flexible work arrangements, work- and family-related management training, and work and family resource libraries. The bank offers a variety of flexible work arrangements, including part-time work, job sharing, flextime, flexibility in the workplace, and modified workweeks. The bank is one of Canada's largest employers and has more employees in job-sharing arrangements than any other Canadian employer. Job sharers are eligible for full benefits. The bank estimates that over one-third of its employees are using some kind of flexible work schedule. The bank has been fine-tuning its policies by undertaking research to determine the obstacles employees and managers encounter in setting up flexible work arrangements. A large study in 1998 of 1,700 of the bank's employees revealed that the bank's flexible work arrangements increased productivity, were supported by managers, and did not keep employees from being promoted. Over 94 percent of flex workers were very satisfied with their working arrangements. The bank has calculated that 40 percent of the customer experience can be traced to employee behaviors, thus it estimates that its flexible work arrangements added $130 million to its bottom line in 1997 (for more information, see Collins 1997; Myth-Busting Study 1998; Olmstead and Smith 1994, 63; Verespej 1999b; Wong 1999).

COMPUTER MANUFACTURERS AND SOFTWARE FIRMS

Hewlett-Packard

This firm adopted flextime in 1971 and is still a leader in work/family programs. Over 85 percent of the employees are using some form of flexible scheduling. Employees in certain departments are eligible for compressed workweeks; other options include job sharing, part-time employment, alternative work schedules, and telecommuting. The company has developed written guidelines, training, and networks of peers to help managers move into the era of the "virtual office." Telecommuters must agree to have their work space approved by the company and the company retains the right to make inspections during normal business hours. Hewlett-Packard has also created informal flexibility through the use of flexible time off (including paid time-off banks) and unpaid leave. There are formal guidelines, but all employees can participate. Managers receive training in work-life issues, and most employees indicate they feel comfortable taking time off for family problems. The company tries to combine some of its formal programs with informal scheduling adjustments to accommodate temporary changes experienced by employees (for more information, see Busenbark 1996; Himmelberg 1998; O'Connell 1996; Sims, Joroff, and Becker 1996; Catalyst 1998; Work and Family 1996).

IBM

This company has been a leader in implementing work/family initiatives for many years, and has been extending its efforts worldwide. One of the company's most striking benefits is its leave for childbirth. The company guarantees mothers and fathers three years of time off, although they retain the right to ask a parent to come back part time after one year if business needs require it. Flexible work arrangements include flextime, compressed workweeks, job sharing, and telecommuting. IBM has been moving sales, marketing, and consulting employees into the telecommuting environment, both to save on real estate costs and to respond to demands from employees for more flexibility in their work lives. IBM feels the move to alternative work sites has been extremely successful on all fronts. Telecommuters are provided with phone lines, laptop computers, software support, fax–printer units, help lines, and full technical backup at the nearest corporate facility. Roughly 20 percent of IBM's worldwide workforce is trained and equipped for telecommuting (for more information, see Apgar 1998; O'Connell 1996; 100 Best Companies 1999).

Lotus Development Corporation

Lotus estimates that its flextime, job sharing, and telecommuting programs are used by about one-third of its employees. The company has created a software tool for employees to use that helps create alternative schedules and assists with work/life issues. The company is somewhat unusual in its offer of four weeks paid paternity leave for fathers (in addition to benefits for mothers). Lotus also invests in a variety of child-care programs for children of employees (for more information, see 100 Best Companies 1999).

EDUCATION

Princeton University

The university began investigating work-life issues in 1989 and initially targeted flextime arrangements and expansion of sick leave (to include care for family members) as areas for action. The university now has a formal policy that supports flextime, and employees can work part time, compress their workweeks, or job share in certain departments. Princeton University has a Work/Life Task Force (part of the Standing Committee on the Status of Women, which reports to the president of the university). The university is actively promoting the expansion of flexible work arrangements and is focusing on additional areas, such as eldercare (for more information, see Friedman, Rimsky, and Johnson 1996).

University of North Carolina

The university began surveying faculty, staff, and students in the late 1980s to gain a better understanding of work-life needs. Over the years changes have been made to leave policies and there is now information support in areas such as child-care referrals and eldercare resources and referrals. The university offers several flexible scheduling option, which include flextime, a compressed work-week, job sharing, and working from home. The university has found that although it has a formal policy on flexible work options, managers are reluctant to make adjustments. Thus, this area has been targeted as a special training area for managers in an effort to sensitize them to work-life issues and to better communicate university policies and practices. Alternative work arrangements are expected to achieve a much higher profile in the overall human resources strategy (for more information, see Friedman, Rimsky, and Johnson 1996).

GOVERNMENT

General Services Administration (GSA)

The federal government has been experimenting with the concept of telecenters and operates several in the Washington, D.C., metropolitan area. The GSA is also subsidizing some state-sponsored telecenters. The federal government has been pursuing telecenters as a means to cut down on air pollution (by having workers commute less) and increase productivity (by helping commuters spend time more productively). The idea behind telecenters is to provide workers with more or better amenities than a home office, and to be closer to home than a main office. Telecenters are facilities with workstations, telephones, photocopiers, fax machines, and a couple of conference rooms. In other words, they are similar to well-stocked small offices. They are expected to provide cost-effective access to high-tech equipment. Telecenters were envisioned as places an employee might come to once or twice a week. Some government agencies have used the centers for short-term team projects. The overall experience with telecenters has been mixed. The successful telecenters are being used by government employees; in areas where telecenters were expected to recruit private-sector tenants the experience has not been positive. However, it is probably too soon to determine how this concept will evolve (for more information, see Durkin 1997).

Inland Revenue

This department is primarily responsible for collecting a wide variety of taxes in the United Kingdom. Inland Revenue employs a variety of flexible work arrangements to meet what it calls business and equity needs. The department has been concerned for many years with providing employment opportunities for women. Flexible work arrangements help reduce labor turnover and contribute to work-life balance. All staff can apply to work part time; the department offers part-year contracts and flexible working hours as well. In addition, Inland Revenue allows both men and women to take formal "career breaks" from the department (for more information, see Corby 1997; Benefits of Flexible Working Patterns 1993).

State of California

The state has been a pioneer in many flexible work arrangements and offers a number of options to state employees. One of the most interesting is the Reduced Work Load Program available to public school teachers. This is a form of phased retirement. It was introduced to allow teachers nearing retirement to ease out of their careers while offering the state the opportunity to phase in new teachers. Teachers meeting certain criteria can negotiate to reduce their schedule to half time. The state is able to reduce its salary costs with this program, as the salaries of its experienced teachers are typically much higher than the salaries of the new teachers hired part time to pick up the uncovered teaching hours (for more information, see Olmsted and Smith 1994).

Oxfordshire County Council

The council is responsible for 80 percent of public services in the county, including education, social services, libraries, museums, roads, emergency services, and so on. The council is a leader in offering flexible work arrangements to employees. Nearly two-thirds of the female employees work part time, and the council is experimenting with telecommuting. The council is encouraging telecommuting as an add on to other flexible arrangements. An employee who is working part time in an office might wish to spend part of that work time telecommuting from home. The council has a generous paternity-leave policy (up to forty-five weeks of leave for new fathers), and also a number of other interesting options. Among them are part-time management development courses, work-life training programs, and job-sharing arrangements. Telecommuting employees receive an allowance (which is taxable) to cover costs involved in working from home (for more information, see Hogg and Harker 1992).

HEALTH-CARE INDUSTRY

Baxter International

This is a global medical product and services company. Baxter implemented a formal program for flexible scheduling in 1997. Policies determine how employees apply to the program as well as how managers determine whether to authorize participation. Workload, use of resources, and importance of physical presence in an office are the deciding factors. Employees receive guidance in submitting proposals for flexible arrangements, and managers receive training in analyzing requests. The most frequently requested options are telecommuting and a compressed workweek. Roughly 10 percent of the employees use some form of alternate scheduling. The company has begun an internal job-posting program that indicates the kinds of alternative work arrangements a given position might be able to accommodate (job sharing, part time, telecommuting, etc.) This also raises the profile of flex work with managers (for more information, see Busenbark 1996; Campbell 1998; Case Study 1997; Klieman 1998).

INSURANCE

Aetna

Flexible work arrangements are becoming increasingly popular at this insurance company as a result of a variety of "tool kits," training, and incentive programs. Aetna can document increased productivity and employee retention as a result of its telecommuting program. Productivity levels increased 20 to 50 percent among 600 telecommuters in claims processing and member services. The company also found that it cut in half the number of resignations by new mothers when it extended its unpaid parental leave to six months. The company believes it was able to save $1 million per year in hiring and training expenses. Over two-thirds of Aetna's employees are using a flexible work schedule (for more information, see Carter 1998; Martinez 1997; 100 Best Companies 1999).

Travelers

This insurance company implemented the first phase of a telecommuting program in 1987 and involved information-systems division personnel hand selected by managers. They worked at home four-and-a-half days a week and in the office half a day. Later that same year the program was extended to include additional staff in the same division. These staff worked at home from one to three days a week. In 1988 telecommuting was implemented organizationwide. It is entirely voluntary, but restricted to jobs where performance can be measured, where little face-to-face contact is required, where access to off-line equipment or files is not necessary, where supervisor responsibilities are minimal or nonexistent, and where tasks focus on research, writing, analyzing, or programming. To be eligible, employees must meet experience criteria and have their manager's approval. Travelers has a furniture package it delivers to telecommuters that is ergonomically correct (for more information, see Sims, Joroff, and Becker 1996).

MANUFACTURING

Pella Corporation

Pella is a pioneer in the job-sharing experience. The company first experimented with job sharing in 1977 in response to an employee request. The company was interested in the concept as a way to reduce absenteeism and cope with overstaffing on production lines (it manufactures windows). Since that time the program has become very popular and absenteeism rates have improved dramatically. Overstaffing of production lines (in order to compensate for absenteeism) has been eliminated. The program is open to current full-time employees in production positions and employees in clerical positions. Eligible employees are responsible for finding their own partners, but the company assists by functioning as a clearinghouse for interested parties. Employees must agree to participate for a minimum of six months, and anyone who drops out cannot rejoin the program for a full year. The company provides full benefits to job sharers (for more information, see Olmsted and Smith 1994).

Steelcase

The furniture manufacturer offers a variety of work/family programs. The company emphasizes tools that enable employees to make educated decisions, solve problems, and implement their own solutions. The company attempts to empower employees so that they are better consumers of programs offered by the company. The company began a job-share and flextime program in 1988 and has expanded to telecommuting. Steelcase has determined that job sharing has lowered absenteeism, reduced employee turnover, improved morale, and improved job coverage. The personnel department helps interested employees find partners. Although the program was initially open only to employees in clerical positions, it has been expanded to include all employees, including production personnel (for more information, see Cutcher-Gershenfeld, Kossek, and Sandling 1997; Olmstead and Smith 1994).

United Technologies

In 1998 this manufacturing company was awarded the Opportunity 2000 award by the U.S. Department of Labor for its comprehensive workforce programs. In part, the award recognized United Technology's policies and programs in the area of work-life initiatives and family-friendly environments. The company offers sixteen weeks of job-protected family-leave time off each year and encourages the use of flextime, job sharing, telecommuting, and other alternative work arrangements. The company also provides paid time off, tuition, textbooks, and stock shares upon graduation for employees completing a degree (for more information, see United Technologies Receives Top U.S. Department of Labor Award 1998).

PERSONAL HEALTH CARE PRODUCTS

Johnson & Johnson

The company introduced its Balancing Work and Family program in 1989. The program consists of several components, including family-care leave, flexible work schedules, part-time work, job sharing, and telecommuting. Johnson & Johnson provides work/family training for supervisors and managers. The company is somewhat unusual in its willingness to evaluate its work-life programs. There have been few other systematic program evaluations. Much of the literature on work/family programs is based on managers' perceptions of programs and other anecdotal evidence. Data collected by Johnson & Johnson in surveys of four companies in 1990 and 1992 indicated that its Balancing Work and Family program did not affect absenteeism or employee turnover one way or the other. However, the rate of absenteeism among employees who used flextime and made use of leave policies was actually less than the rate for the workforce as a whole. Employees felt their supervisors and their general work environments had become more supportive of their personal and family needs in the early 1990s. Employees also felt their supervisors were becoming more accepting of flexible schedules. The surveys revealed that employees wanted more control over their own schedules, and that supervisors who are supportive of work-life initiatives have a great impact on how competently employees feel they are balancing their work and family lives. Johnson & Johnson continues to offer generous leave policies (one year for new mothers) as well as a variety of flexible work options (flextime, compressed work-weeks, job sharing, telecommuting, and part-time work) (for more information, see An Evaluation of Johnson & Johnson's Work–Family Initiative 1993; 100 Best Companies 1999).

PHARMACEUTICALS

DuPont

Flexible scheduling practices have evolved gradually at this company, but are built around seven principles. Flexible work practices should deliver value to DuPont's four stakeholders (customers, employees, stockholders, and the public); practices should be designed and implemented to accommodate individual needs without impacting team effectiveness; employees should be compensated in accordance with hours worked; performance should be measured by the quality and quantity of work performed (not number of hours worked, when work was performed, or where it was performed); flexible work practices should be reviewed and continuously improved or discontinued if appropriate; flexible work practices should not have a negative effect on career advancement, use of leave policies, or raises; and a commitment to high standards of safety, ethics, and legal requirements must continue. Close to 40 percent of employees use flextime, and many others telecommute, job share, work part time, or work a compressed workweek. Supervisors get good marks at DuPont from employees for support of family/work initiatives (for more information, see Busenbark 1996; 100 Best Companies 1999).

Merck

This company has made a commitment to having leaders in place who understand and value Merck's work-life initiatives and are capable of providing the atmosphere and flexibility to help the company achieve its objectives. Merck feels that flexibility enables the company to meet its business demands and states that flexibility is supported by senior management. When new jobs are posted internally, managers are expected to indicate what kinds of flexible work arrangements might be compatible with the position. Alternative scheduling arrangements include flextime, compressed workweeks, job sharing, telecommuting, and part-time work. Ironically, when Merck was listed in *Working Mother* magazine as one of the ten best places to work in 1995 there was significant employee backlash. The company was faulted for relentless workload demands in spite of family-friendly initiatives. As a result, Merck now invests more time in surveying employees and developing action plans to improve the work environment based on employee feedback. One example is the way Merck handled reports it was expecting its sales force to write. A focus-group discussion revealed that salespeople spent significant amounts of time evenings and weekends working on required reports because they didn't want report writing to eat into their sales time. Merck reduced the number of required reports by more than half. As a result, salespeople had more time for clients and family (for more information, see Caudron 1998; Levine and Pittinsky 1997; 100 Best Companies 1999; Catalyst 1998).

Schering AG

This large German chemical and pharmaceutical company introduced flextime in 1972. Flextime and part-time work has enabled Schering to recruit and retain skilled employees. Child care is in short supply in Germany, so the company offers contracts for half-day work, work for one week on and one week off, and a reduced-hour week (three or four day workweek). About half of all part-time employees choose the half-day option. Over 80 percent of Schering employees use some form of flexible scheduling (for more information, see Hogg and Harker 1992; Verespej 1999a).

PROFESSIONAL SERVICES

Arthur Andersen

This firm has been increasing the number of work-life programs and benefits it offers. The company developed a national policy with guidelines of alternative work options. The policy formalizes many informal arrangements that had been in place for years, and is designed to track utilization of flexible arrangements. The company requires prospective telecommuters to attend training sessions where employees learn time-management techniques and teamwork skills for the virtual environment. Arthur Anderson performs an initial inspection of home offices to make sure safety standards are being met. In an effort to make sure telecommuters do not become isolated, some offices host informal lunches for telecommuters. The performance and learning division of Arthur Andersen offers training aimed at managers of teleworkers. Topics covered include communicating with remote workers, leading remote teams, and in general brushing up on basic management skills, such as managing by results.

Arthur Andersen also employs the hoteling concept for telecommuters. Any employee who teleworks must sign up for work space through an on-line database. The company is attempting to avoid any expansion of office space, so teleworkers become part of the hoteling pool. Each hoteling space has an outlet and phone line to connect a laptop to the network. Employees can forward their phone calls to their home office or anywhere in the hoteling space, and portable files, drawers, reference books, and office supplies are available. The company estimates that by providing office space on an as-needed basis to telecommuters, it has been able to fit 25 percent more employees into the same space (for more information, see Fister 1999; Grensing-Pophal 1999; 100 Best Companies 1999; Tergesen 1998).

Ernst and Young LLP

Although Ernst and Young offers a broad array of consulting services, its history as an accounting firm is related in an interesting way to the growth of flexible work arrangements. Public accounting firms have traditionally experienced a high level of turnover, as the work has been characterized by long hours, frequent travel, and pressure to advance in an "up or out" philosophy. However, during the 1980s a focus on customer service and workforce demographics converged and contributed to a desire by accounting firms to reduce employee turnover. The result was an emphasis on flexible work arrangements, work-life balance initiatives, and flexible career paths. Telecommuting, hoteling, part-time work, and flextime have all been adopted by accounting firms.

Ernst and Young maintains three internal databases that assist employees with work-life issues: a database on flexible work arrangements, one on work-life balance, and one on networking for women. The intent is to help employees make informed decisions about work and career paths and personalize their schedules. The company is a leader in telecommuting and also has opportunities for alternate work arrangements through use of flextime, job sharing, and part-time work. The company created an office for retention that can also help with flexible work arrangements, networking, and mentoring. Ernst and Young is working to help erode employee fears about using flexible work arrangements. The flexible work arrangements database contains profiles of 400 employees (from staff to partners) who telecommute, job share, work part time, or work a compressed workweek. One extremely valuable feature of the database is that it helps employees interested in an alternative arrangement locate individuals in upper management who will act as advocates in explaining to the employee's boss how a flexible arrangement might work.

Ernst and Young was also a pioneer in the hoteling flexible work arrangement. The company implemented the first computerized hoteling system in an office in Chicago's Sears Tower in 1992. The system's database maintains a profile for each consultant (which includes items such as the files and other materials a consultant needs for his or her work) (for more information, see Alonzo 1998; Connor, Hooks, and McGuire 1997; Coolidge 1997; 100 Best Companies 1999; Wood 1998).

RETAIL

Boots the Chemist

This large U.K. drugstore chain has dramatically reduced employee turnover through family-friendly policies. Roughly 30 percent of its store managers and 94 percent of its supervisors are women. In 1989 only 7 percent of the female employees returned to work after taking maternity leave. The company introduced flexible working arrangements, and in 1992, 49 percent of the women returned, while in 1996 the number increased to 75 percent of the female staff. The company estimates that 40 percent of the time in the human resources department is spent on recruitment and associated activity. For every yearly reduction of 1 percent in staff turnover, the company believes it saves approximately £1 million by eliminating recruitment, training, uniforms, and associated administrative costs. The types of flexible work options offered by the company include job sharing, flextime, career breaks, part-time work, and a "working mother's contract," which includes flexible working hours and allows mothers to take time off during school holidays and term breaks (for more information, see Benefits of Flexible Working Patterns 1993; Jourdan 1995; Women Work 1996).

Eddie Bauer

This clothing chain has worked aggressively to make sure that its extensive range of work/family benefits is available to all of its 12,000-plus employees. The company takes care to offer programs that give more flexibility to employees, whether they are married or single, parents or nonparents. Balance between home life and work life is part of the corporate culture at this company. In 1986 the company became one of the first in the country to offer paid parental leave to both mothers and fathers. In 1996 it introduced Balance Day, a bonus day off for all employees to take care of their personal needs (which is in addition to accrued vacation, three personal days a year, holidays, and sick leave). The company offers a Customized Work Environment program that includes options such as job sharing, a compressed workweek, and telecommuting (for more information, see Faught 1997; Levine and Pittinsky 1997).

JCPenney

In 1997 this company had 200 employees taking orders for catalog sales working at home. The telecommuters work regular part-time schedules of twenty hours per week. The company provides workstations and handles the arrangements for telecommunications (using leased high-speed lines to connect the telecommuters' homes with the company mainframe). The program has cut employee turnover and absenteeism, and has improved customer service. The program also saves office space and has improved the company's ability to deal with fluctuating call volumes. JCPenney initially recruited employees from its in-house telemarketing staff. The employees are supervised by phone, e-mail, and twice-monthly visits. Employees working at the company headquarters are also able to take advantage of flexible work options, including telecommuting, flextime, and a compressed workweek (for more information, see Earls 1997; Harler 1997; Wells 1999).

Patagonia

This outdoor clothing and accessories company makes flextime arrangements available to all employees, not just employees with children. Extended leaves of absence are handled formally, but other spontaneous schedule changes are managed with an honor system. The example given by the company relates to surfing: If employees want to surf in the middle of the day, that's fine as long as the work will be made up and no deadlines are missed. The company hires people who want balance in their lives and feels that an enriching personal life makes a more productive employee. Flexible work options include flextime, compressed workweeks, job sharing, telecommuting, and part-time work. The company offers eight weeks of paid leave for all new parents (as long as they have been with the company at least two years). A unique opportunity offered by Patagonia is an environmental internship program that functions as a corporate sabbatical. The program permits employees to take two months off (with full pay) to work for a nonprofit environmental organization (for more information, see Coolidge 1996; 100 Best Companies 1999; Solomon 1998; Wood 1998).

SERVICE INDUSTRY

Marriott

Major foodservice and hospitality companies with a huge number of lower-level positions are establishing special programs and policies to improve recruitment and retention of employees in such positions. Marriott is offering flexible work hours, bonuses for retention, and special child-care supports. In competing for employees, Marriott realized it had to offer more in the way of flexible work arrangements. The company created a Worklife and Wellness Advisory Board to explore the benefits and problems associated with the workplace and to create guidelines for managers. Marriott is increasing the number of programs that promote flexibility, and is taking care to educate its employees about alternative work offerings. The company is also tracking the way in which programs such as flextime, compressed workweeks, job sharing, telecommuting, and part-time work are utilized. Marriott is a relative newcomer to telecommuting as an option for employees in clerical and managerial positions, but the number of employees working from home has increased substantially. Company studies indicate that telecommuting has improved job satisfaction and increased productivity (for more information, see Lambert 1999; 100 Best Companies 1999; Telecommuting's Time Has Come 1999).

United Airlines

United Airlines was an early adopter of remote work programs. In an effort to improve the work/family life balance and reduce turnover without raising labor costs, the company has moved hundreds of low-paying reservations jobs from large cities to smaller, more affordable towns. Commuting distances are minimal, as employees are working in neighborhood satellite offices, essentially a type of telecenter. The airline uses a form of automated call distribution developed by AT&T. When a customer telephones, the call is automatically routed through United's network to the first available agent across multiple offices. In terms of alternate work schedules, United formalized its programs when it became an employee-owned business in 1994. The company developed a human resource flexibility manual that provides guidance to units attempting to see which flex options will work best for them. Workers are most interested in varieties of compressed workweeks, and want to spend fewer days at work without reducing their compensation (for more information, see Flynn 1996; Manire 1997; Sheley 1996; United Rates High with Workers 1996).

TELECOMMUNICATIONS

AT&T

This company has been one of the leaders of the telecommuting movement. In 1989, in response to union demands for a more family-friendly contract, the company began experimenting with telecommuting and other flexible work options. Because managers were concerned about the impact of telecommuting on productivity, the first area chosen for a program was sales. In this area managers could easily measure productivity, and they were surprised to see a sales gain of 20 to 40 percent. AT&T used these data to convince other more traditional and conservative managers that telecommuting could work in their departments.

The percentage of AT&T managers who regularly telecommute increased from 8 percent in 1994 to 29 percent in 1999, although there has been some recent fluctuation in that number. Anecdotal evidence indicates that some employees are having trouble adjusting to more-frequent telecommuting. AT&T initially tried to pressure employees to work at home. That effort was a failure and the company now lets department heads make the decision about whether to encourage telecommuting in their departments. The company has learned more about the kinds of jobs and personalities that are a good fit for telecommuting as well. AT&T offers employees several training courses related to telecommuting. Telecommuting employees are required to sign an agreement in which they stipulate location, hours, assignments, output, equipment to be provided by the company, reimbursable expenses, and how often they will check their voicemail. The company estimates that the cost savings due to telecommuting (reductions in necessary office space and reducing overhead) were $550 million from 1991 through 1998. AT&T plans to reduce annual occupancy costs by $200 million, and telecommuting figures prominently in this plan. The company also estimates that employees in some telecommuting units gain an average of five weeks per year of productive time as a result of not commuting.

In addition to telecommuting, AT&T offers flextime, compressed workweeks, job sharing, and part-time work. The company also has several innovative family-leave programs. Leave for newborn or adopted children is available for up to twelve months, and employees are also eligible to take up to twelve months of unpaid leave in a two-year period to care for a family member. The company permits a gradual return to work for new mothers or employees returning from a family-care leave (for more information, see Apgar 1998; Dobrian 1999; Lazzareschi 1997; Leonhardt 1999; 100 Best Companies 1999).

British Telecommunications PLC

The United Kingdom's largest telecommunications provider is attempting to persuade 10 percent of its office staff (10,000 employees) to work from home by the end of the year 2000. The company estimates it could save £134 million per year in costs if it is successful, as well as lessen employee stress and save commuting time and fuel. Roughly 4,000 employees are already working regularly from home. British Telecommunications is offering to pay for office furniture, computers, fax machines, and high-speed communications lines. The company provides a help desk for employees who experience technical difficulties. All senior managers have Web sites through which they can be contacted. Some staff will be provided with videoconferencing equipment. Supervisors are expected to counsel prospective telecommuters regarding some of the problems they are likely to experience (for more information, see Cane 1999; Cane and Hargreaves 1999).

REFERENCES

100 best companies. 1999. *Working Mother*, October, entire issue.

The 100 best companies to work for in America. 1998. *Fortune*, 12 January, 69–95.

Alonzo, V. 1998. Ernst and Young LLP. *Incentive* 172 (6): 26–27.

An evaluation of Johnson & Johnson's work–family initiative. 1993. New York: Families and Work Institute.

Apgar, M. 1998. The alternative workplace: Changing where and how people work. *Harvard Business Review* 76 (3): 121–132.

Benefits of flexible working patterns. 1993. *Industrial Relations Review and Report* 550 (December): 2–3.

Busenbark, G. 1996. Stretching out the clock. *Financial Executive* 12 (1): 17–23.

Butruille, S. G. 1990. Corporate caretaking. *Training and Development Journal* 44 (4): 48–55.

Campbell, A. 1998. Baxter healthcare gets to the root of the issue. *HR Focus* 75 (8): S9–S10.

Cane, A. 1999. BT aims to turn a tenth of its staff into teleworkers. *Financial Times*, 12 May, 1.

Cane, A., and D. Hargreaves. 1999. Pioneer teleworkers feel at home. *Financial Times*, 12 May, 8.

Carter, J. 1998. Flexible benefits keep workers happy, loyal. *Rocky Mountain News*, 9 September, 19D.

Case study: One company's delicate balancing act. 1997. *Business Week*, 15 September, 102–104.

Catalyst. 1998. *Two careers, one marriage: Making it work in the workplace*. New York: Catalyst.

Caudron, S. 1998. The only way to stay ahead. *Industry Week*, 17 August, 98–102.

Collins, R. 1997. Flex appeal *Canadian Banker* 104 (3): 12–16.

Connor, M., K. Hooks, and T. McGuire. 1997. Gaining legitimacy for flexible work arrangements and career paths: The business case for public accounting and professional services firms. In *Integrating work and family: Challenges and choices for a changing world*, edited by S. Parasuraman and J. H. Greenhaus. Westport, Conn.: Quorum Books.

Coolidge, S. D. 1996. Family-friendly firms see bottom-line benefit. *Christian Science Monitor*, 17 October, 1.

Coolidge, S. D. 1997. Corporations flex for the family but critics say they still falter on work-life issues; key is changing culture at work. *Christian Science Monitor*, 2 September, 8.

Corby, S. 1997. Equal opportunities and flexibilities in the United Kingdom's public services. *Review of Public Personnel Administration* 17 (3): 57–68.

Cottle, M. 1999. Talking up telecommuting. *New York Times*, 8 August, sect. 3, p. 10.

Crisis in the motor industry: How flexibility works for BMW's German staff. 1998. *The Guardian*, 23 October, 25.

Cutcher-Gershenfeld, J., E. E. Kossek, and H. Sandling. 1997. Managing concurrent change initiatives. *Organizational Dynamics* 25 (3): 21–36.

Dobrian, J. 1999. Long-distance workers suit long-distance companies. *HR Focus* 76 (12): 11–12.

Durkin, T. 1997. Telecenters are no joke—seriously. *Telecommuting Review* 14 (6): 2–10.

Earls, A. R. 1997. True friends of the family. *Computerworld* 31 (7): 84–84.

Faught, L. 1997. At Eddie Bauer you can work and have a life. *Workforce* 76 (4): 83–90.

Fister, S. 1999. A lure for labor. *Training* 36 (2): 56–62.

Flynn, G. 1996. United Airlines new telecommuting program soars. *Personnel Journal* 75 (2): 24.

Friedman, D. E., and E. Galinsky. 1992. Work and family issues: A legitimate business concern. In *Work, families, and organizations*, edited by S. Zedeck. San Francisco: Jossey-Bass.

Friedman, D. E., C. Rimsky, and A. A. Johnson. 1996. *College and university reference guide to work–family programs: Report on a collaborative study*. New York: Families and Work Institute.

Galinsky, E., D. E. Friedman, and C. A. Hernandez. 1991. *The corporate reference guide to work–family programs*. New York: Families and Work Institute.

Gillian, F. 1997. A bank profits from its work/life programs. *Workforce* 76 (2): 49.

Grensing-Pophal, L. 1999. Training supervisors to manage teleworkers. *HRMagazine* 44 (1): 67–72.

Harler, C. 1997. Telecommuting: Making the commitment work. *Managing Office Technology* 42 (2): 18–21.

Hein, K. 1996. Family values: Corporations find family programs increase employee motivation as well as the bottom line. *Incentive* 170 (12): 23–27.

Himmelberg, M. 1998. Flextime muscles its way into workplace. *Orange County Register*, 23 February, D10.

Hogg, C., and L. Harker. 1992. *The family-friendly employer: Examples from Europe*. New York: Daycare Trust, in association with Families and Work Institute.

Jourdan, T. 1995. Nice work if you can get it. *The Scotsman,* 30 January, 15.

Klieman, C. 1998. More options, happier workers. *Chicago Tribune,* 27 September, C1.

Lambert, S. J. 1999. Lower-wage workers and the new realities of work and family. *Annals of the American Academy of Political and Social Science* 562: 174–190.

Lazzareschi, C. 1997. Telecommuters still feel pull of office. *Los Angeles Times,* 13 September, D1.

Leonhardt, D. 1999. Telecommuting to pick up as workers iron out kinks. *New York Times,* 20 December, C6.

Levine, J. A., and T. L. Pittinsky. 1997. *Working fathers: New strategies for balancing work and family.* Reading, Mass.: Addison-Wesley.

Lobel, S. A. 1996. Four methods for proving the value of work-life interventions. *Compensation & Benefits Review* 28 (6): 50–57.

Manire, R. W. 1997. Remote access: The "drive to work" in the information age. *Telecommunications* 31 (1): 50–55.

Martinez, M. N. 1997. Work-life: programs reap business benefits. *HRMagazine* 42 (6): 110–114.

Myth-busting study reveals flexible work arrangements growing in popularity. 1998. Canada Newswire, 15 May.

O'Connell, S. E. 1996. The virtual workplace moves at warp speed. *HRMagazine* 41 (3): 50–53.

Olmsted, B., and S. Smith. 1994. *Creating a flexible workplace: How to select & manage alternative work options.* 2d ed. New York: AMACOM.

Schwartz, D. B. 1994. *An examination of the impact of family-friendly policies on the glass ceiling.* New York: Families and Work Institute.

Sheley, E. 1996. Flexible work options: Factors that make them work. *HRMagazine* 41 (2): 52–59.

Sims, W., M. Joroff, and F. Becker. 1996. *Managing the reinvented workplace.* Houston, Tex.: International Facility Management Association; Norcross, Ga.: International Development Research Council.

Solomon, C. M. 1991. 24-hour employees. *Personnel Journal* 70 (8): 56–63.

Solomon, C. M. 1998. Women are still undervalued: Bridge the parity gap. *Workforce* 77 (5): 78–86.

Telecommuting's time has come. 1999. *Nation's Restaurant News* 33 (44): 24–30.

Tergesen, A. 1998. Making stay-at-homes feel welcome. *Business Week,* 12 October, 155–156.

United rates high with workers after moving office to Rockford. 1996. *Chicago Sun-Times,* 23 December, 43.

United Technologies receives top U.S. Department of Labor award. 1998. *PR Newswire,* 1 October.

Verespej, M. A. 1999a. Why they're the best. *Industry Week,* 16 August, 102–109.

Verespej, M. A. 1999b. Work vs. Life. *Industry Week,* 19 April, 37–42.

Wells, S. J. 1999. Using rush hour to your advantage. *HRMagazine* 44 (3): 26–32.

Women work: Case study: Boots the Chemist. 1996. *The Independent,* 3 December, W1.

Wong, N. 1999. The key is to find the right partner. *Workforce* 78 (4): 112–113.

Wood, N. 1998. Singled out. *Incentive* 172 (7): 20–23

Work and family: Best practices from 10 leading companies. 1996. *Business Week*, 16 September, 74–80.

CHAPTER 5

The Future of Workplace Flexibility

This chapter examines newly emerging workplace options such as annual hours contracts, paid time off (PTO), and leave banks. It also discusses trends that will affect the need for expanded flexibility and unresolved issues relating to flexibility.

Annual hours contracts, sometimes referred to as annualized hours schemes or flexiyear schedules, are a work option where the employee and the employer negotiate the number of hours worked within a year (Ronen 1984; Annual Hours Bring Widespread Change to Chemicals 1996; A Workstyle Revolution? 1999). Annual hours contracts can apply to part-time or full-time workers (Annual Hours Bring Widespread Change to Chemicals 1996). Workers are guaranteed a certain number of work hours (Wheatley 1997).

Although annual hours were first introduced in Sweden in the mid-1970s, the use of this arrangement did not become more widespread until it was adopted by employers in the United Kingdom (Olmsted and Smith 1994). Goss (1997) has analyzed the benefits and drawbacks of annual hours from the perspective of both the employer and the employee. This scheme helps employers handle workflow, especially cyclical fluctuations, since it allows employees to work longer during peak times and fewer hours during slower periods. It allows firms to reduce overtime costs, while retaining core staff. From the perspective of employees, annual hours are preferable to being laid off during slack periods. Cooper and Lewis (1993) identified other advantages and disadvantages. Annual hours contracts can help employees balance work and home responsibilities. For example, employees with children can reduce their work time when their children are on school vacation. They also have the stability of a monthly salary, since they receive a regular salary based on annual hours worked instead of the number of hours worked that month. However, some workers have found it difficult to arrange for child care, especially if they are asked to work long hours at short notice. Some workers regret the loss of overtime pay.

Annual hours have been most closely associated with industry, particularly those involving continuous processes. However, a 1993 study of annual hours contracts conducted by the United Kingdom's Institute of Personnel and Development found that the use of annual hours contracts was growing and expanding to the service industries (Flexible Working Hours—A Survey of Practice 1996). A 1999 survey regarding flexible employment practices in the United Kingdom found that almost one-third of the U.K. employers responding planned to implement annual hours contracts within the next three years (A Workstyle Revolution? 1999). Recently, a leading bank in the United Kingdom announced that all branch staff were moving to annual hours contracts, evidence that this scheme is gaining popularity among the retail sectors as a strategy to extend coverage during extended hours (NatWest to Put All Branch Staff on Annualised Hours 1999).

Two other emerging workplace trends are paid time off and leave banks. Paid time off allows workers to pool their vacation, sick, and personal days (Dumas 1996; Paid Leave Improves Attendance 1998). This practice has also been referred to as a time-off pool system (Time-Off Transitions 1999). Employees can use these days for any reason. Most employers allow unused days to carry over from one year to the next. A 1994 survey of 360 companies, conducted by Hewitt Associates, found that approximately 17 percent of these 360 firms already had a PTO policy in place and more than 10 percent of firms had plans to establish a PTO program (Dumas 1996). Studies have shown that PTOs can dramatically reduce unscheduled absenteeism, in some cases by as much as 40 percent (Dumas 1996; Paid leave Improves Attendance 1998). A related trend, leave banks, allows workers to donate vacation time to a leave bank (Dumas 1996). Workers who have used up all of their own vacation, sick, or personal days can draw additional paid days off from the leave bank in order to cover medical and family emergencies. Companies have found that this is a popular benefit that generates significant goodwill while requiring minimal administrative costs (Dumas 1996). Both PTOs and leave banks benefit workers by giving them paid time off.

Workplace flexibility is not a fad. It is a business strategy that is here to stay. As one British leader in the area of human resource management remarked, "The 9 to 5 job is a thing of the past" (Flexibility Now Key to Survival Says U.K.'s Top Employers 1996). The traditional five-day, forty-hour workweek is being replaced by several variations of the workday, the workweek, and the workplace. As noted in Chapters 1 through 3, several trends will affect the need for expanded flexibility: the downshifters, defined as a new breed of workers who want to slow down at work so they can speed up other areas of their lives; organizational change (the movement away from hierarchies); the expansion of technology; concern about labor shortages (especially the demographics of the twenty-first century); and, in Europe, a push from the European Commission. As a result of these factors, the need for workplace flexibility is becoming increasingly viewed as an issue for all employees, not just women. More companies are realizing that all workers have a need for flexible work. Consequently, many work/family programs have been renamed work-life programs (The Childless Employee 1996; Shellenbarger 1998).

However, there are several unresolved issues relating to flexibility. The first issue is equity. In the United States research has indicated that not all workers have access to family-friendly work benefits. Workers who are highly educated, higher paid, and in professional occupations are more likely to have options such as flexible scheduling or telecommuting. A 1997 Conference Board study found that many lower-wage employees have no access to flexible work options. Shift work may preclude the use of an option such as flextime and constraints such as the inability to afford a personal computer in order to work from home hinder their ability to take advantage of flexible work options in place (Lower-Wage Employees 1997). This Conference Board survey focused on assessing how well flexible work arrangements and other work/family/life programs met the needs of lower-wage earners. Lower-wage earners were defined as those full-time workers earning an annual salary of no more than $20,000. Approximately forty companies representing several industrial sectors (financial services, communications, manufacturing, and health care) participated in the survey. All the firms in the study had implemented work/family/life programs. More than 40 percent of the organizations responding believed that lower-wage employees benefited less from work/family programs. Telecommuting was the flexible work option most difficult for lower-wage earners to utilize.

Joel Kugelmass (1995), author of *Telecommuting: A Manager's Guide to Flexible Work Arrangements*, also noted that in the United States flextime and telecommuting are often offered only to professional employees. His book focuses on three alternative work arrangements: flextime, flexiplace (remote work), and telecommuting. Kugelmass pointed to research conducted at the City University of New York, the site of renowned researcher Kathleen Christensen's National Project on Home-Based Work. Christensen found that clerical and professional workers are treated differently. There is more autonomy for professional workers than for clerical. Christensen found that clerical workers are often subjected to extensive monitoring by computer and phone.

Other researchers have argued that some flexible workplace schemes promote gender inequality. Barbara Bergmann (1997) maintains that options such as part-time work and extended maternity leaves reinforce the traditional division of labor, most frequently the view that women serve as primary caregivers. In addition, she points out that many work/family policies are targeted to legally married heterosexual couples with children, excluding the needs of unmarried couples with children and homosexual couples with children.

Two studies in the United Kingdom, commissioned by the Equal Opportunities Commission (EOC), highlighted other equity issues relating to workplace flexibility (Flexible Working 1996). The first study commissioned by the EOC analyzed overall trends in flexible employment in four industries: agriculture, construction, distribution, and other services. The study concluded that "within these industries women were disproportionately employed in flexible jobs with the poorest conditions and the lowest pay" (p. 19). The second study focused on flexible working arrangements in the retail and finance sectors. This study revealed that some flexible workers had limited access to training and promotion and were excluded from some parts of their companies' benefits packages. A study of flexible work in fourteen European countries also found that many firms are not providing flexible workers equal access to salary increases, career advancement, training and development opportunities, and other benefits (Brewster 1997).

Another unresolved issue that relates to workplace flexibility is education and training. Flexible work arrangements must address the need for skills training. Training is needed for both managers and employees in order for workplace flexibility to succeed (Training Required for Work Flexibility to Succeed 1996). Supervisors must learn how to evaluate requests for flexibility, how to determine which flexible option is most appropriate for a given situation, and how to evaluate the performance of employees working remotely, on flextime, or sharing a job (Olmsted 1990–1991). At the same time, flexible workers need to know what is required of them.

Finally, a major issue that needs to be addressed is the need for more data evaluating flexible work arrangements. Dana Friedman (1991) noted that companies have not typically conducted research on work/ family issues because of the cost and complexity involved. David Ralston (1989) documented the need for improved methodology and more rigorous research design in flextime studies. Christensen and Staines (1990) reiterated this plea for better-constructed studies as part of their review of the literature relating to flextime and work/family conflict. Marni Ezra (1996) found that few empirical studies have been conducted on flextime and even fewer have been conducted on the impact of flextime on employees' home lives.

Gottlieb, Kelloway, and Barham (1998) also concluded that much of the research on the effects of flexible work arrangements "lacks methodological rigor" and that many studies have relied "solely on anecdotal evidence with no 'hard data' or statistical analysis" (p. 101). These three researchers expressed other concerns about the research that has been conducted on the effectiveness of flexible work arrangements. For example, some studies asked workers whether they thought their productivity and work performance had improved as a result of choosing a flexible work arrangement. Gottlieb, Kelloway, and Barham caution that workers may overstate their productivity, especially if they want to retain these benefits. In addition, these researchers noted that many research studies have failed to include controls that can separate productivity gains attributable to a flexible work arrangement from productivity gains attributable to the characteristics of workers opting for flexibility.

A 1993 study conducted by the Conference Board concluded that interest in evaluation is growing and evaluative studies are being used to improve flexible work programs, rather than to justify these programs (Evaluating Programs 1993). Some of the respondents in the survey pushed for rigorous data collection, particularly quantitative data that would support the business case for flexibility. Edward Shepard (1996) has argued that better empirical studies documenting the benefits of flexibility could provide an impetus for the development of public policy on flexibility, including the development of incentives such as tax breaks for flexible employers.

Dana Friedman (1991) outlined some work/family issues meriting additional research. In particular, she stressed the need for work/family research that is interdisciplinary, longitudinal, comparative, and visionary. She identified many gaps in the literature and directions for future research. One of her most interesting suggestions was that work/ family issues should be studied in unsupportive environments. Most research has involved companies that have been supportive of workplace flexibility. Another insightful suggestion was that future research should focus on work/family issues in an aging society. This directive is particularly relevant as we approach the mass retirement of the baby boom generation. Friedman summed up the importance of evaluation, concluding that "more evaluation of work/family programs can help strengthen the effectiveness of company responses" (p. 60).

In the summer of 1999, Shirley Dex and Fiona Scheibl published a literature review on studies linking family-friendly policies to business performance. Their review of the literature covered both American and British studies. Dex and Scheibl's article presents a set of performance measures that can be used for evaluating the effectiveness of workplace flexibility. Their article will no doubt impact future research evaluating the costs and benefits of flexibility and will help researchers devise evaluative measures. In the near future, there is promise that more rigorous and longitudinal studies will be conducted on workplace flexibility. While there is a need for better quantitative data, well-designed qualitative data will also be valued.

REFERENCES

Annual hours bring widespread change to chemicals. 1996. *IRS Employment Review*, October, 3.

Bergmann, B. R. 1997. Work–family policies and equality between women and men. In *Gender and family issues in the workplace*, edited by F. D. Blau and R. G. Ehrenberg. New York: Sage.

Brewster, C. 1997. Flexible working in Europe: A review of the evidence. *Management International Review* 37 (1): 85–103.

The childless employee. 1996. *Work–Family Roundtable* 3 (2): entire issue.

Christensen, K. E., and G. L. Staines. 1990. Flextime: A viable solution to work/family conflict? *Journal of Family Issues* 11 (4): 455–476.

Cooper, C. L., and S. Lewis. 1993. *The workplace revolution: Managing today's dual-career families*. London: Kogan Page.

Dex, S., and F. Scheibl. 1999. Business performance and family-friendly policies. *Journal of General Management* 24 (4): 22–37.

Dumas, L. S. 1996. The new flexibility: Two hot workplace trends—PTOs and leave banks—could give you more time off. *Working Mother*, July–August, 28–32.

Evaluating programs. 1993. *Work–Family Roundtable* 3 (2): entire issue.

Ezra, M. 1996. Balancing work and family responsibilities: Flextime and child care in the federal government. *Public Administration Review* 56 (2): 174–179.

Flexible working hours—a survey of practice. 1996. *IRS Employment Review*, May, 4–10.

Flexible working: The impact on women's pay and conditions. 1996. *Equal Opportunities Review*, January–February, 19–24.

Flexibility now key to survival says U.K.'s top employers. 1996. *Management Services* 40 (1): 8.

Friedman, D. E. 1991. *Linking work–family issues to the bottom line*. New York: The Conference Board.

Goss, D. 1997. *Human resource management: The basics.* London: International Thomson Business Press.

Gottlieb, B. H., E. K. Kelloway, and E. J. Barham. 1998. *Flexible work arrangements: Managing the work–family boundary.* Chichester, England: Wiley.

Kugelmass, J. 1995. *Telecommuting: A manager's guide to flexible work arrangements.* New York: Lexington Books.

Lower-wage employees. 1997. *Work–Family Roundtable* 7 (3): entire issue.

NatWest to put all branch staff on annualised hours. 1999. *People Management* 5 (2): 16.

Olmsted, B. 1990–1991. Flexible work arrangements: A sea of change for managers: Flexibility is the key for staffing and scheduling in the 1990s. *Employment Relations Today* 17 (4): 291–296.

Olmsted, B., and S. Smith. 1994. *Creating a flexible workplace: How to select & manage alternative work options.* 2d ed. New York: AMACOM.

Paid leave improves attendance. 1998. *Professional Safety* 43 (4): 1.

Ralston, D. A. 1989. The benefits of flextime: Real or imagined? *Journal of Organizational Behavior* 10: 369–373.

Ronen, S. 1984. *Alternative work schedules: Selecting . . . implementing . . . and evaluating.* Homewood, Ill.: Dow Jones Irwin.

Shellenbarger, S. 1998. For harried workers, time off is not just for family affairs. *Wall Street Journal,* 11 November, B1.

Shepard, E. M. 1996. Flexible work hours and productivity: Some evidence from the pharmaceutical industry. *Industrial Relations* 35 (1): 123–139.

Time-off transitions. 1999. *Credit Union Management* 22 (8): 9.

Training required for work flexibility to succeed. 1996. *Employee Benefit Plan Review* 51 (3): 34.

Wheatley, M. 1997. Open all hours. *Management Today,* September, 68–70.

A workstyle revolution? 1999. *Management Services* 43 (9): 4.

CHAPTER 6

Resources

This chapter identifies some useful resources for the flexible worker, the organization seeking to implement flexibility, and students and researchers studying flexibility. Resources are grouped by broad categories: books, periodicals, nonprint materials, and secondary datasets.

BOOKS, REPORTS, AND THESES

The following resources are recommended as part of a core collection on workplace flexibility.

American Institute of Certified Public Accountants (AICPA) Women and Family Issues Executive Committee and the AICPA Management of an Accounting Practice Committee, in collaboration with Barney Olmsted. 1997. *Flexible work arrangements in CPA firms*. New York: AICPA.

Several factors are driving flexibility in the accounting profession. In 1995 more than half of all graduates hired by CPA firms were women. Other factors include an increase in dual-career families and greater interest (especially among younger accountants) in work/family balance. Part-time work is the most common option in accounting firms, followed by flextime. This report explains how flexible work arrangements can help accounting firms.

Axel, H. 1992. *Redefining corporate sabbaticals for the 1990s*. New York: The Conference Board.

This is the only comprehensive work on corporate sabbaticals. Axel traces the history of worker sabbaticals, examines the advantages and disadvantages of these sanctioned leaves, and profiles companies with sabbatical and related leave programs.

Bailyn, L. 1993. *Breaking the mold: Women, men, and time in the new corporate world*. New York: Free Press.

Bailyn questions whether there are better ways of working. She asks why so many professionals are expected to work such long hours and to put in so much face time. She argues for a fundamental change in corporate culture, one where employees needs are not considered peripheral.

Bastian, J. 1994. *A matter of time: From work sharing to temporal flexibility in Belgium, France and Britain*. Aldershot, England: Avebury.

Bastian compares working-time policies in Belgium, Britain, and France during the past fifteen years. He analyzes work sharing as a strategy for reducing unemployment.

Becker, F., A. J. Rappaport, K. L. Quinn, and W. R. Sims. 1993. *New working practices: Benchmarking flexible scheduling, staffing and work location in an international context*. Ithaca, N.Y.: Cornell University, International Workplace Studies Program.

In 1993 the authors conducted a benchmarking study of sixteen international organizations. The study's focus was flexible work options. The options studied were flexible work schedules, flexible staffing, and flexible work location. The flexible work-scheduling options that the authors examined included flextime, job sharing, compressed workweek, and regular part-time work. This is an excellent source of data on worldwide trends relating to flexible scheduling.

Biernat, B. A. 1997. Employed parents' preference for reduced job hours in relation to job and family characteristics. Ph.D. diss., University of Minnesota.

This is an important dissertation, since there has been a paucity of studies on parents' preference for job hours. Biernat studied approximately 200 working (full-time employed) parents of children under age eighteen from two computer-related companies in the Minneapolis area. Almost 60 percent of parents indicated that they would prefer reduced hours (even with a corresponding reduction in salary) if job security, benefits, and career advancement were guaranteed. The dissertation includes an extensive literature review on studies relating to job/family conflict.

Bond, J. T., E. Galinsky, and J. E. Swanberg. 1998. *The 1997 national study of the changing workforce*. New York: Families and Work Institute.

Like previous institute surveys, the 1997 National Study of the Changing Workforce used a nationally representative sample of the U.S. workforce. The authors were able to identify workplace trends by comparing data to the institute's 1992 National Study of the Changing Workforce and the 1977 Quality of Employment Survey. They concluded that the workplace has become more supportive during the five-year period from 1992 to 1997.

Bosch, G., P. Dawkings, and F. Michon, eds. 1993. *Times are changing: Working time in 14 industrialised countries*. Geneva: International Institute for Labour Studies.

The chapters in this edited volume trace workplace trends (including working-time flexibility) in Australia, Austria, Belgium, Canada, France, Germany, Hungary, Italy, Japan, The Netherlands, Sweden, the United Kingdom, the United States, and the USSR. Sweden provides one of the most interesting case studies. A range of flexible options gives Swedish workers the ability to have different working hours throughout different phases of their life.

Bravo, E. 1995. *The job/family challenge*. New York: Wiley.

Bravo is the executive director of 9 to 5, the National Association of Working Women. 9 to 5 was established in 1973. Bravo profiles some companies that have been models in the area of flexibility. In addition, she explains how flexibility helps the bottom line. She outlines the advantages and disadvantages of several types of flexibility. Finally, she offers solutions for strengthening the Family and Medical Leave Act.

Catalyst. 1989. *Flexible work arrangements: Establishing options for managers and professionals.* New York: Catalyst.

This was a landmark study, since it represented the first qualitative study of flexible work arrangements at the managerial and professional levels in U.S. companies. It examined three types of flexibility: part-time work, job sharing, and telecommuting. More than fifty companies participated, ranging in size from a major corporation with 400,000 employees to a small firm with 300 employees.

Catalyst. 1993. *Flexible work arrangements II: Succeeding with part-time options.* New York: Catalyst.

This study was a follow up to Catalyst's important 1989 study, *Flexible Work Arrangements: Establishing Options for Managers and Professionals.* This new study involved two phases: (1) interviews with human resource professionals from seventy companies (including some companies that had participated in the 1989 study), and (2) interviews with employees who had used flexible arrangements. The companies selected represented a range of sizes, geographic locations, and industries. Catalyst found that flexible work arrangements were more common and formal (in terms of policy and tracking) than in 1989. Based on these interviews, Catalyst developed recommendations for both companies and employees.

Catalyst. 1996. *Making work flexible: Policy to practice.* New York: Catalyst.

This manual has been designed to help organizations implement flexible work arrangements. It includes worksheets, examples of real-world guidelines for flexible arrangements, and sample pages from actual corporate brochures, memos, and handbooks relating to flexibility.

Catalyst. 1998. *A new approach to flexibility: Managing the work/time equation.* New York: Catalyst.

This is the first in-depth study of part-time employment among professionals in the United States. More than 2,000 people participated in this study through surveys, interviews, and focus groups. Participants included part-time professionals, their supervisors, their coworkers, their clients, and human resource professionals in four companies. Two of these firms had a long history of workplace flexibility, while the other two companies had recently introduced flexibility.

Catalyst. 1998. *Two careers, one marriage: Making it work in the workplace*. New York: Catalyst.

According to data from the U.S. Bureau of Labor Statistics, dual-earner families made up 45 percent of the U.S. workforce in 1996. The purpose of this national study of dual-earner marriages was to identify actions companies can take to attract and retain members of dual-earner couples. One of the important findings of this study is that both men and women want greater workplace flexibility and both want more control over the pace of their career advancement.

Cooper, C. L., and S. Lewis. 1993. *The workplace revolution: Managing today's dual-career families*. London: Kogan Page.

The authors' research indicates that dual earners who work in inflexible organizations are less satisfied with their jobs and experience higher levels of stress than dual earners who work in flexible organizations. Their book is based on research involving more than 400 dual-earner spouses in a range of occupations.

Dinnocenzo, D. A. 1999. *101 tips for telecommuters: Successfully manage your work, team, technology and family*. San Francisco: Berrett-Koehler.

Dinnocenzo has been a telecommuter for many years. She operates her own consulting firm, offering services and products to individual telecommuters as well as to organizations employing telecommuters. This is an excellent practical manual, covering all aspects of telecommuting. It includes several useful appendices that lead users to additional resources on telecommuting.

Edelman, K. A., ed. 1996. *Building the business case for workplace flexibility: A conference report*. Report no. 1154-96-CH New York: The Conference Board.

This report is based on excerpts of speeches delivered at the Workplace Flexibility Conference held in New York in September 1995. It documents that workplace flexibility has moved beyond an accommodation made for select employees to a business strategy for retaining workers and achieving other measurable benefits including productivity gains, improved customer satisfaction, and reduced absenteeism and turnover.

Estess, P. S. 1996. *Work concepts for the future: Managing alternative work arrangements*. Menlo Park, Calif.: Crisp.

This book focuses on flextime, telecommuting, compressed work-weeks, part-time work, job sharing, and phased retirement. Estess has created a practical guide for managers. She outlines the benefits of alternative work arrangements, explains how managers can remove barriers to the implementation of these options, and explains how supervisors can manage individual performance as well as departments on alternative arrangements.

An evaluation of Johnson & Johnson's work–family initiative. 1993. New York: Families and Work Institute.

Johnson & Johnson introduced its Balancing Work and Family Program in 1989. The program consists of several flexible work options, including flextime, job sharing, part-time work, telecommuting, and family leave. This report presents the findings of employee surveys conducted at four Johnson & Johnson companies. Johnson & Johnson's willingness to evaluate its work-life program is significant, since there have been few systematic program evaluations.

Ferber, M. A., B. O'Farrell, and L. R. Allen, eds. 1991. *Work and family: Policies for a changing work force*. Washington, D.C.: National Academy Press.

This report is the work of twelve experts (including both researchers and practitioners) in the area of work and family. These experts served on the National Research Council's (U.S.) Panel on Employer Policies and Working Families. The purpose of the report was to assess the research on employer policies and working families. The panel also looked at work and family issues in Europe.

Fried, M. 1998. *Taking time: Parental leave policy and corporate culture*. Philadelphia: Temple University Press.

This is a case study of parental leave in a large U.S. corporation. Fried looks at the relationship between corporate culture and leave taking.

Friedman, D. E. 1991. *Linking work–family issues to the bottom line*. New York: The Conference Board.

This report is the synthesis of a 1988 symposium on work/family issues and findings from more than eighty other studies. In 1983 the Conference Board established a Work and Family Center and created a Work and Family Research Council to support research on work/

family issues. Friedman concluded that flextime can reduce tardiness and absenteeism and improve employee morale.

Friedman, D. E., and T. Brothers, eds. 1993. *Work–family needs: Leading corporations respond.* New York: The Conference Board.

This report is based on Work–Family Issues and the Work Ethic, a 1992 conference cosponsored by the Families and Work Institute. One of the conclusions was that companies without work/family programs are less successful at recruiting and retaining valuable staff.

Friedman, D. E., C. Rimsky, and A. A. Johnson. 1996. *College and university reference guide to work–family programs: Report on a collaborative study.* New York: Families and Work Institute.

This report highlights the findings of a joint study on family-supportive policies at 375 U.S. colleges and universities. The study was conducted by the Families and Work Institute and the College and University Personnel Association Foundation. This report includes survey data and case studies.

Galinsky, E., J. T. Bond, and D. E. Friedman. 1993. *The changing workforce: Highlights of the national study.* New York: Families and Work Institute.

The National Study of the Changing Workforce was a nationally representative study of approximately 3,400 American workers. The study was developed by the Families and Work Institute and sponsored by several major corporations. One of the issues that the study addressed was how workers managed both work and home obligations.

Gooler, L. E. 1996. Coping with work–family conflict: The role of organizational support. Ph.D. diss., City University of New York.

Gooler looked at the impact of perceived and actual organizational support, including flexible work arrangements and alternative work schedules, on work/family conflict. Data are drawn from a survey of approximately 800 workers from several companies in different industries. Gooler includes a good literature review of studies on work and family relationships.

Gore, A. 1997. *Turning the key: Unlocking human potential in the family-friendly federal workplace: A status report on federal workplace family-friendly initiatives.* Washington, D.C.: GPO.

The federal government has been a leader in the area of workplace flexibility. This report provides a good summary of government initiatives in the areas of job sharing, career part-time employment, alternative work schedules, and telecommuting.

Gottlieb, B. H., E. K. Kelloway, and E. J. Barham. 1998. *Flexible work arrangements: Managing the work–family boundary*. Chichester, England: Wiley.

These three researchers, who are affiliated with the Canadian Aging Research Network, have done the most extensive analysis of flexible work arrangements in Canada. CARNET has conducted threes studies relating to the workplace: the 1993 Work and Family Survey, the 1994 Work and Home Life Survey, and the 1995 Workplace Flexibility Study. The results of these surveys have been summarized in *Flexible Work Arrangements*. Flextime emerged as the most prevalent types of flexible work arrangement in Canada. In addition to summarizing data from these three surveys, the authors review the published literature on flexible work arrangements.

Gray, M., N. Hodson, and G. Gordon. 1993. *Teleworking explained*. Chichester, England: Wiley.

This has been written as a practical guide for teleworkers and managers. It is aimed at managers in medium- to large-size corporations. The book looks at the theoretical issues associated with telecommuting, explains how to calculate the costs and benefits, and gives practical advice on establishing a telecommuting program.

Hewlett, S. A., and C. West. 1998. *The war against parents: What we can do for America's beleaguered moms and dads*. Boston: Houghton Mifflin.

The authors, with the support of the National Parenting Association, conducted a national survey of the needs and concerns of American parents. The survey, administered by independent pollsters, was carried out the summer of 1996 and targeted parents whose household income ranged between $20,000 and $100,000. Hewlett and West also conducted a series of focus groups with parents. The authors found that the overwhelming need was for workplace policies that would give parents more time.

Hochschild, A. R. 1997. *The time bind: When work becomes home and home becomes work*. New York: Henry Holt.

Hochschild's book is based on her extensive study of a company that was ranked as one of the top family-friendly firms in the United States. This company had a range of work/family programs, including flextime, job sharing, and part-time positions. However, Hochschild found that although these programs allowed employees to reduce their work time, almost no employees did so. Her book is an attempt to find out why working parents and other employees did not take advantage of opportunities to reduce their hours at work.

Hogg, C., and L. Harker. 1992. *The family-friendly employer: Examples from Europe.* New York: Daycare Trust, in association with Families and Work Institute.

This book profiles twenty-five corporate initiatives in seven European countries (Belgium, Denmark, France, Germany, Ireland, The Netherlands, and the United Kingdom) to help workers balance work and family responsibilities. While many initiatives relate to child care, some of the schemes are examples of flextime, part-time work, teleworking, and family leave.

Hollister, N. 1995. *The mobile office: Towards the virtual corporation.* London: Financial Times Telecommunications and Media Publishing.

Hollister's use of the term "mobile office" includes both hot desking and teleworking. Both are part of the trend toward a virtual corporation.

Hunnicutt, B. K. 1996. *Kellogg's six-hour day.* Philadelphia: Temple University Press.

In the 1930s, the W. K. Kellogg Company was the world's largest manufacturer of ready-to-eat cereals and employed almost 1,500 workers. The company was a leader in industrial reform. It was one of the first companies to introduce the eight-hour day and the five-day workweek. This is a fascinating account of Kellogg's experiment with work sharing during the 1930s and the 1940s.

Huws, U. 1995. *Follow-up to the white paper.* Luxembourg: Office for Official Publications of the European Communities.

Section A of this publication focuses on teleworking. It discusses the role of the new information technologies in making Europe competitive in the twenty-first century and in creating new employment in the European Union. Huws breaks teleworking into five types: (1) home-based teleworking, (2) mobile teleworking, (3) teleworking on remote sites controlled by the employer, (4) teleworking from telecottages or telecenters, and (5) the development of telematic links between organizations. She discusses the costs and benefits associated with each type.

Huws, U., W. B. Korte, and S. Robinson. 1990. *Telework: Towards the elusive office*. Chichester, England: Wiley.

The authors provide an excellent literature review on teleworking as well as a concise history of the movement. This is an important source, since it provides detailed data on important European surveys relating to teleworking.

Jackson, P. J., and J. M. Van der Wielen. 1998. *Teleworking: International perspectives: From telecommuting to the virtual organisation*. London: Routledge.

This volume grew out of the 1996 workshop, New International Perspectives on Telework, which was held at Brunel University. This was an interdisciplinary workshop that drew together researchers in management, sociology, economics, anthropology, philosophy, and transportation studies. The volume includes twenty-one chapters organized into four parts. Part 1 focuses on the evolution (both practical and theoretical developments) of teleworking. Part 2 focuses on managerial issues. Part 3 focuses on the planning and integration of teleworking. Part 4 looks at examples from North America and Europe.

Korte, W. B., and R. Wynne. 1996. *Telework: Penetration, potential and practice in Europe*. Amsterdam: IOS Press.

This book presents the results of the TELDET Project. Funded by the European Commission, this project began in January 1994 and concluded in June 1995. It had three objectives: (1) to survey the penetration, potential, and practice of teleworking in Europe; (2) to provide European case studies on teleworking; and (3) to analyze the conditions for the development of teleworking in Europe.

Kugelmass, J. 1995. *Telecommuting: A manager's guide to flexible work arrangements*. New York: Lexington Books.

Kugelmass focuses on three alternative work arrangements: flextime, flexiplace (remote work), and telecommuting. He traces the history of these studies, analyzes the benefits of flexibility, discusses logistical problems relating to these work options, and profiles some companies that have been leaders in workplace flexibility.

Langhoff, J. 1997. *The business traveler's survival guide: How to get work done while on the road*. Newport, R.I.: Aegis.

Langhoff, one of the nation's experts on telecommuting, has designed this practical manual for road warriors. She provides lots of sound advice on equipment, security, groupware, teleconferencing, and remote working. There are even tips for those working abroad.

Langhoff, J. 1999. *The telecommuter's advisor*. 2d ed. Newport, R.I.: Aegis.

This is the second edition of veteran telecommuter June Langhoff's best-selling guide to the nuts and bolts of telecommuting. Langhoff has been telecommuting since 1982 and is recognized as a national expert on the topic. *The Telecommuter's Advisor* provides all the information needed for working from any remote location. Langhoff explains how to set up a home office, provides advice on equipment (including phone options), and includes chapters on managing modem, e-mail, fax, and voicemail. She also outlines the various technologies (from groupware to Web conferencing) that can help telecommuters who work in teams. Many helpful appendixes are provided, including a listing of resources, a survey to determine one's aptitude for telecommuting, advice on getting started, a list of companies with formal or informal telecommuting programs, and a list of jobs held by telecommuters.

Levine, J. A., and T. L. Pittinsky. 1997. *Working fathers: New strategies for balancing work and family*. Reading, Mass.: Addison-Wesley.

Levine is the foremost authority on the importance of workplace flexibility for men. He conducts seminars on combining work and family to major corporations. Pittinsky is a researcher at the Families and Work Institute. *Working Fathers* is the first practical guide to creating a father-friendly workplace.

Meade, J. 1993. *Home sweet office: The ultimate out-of-office experience: Working your company job from home*. Princeton, N.J.: Peterson's.

This is a great practical how-to manual that is interspersed with interesting anecdotes.

Miranda, E. J., and B. E. Murphy. 1993. *Work–family: Redefining the business case.* Report no. 1050. New York: The Conference Board.

This report is based on speeches given by executives at the Conference Board's conference, Redefining the Business Case, held in 1993. The conference was cosponsored by the Families and Work Institute. Several leading family-friendly companies are profiled.

Moorcroft, S., and V. Bennett. 1995. *European guide to teleworking: A framework for action.* Dublin: European Foundation for the Improvement of Living and Working Conditions.

The foundation has researched teleworking since 1982. This book is a practical guide to teleworking and provides a comprehensive cross-national guide for all the member states of the European Union. It addresses issues such as hardware selection, software selection, security, insurance, health, and safety. Useful appendixes include a directory of organizations involved with teleworking as well as consultants, trade unions, and government agencies; a selective bibliography; and sample questions that can be used by managers and participants in telework pilots.

Murphy, E. 1996. *Flexible work.* London: Director Books.

Murphy is director of the Home Office Partnership, an organization that has introduced flexibility into a range of British firms. Murphy identifies the factors driving flexibility, reports on the status of flexibility in the United Kingdom, and provides examples of flexible employers.

Nilles, J. M. 1994. *Making telecommuting happen: A guide for telemanagers and telecommuters.* New York: Van Nostrand Reinhold.

The first part of this book focuses on management issues (policies, site location, technology requirements, costs and benefits). The second part focuses on establishing a home office. Appendixes provide sample forms such as an employer/employee agreement on the terms of telecommuting.

Nilles, J. M. 1998. *Managing telework: Strategies for managing the virtual workforce.* New York: Wiley.

This is the definitive guide to managing telework, written by the acknowledged father of telecommuting. Nilles has almost three decades of experience with telecommuting. His book covers all aspects of managing a virtual workplace, including home-based telecommuting and center-based telecommuting.

O'Hara, B. 1993. *Working harder isn't working*. Vancouver, British Columbia: New Star Books.

O'Hara worked as an employment counselor at one phase of his career. He established an organization to lobby for a reduction in the standard workweek in Canada. He then went on to establish Work Well, an organization that promotes flexible work options. This book looks at strategies for reducing work hours.

O'Hara, B. 1994. *Put work in its place: How to redesign your job to fit your life*. 2d ed. Vancouver, British Columbia: New Star Books.

O'Hara predicts that it may take fifteen years before flexible work schedules are widely available. This book focuses on job sharing and career part-time work.

O'Hara, B., and G. Williams. 1990. *A manager's guide to phased retirement*. Victoria, British Columbia: Work Well Publications.

Work Well was established in 1985. This center provides assistance to both workers and employers considering flexible work arrangements. The authors provide a good history of phased retirement, identify the elements of a formal phased-retirement program, and make the business case for implementing phased retirement.

Olmsted, B., and S. Smith. 1994. *Creating a flexible workplace: How to select & manage alternative work options*. 2d ed. New York: AMACOM.

The first edition of this book won the Society for Human Resource Management's 1990 award for best book of the year. This is an essential guide to implementing flextime, compressed workweeks, job sharing, phased retirement, telecommuting, part-time options, voluntary reduced work time, work sharing, sabbaticals, and other leaves.

Olmsted, B., and S. Smith. 1996. *The job sharing handbook*. Rev. ed. San Francisco: New Ways to Work.

This essential handbook on job sharing leads interested job sharers through the process of finding a partner, proposing a job-sharing scheme, devising a schedule, and working out problems. It also contains profiles of job sharers. First published in 1983, it is the definitive manual on job sharing.

Olmsted, B., and S. Smith. 1997. *Managing in a flexible workplace*. New York: American Management Association.

The authors are affiliated with New Ways to Work, an organization that has promoted alternative work schedules since 1976. This book reiterates the process in implementing flexibility that was defined in their earlier book, *Creating a Flexible Workplace*. This is an indispensable guide to implementing and managing flextime, compressed workweeks, telecommuting, part-time work, job sharing, voluntary reduced work time, work sharing, phased retirement, sabbaticals, and other leaves.

O'Reilly, J., and C. Fagan, eds. 1998. *Part-time prospects: An international comparison of part-time work in Europe, North American and the Pacific Rim*. London: Routledge.

This edited volume brings together fourteen scholarly papers on the growth of part-time work in industrialized countries. Many of the chapters are comparative, looking at similarities and differences across countries.

Parasuraman, S., and J. H. Greenhaus, eds. 1997. *Integrating work and family: Challenges and choices for a changing world*. Westport, Conn.: Quorum Books.

The twenty-one chapters in this book are grouped under five themes: (1) environmental factors impacting work and family, (2) different perspectives of work/family issues, (3) legal and cultural perspectives on work/family issues, (4) the impact of career development programs on employees and their families, and (5) cultural barriers to achieving a more effective integration of work/family issues.

Perlow, L. A. 1997. *Finding time: How corporations, individuals and families can benefit from new work practices*. Ithaca, N.Y.: ILR Press.

This book is based on Perlow's four-year study of product development engineers at a Fortune 500 company. She studied engineers' use of time in depth and the effect of work on engineers themselves, their families, and the corporation. The group of engineers that Perlow studied was under pressure to develop a product and get it to market as soon as possible. Perlow found that the work culture rewarded long hours at work.

Piskurich. G. 1998. *An organizational guide to telecommuting: Setting up and running a successful telecommuter program.* Alexandria, Va.: American Society for Training and Development.

This is an excellent practical manual for establishing a telecommuting program. Piskurich provides a brief history of telecommuting, explains the rationale for telecommuting, discusses the need for firms to develop a telecommuting vision, and outlines the nuts and bolts of developing telecommuting policies and procedures. He has compiled several useful appendixes, including assessment tools, examples of telecommuters' contracts, and sample evaluation surveys.

Pleck, J. H. 1994. *Family-supportive employer policies and men: A perspective.* Working paper series no. 274. Wellesley, Mass.: Wellesley College, Center for Research on Women.

Pleck examines the relevance of family-friendly policies to men. There has been a trend toward greater father involvement in child care and housework. Consequently, family-friendly policies would benefit men.

Pratt, J. H. 1993. *Myths and realities of working at home: Characteristics of homebased business owners and telecommuters.* Dallas: Joanne H. Pratt Associates.

This is a groundbreaking study of the work habits and attitudes of telecommuters.

Reid, A. 1993. *Teleworking: A guide to good practice.* Manchester, England: Blackwell.

Reid traces the history of teleworking. The chapter on telecottages and satellite offices is particular useful for those studying European teleworking. He includes some interesting examples of teleworking projects.

Reynolds, T., and D. Brusseau. 1998. *Cyberlane commuter.* Chula Vista, Calif.: Black Forest Press.

Reynolds and Brusseau have created an excellent practical manual for individuals who want to telecommute via a high-speed network.

Both authors now serve as consultants to firms implementing telecommuting.

Rogak, L. A. 1994. *Time off from work: Using sabbaticals to enhance your life while keeping your career on track*. New York: Wiley.

This is a practical guide to planning a sabbatical. The author interviewed more than forty professionals who took a break from work.

Ruppel, C. P. 1995. Correlates of the adoption and implementation of programmer/analyst telework: An organizational perspective. Ph.D. diss., Kent State University.

Ruppel examines why telecommuting has not been more widely adopted and implemented. She identifies factors related to the adoption and implementation of telecommuting. Her study focuses on telecommuting among programmer/analysts in information-systems departments and information-systems firms.

Saltzman, A. 1991. *Down-shifting: Reinventing success on a slower track*. New York: HarperCollins.

Saltzman interviewed business managers, engineers, doctors, lawyers, journalists, and professors who have slowed down their careers. These downshifters represented a variety of occupations and came from a wide range of geographic regions.

Schepp, D., and B. Schepp. 1995. *The telecommuter's handbook: How to earn a living without going to the office*. 2d ed. New York: McGraw-Hill.

In 1990, when the Schepps published the first edition of this book, they found that many corporations were hesitant to talk about their telecommuting initiatives or were not familiar with the concept. Five years later things were completely different. Companies were immediately familiar with the term and many companies were proud of their telecommuting initiatives and eager to talk about it.

Schwartz, D. B. 1994. *An examination of the impact of family-friendly policies on the glass ceiling*. New York: Families and Work Institute.

Schwartz focuses on the career advancement of women who use family-friendly policies, such as leaves and flexible work arrangements. She outlines the need for additional research in specific areas.

Shellenbarger, S. 1999. *Work & family: Essays from the "Work & Family" column of the* Wall Street Journal. New York: Ballantine Books.

This is a wonderful collection of 100 of Shellenbarger's essays from the Work & Family column of the *Wall Street Journal*. Shellenbarger's popular column is one of five regular marketplace page columns and has a wide readership. All the essays reprinted here were originally published between 1994 and 1998. They are grouped into broad topical categories, including chapters on balancing work and family, negotiating workplace flexibility, and family-friendly companies. The volume concludes with a brief list of recommended resources.

Simmons, S. 1996. *Flexible working: A strategic guide to successful implementation and operation*. London: Kogan Page.

This is an excellent source of data on teleworking in the United Kingdom. Simmons breaks down teleworking into four types: (1) home-based telework, (2) satellite offices/touchdown/drop-in centers, (3) nomad telework, mobile work, or itinerant work, and (4) neighborhood office and telecenters.

Sims, W., M. Joroff, and F. Becker. 1996. *Managing the reinvented workplace*. Houston, Tex.: International Facility Management Association; Norcross, Ga.: International Development Research Council.

Becker and Sims are directors of Cornell University's International Workplace Studies Program. Joroff is director, research and special programs, School of Architecture, Massachusetts Institute of Technology. This report looks at the experiences of more than twenty-five companies that have been innovative in implementing alternative work options. The authors combined these case studies with interviews with managers, discussions at a series of workshops on new workplace strategies, and their own experiences as consultants and researchers. This book presents best practices to organizations that have implemented or plan to implement alternative workplace options. The authors identify key issues managers face when implementing alternative workplace strategies, explore how leading companies have managed alternative workplace programs, and identify the new skills, roles, and attitudes required of professionals to manage this reinvented workplace.

Speeth, L. M. 1992. The attributes of successful managers of telecommuters and successful telecommuting programs. Ph.D. diss., Golden Gate University.

This important dissertation provides insight into the factors that make telecommuting programs successful. Most research has focused on the telecommuter or the organization, not the manager. Speeth identifies managers of telecommuters in an effort to identify the attributes of successful telemanagers and factors contributing to the success of a telecommuting program.

Stanworth, C. 1996. *Working at home: A study of homeworking and teleworking*. London: Institute of Employment Rights.

This is a good analysis of obstacles to the growth of telecommuting in the United Kingdom.

Swank, C. 1982. *Phased retirement: The European experience*. Washington, D.C.: National Council for Alternative Work Patterns.

This is an in-depth study of phased retirement in Western Europe. It summarizes the rationale for implementing phased retirement, discusses problems organizations experienced, and addresses barriers to introducing this scheme.

Thompson, B. B. 1996. *Telecommuting pluses & pitfalls*. Brentwood, Tenn.: M. Lee Smith.

Most of this report focuses on the legal issues that employers need to consider before implementing a telecommuting program.

Tilly, C. 1996. *Half a job: Bad and good part-time jobs in a changing labor market*. Philadelphia: Temple University Press.

This is an extremely important work on part-time employment. Tilly makes the important distinction between two types of part-time jobs: secondary part-time jobs and retention part-time jobs. Tilly's research is based on a study of part-time workers in two metropolitan areas: Boston and Pittsburgh.

Wilson, A. 1991. *Teleworking: Flexibility for a few*. Sussex, England: Institute of Manpower Studies.

Wilson examined teleworking in six U.K. firms. He conducted interviews with senior managers involved in implementing or managing teleworking schemes. Except for IBM, all teleworking was home based.

PERIODICALS

The following is a selective listing of magazines, journals, and newsletters that frequently feature articles on topics relating to workplace flexibility. The listing of a title in the section does not constitute an endorsement of the periodical by the authors or Quorum Books.

Compensation and Benefits Review
American Management Association
1601 Broadway
New York, NY 10019–7420
Bimonthly

Employee Benefit Plan Review
250 S. Wacker Dr., Ste. 600
Chicago, IL 60606–5834
Monthly

European Industrial Relations Review
Eclipse Group Ltd., Industrial Relations Services
18-20 Highbury Pl.
London N5 1QP, England
Monthly

Home Office Computing
156 W. 56th St., 3rd Floor
New York, NY 10020
Monthly

HR Executive Review
The Conference Board
845 Third Avenue
New York, NY 10022–6601
Quarterly

HR Focus
American Management Association
1601 Broadway
New York, NY 10019–7420
Monthly

HRMagazine
Society for Human Resource Management
1800 Duke St.
Alexandria, VA 22314–3499
Monthly

International Labour Review
ILO Publications, CH-1211
Geneva 22, Switzerland
Bimonthly

Mobile Computing and Communications
6420 Wilshire Blvd.
Los Angeles, CA 90048–5515
Monthly

Public Personnel Management
1617 Duke St.
Alexandria, VA 22314
Quarterly

Telecommute: Today's Magazine for the Workplace of Tomorrow
P.O. Box 14357
Parkville, MO 64152
Monthly

Telecommuting Review
10 Donner Ct.
Monmouth Junction, NJ 08852
Monthly

Training
50 S. Ninth St.
Minneapolis, MN 55402
Monthly

Work–Family Roundtable
The Conference Board
845 Third Avenue
New York, NY 10022–6601
Quarterly

Workforce
P.O. Box 2440
Costa Mesa, CA 92626
Monthly

Working at Home
733 Third Avenue
New York, NY 10017
Quarterly

Working Mother
135 W. 50th St., 16th Floor
New York, NY 10020
Ten issues per year

NONPRINT MATERIALS

Organizations implementing flexible workplace options may find the following videos useful for training purposes. A listing of a video in this section does not constitute an endorsement by the authors or Quorum Books.

Balancing work and family: Challenges and solutions. 1994. Logan: Utah State University. One ninety-minute videocassette.

A better place to work. 1990. Toronto: Ontario Ministry of Labour Video Group. One eighteen-minute videocassette.

Family friendly forum. 1996. Washington, D.C.: U.S. Department of Energy. Two videocassettes totaling two hours, fourteen minutes.

Home-based business: A winning blueprint. 1991. Arlington, Va.: Bell Atlantic. One fifty-five-minute videocassette and accompanying booklet.

Industrial futures. 1990. London: BBC-TV. One fifty-minute videocassette.

The keys to telecommuting success. 1994. Salem: Oregon Department of Energy. One seventeen-minute videocassette and accompanying workbook.

Telecommuting: Management tool for the '90s. 1995. Tri-state version. Phoenix: Arizona Department of Administration, Travel Reduction Programs; Salem: Oregon Department of Energy, Telecommuting Resources; Olympia: Washington State Energy Office, Telecommuting Resources. One thirteen-minute videocassette.

Telecommuting: Supporting your road warriors. 1995. Syosset, N.Y.: Computer Channel. One videocassette and accompanying booklet.

Telecommuting: The future is now. 1994. Washington, D.C.: General Services Administration, Office of Public Affairs, Office of Audiovisual Services. One twelve-minute videocassette.

The virtual office wherever work needs to be. 1995. Haverford, Pa.: Videolearning Resource Group. One twenty-eight-minute videocassette with thirty-five-page leader's handbook.

Working family values. 1988. Oakland: Working Group. One fifty-six-minute videocassette originally broadcast as a PBS television program.

SECONDARY DATASETS

There are many secondary datasets relating to labor and work history. Several datasets exist on this topic in the social sciences. While sociologists may be familiar with them, economists and other academics may not be aware of them. The following are a representative sampling of major national surveys that will be useful to researchers.

Employee Benefit Survey

This is a national survey of employee-benefit-plan features and provisions collected periodically by the U.S. Bureau of Labor Statistics. Many researchers have used these data to track the growth of various work/family policies.

Labour Force Survey

This is the longest-running and most widely used source of statistical information about the employment and labor market behavior of workers in the U.K. economy. It is a quarterly sample survey covering some 60,000 households. It was conducted every two years until 1983. Since 1983 it has been conducted annually. It has been used by researchers to detect changes in employment practices over time. This survey covers individuals in all sizes and types of organizations.

National Longitudinal Survey

This large dataset compiled by the U.S. Bureau of Labor Statistics allows researchers to compare home-based work with non-home-based work. Leading telecommuting researcher Joanne Pratt used this data to develop an extensive sociodemographic profile of telecommuters.

National Study of the Changing Workforce

This is a longitudinal study on workforce attitudes and preferences conducted by the Families and Work Institute.

Quality of Employment Survey

This large national survey of U.S. workers was conducted in 1977. Among the factors it examined were excessive work hours and work/family conflict. Researchers have used these data to assess changes in the development of supportive workplaces.

Survey of Federal Employees

This 1991 U.S. survey provides data on the extent and use of flexible work arrangements by federal workers.

Workforce 2000

Published by the Hudson Institute in 1987, this landmark report predicted future labor shortages and an increasingly diverse workforce.

Workplace Industrial Relations Survey

This nationally representative survey collects data on employers in the United Kingdom. It excludes small businesses.

CHAPTER 7

Strategies for Locating Information

In this chapter we provide some suggestions for locating additional resources relating to workplace flexibility. Relevant organizations, Internet sites, databases, and useful search terms are included. We conclude with a glossary of terms related to all aspects of workplace flexibility.

ORGANIZATIONS

American Management Association
1601 Broadway
New York, NY 10019
(212) 586–8100
http://www.amanet.org

American Society for Training and Development
1640 King Street, Box 1443
Alexandria, VA 22313–2043
(703) 683–8100
http://www.astd.org

American Telecommuting Association
1220 L Street, NW, Suite 100
Washington, DC 20005
(800) 282–4968
http://www.knowledgetree.com/ata.html

Association of Part-Time Professionals
Crescent Plaza
7700 Leesburg Pike, Number 216
Falls Church, VA 22043
(703) 734–7945
http://www.aptp.org

Canadian Telework Association
52 Stonebriar Drive
Nepean, Ontario K2G 5X9, Canada
(613) 225–5588
http://www.ivc.ca

Catalyst
120 Wall Street
New York, NY 10005
(212) 514–7600
http://www.catalystwomen.org

The Conference Board
845 Third Avenue
New York, NY 10022–6679
(212) 759–0900
http://www.conference-board.com

Families and Work Institute
330 Seventh Avenue, 14th Floor
New York, NY 10001
(212) 465–2044
http://www.familiesandwork.com

Formerly Employed Mothers at the Leading Edge (FEMALE)
P.O. Box 31
Elmhurst, IL 60126
(630) 941–3553
http://www.FEMALEhome.org/female.htm

Home Office Association of America
133 East 58th Street, Suite 711
New York, NY 10022
(212) 588–9097
http://www.hoaa.com

International Industrial Relations Association
c/o RELPROF
International Labour Office
CH-1211 Geneva 22, Switzerland
(41–22) 799–6841
http://www.ilo.org/public/english/dialogue/govlab/iira/membership.htm

International Telework Association Council
204 E Street NE
Washington, DC 20002
(202) 547–6157
http://www.telecommute.org

Labor Project for Working Families
Institute of Industrial Relations
2541 Channing Way
Berkeley, CA 94720
(510) 643–6814
http://laborproject.berkeley.edu

National Association for the Cottage Industry
P.O. Box 14850
Chicago, IL 60614
(773) 472–8116

National Association of At-Home Mothers
406 E. Buchanan Avenue
Fairfield, IA 52556
(515) 472–3202
http://www.at-home-mothers.com

National Association of Part-Time and Temporary Employees
5800 Barton, Suite 201
P.O. Box 3805
Shawnee, KS 66203
(913) 962–7740

New Ways to Work
785 Market Street, Suite 950
San Francisco, CA 94103
(415) 995–9860
http://www.nww.org

9 to 5 Working Women Education Fund
231 Wisconsin Avenue, Suite 900
Milwaukee, WI 53203
(414) 274–0925

Telework, Telecottage, and Telecentre Association
Shortwood
Nailsworth GL6 OSH, England
(44) 1203 696986
http://ourworld.compuserve.com/homepages/teleworker/

INTERNET SITES

AT&T Telework Guide

http://www.att.com/ehs/telework/

This site was developed to assist telecommuters. The site highlights the benefits of telework, shares tips and tools to help telecommuters get started, and includes a telecommuting calculator to help measure the environmental impacts of teleworking. Topics such as assessing organizational readiness, implementing a pilot program, and drafting a telework policy are included. Helpful suggestions and tools to assist supervisors and teleworkers embark on a successful telework arrangement are detailed. Issues such as training and setting up a home office are adddressed. Sample surveys to measure and assess the success of the telework program are also available.

Boston College Center for Work and Family

http://www.bc.edu/bc_org/avp/csom/cwf/center/overview.html

The Boston College Center for Work and Family, located within the Wallace E. Carroll School of Management, is a research organization dedicated to increasing the quality of life of working families by promoting the responsiveness of workplaces and communities to their needs. The center uses three core strategies to pursue its mission: research, workplace partnerships, and communication and information services.

British Telecommunications

http://www.wfh.co.uk/wfh/flexible_corp/flexible.htm

This section of the British Telecommunications site has resources for the "flexible corporation" and for individuals working from home. There are case studies and a wealth of practical information.

Canadian Telework Association

http://www.ivc.ca

This is a comprehensive site providing information about and promoting telecommuting. It is international in scope: 66 percent of the members are Canadian, 29 percent are from the United States, and the remainder are from other countries. The site also provides a job matching service.

European Community Telework/Telematics Forum

http://www.telework-forum.org

The European Community Telework/Telematics Forum (ECTF) is the framework across European Union member states for concentration on telework and related telematics applications. The ECTF promotes teleworking and the exchange and dissemination of information between telework projects and organizations interested in telework.

European Telework Online

http://www.eto.org.uk

This site bills itself as the world's largest repository of information and links on telework and related topics. It contains descriptions and links for more than 1,000 items on telework, e-commerce, telecooperation, and related topics.

Fleming LTD

http://www.mother.com/dfleming

This is an interesting site, with articles by guest commentators, links to resources, and news about developments related to telecommuting. The site is maintained by Fleming LTD, a provider of telework consulting services.

Gil Gordan Associates

http://www.gilgordon.com

This site, operating since May 1995, consolidates a wide variety of information from around the world and from many different perspectives on the subjects of telecommuting, teleworking, the virtual office, and related topics. The site is sponsored by Gil Gordon Associates, an expert in the implementation of telecommuting and telework.

June Langhoff's Telecommuting Resource Center

http://www.langhoff.com

This site is maintained by June Langhoff, who is a writer in the area of workstyle, telecommunications, and technology issues for business and the media. It provides advice to potential telecommuters, facts and figures about telecommuting, a calendar of conferences and seminars, and links to other sites for telecommuting.

International Telework Association and Council

http://www.telecommute.org

This site provides a complete guide to setting up a telework program, the Telework America Online Curriculum. There are also recent articles on telecommuting and telework, discussion groups, and much other practical advice.

Pacific Bell

http://www.pacbell.com

The Work at Home section of Pacific Bell's Web site has many useful resources, including an extensive list of online publications.

Smart Valley, Inc.: Telecommute America, California Style

http://www.SVI.ORG/telework/index.html

This site has an excellent Telecommuting Guide, with information on how to set up a telecommuting program plus other practical resources. There are useful links to other Internet sources for telecommuting information.

Telecommuting Jobs

http://www.tjobs.com

This is a job bank for individuals interested in telecommuting. Interested individuals can also post resumes on this site.

Tips for Telecommuters

http://www.allearnatives.com

This site has suggestions for telecommuters who work at home. The site is maintained by the consulting firm ALLearnatives, which offers services in the areas of telecommuting program planning and program implementation. The sections on making a case for telecommuting with employers and what to include in a telecommuting agreement are particularly helpful.

The U.S. General Services Administration Office of Workplace Initiatives

http://www.gsa.gov/pbs/owi/telecomm.htm

The GSA has a very thorough list of government resources and research in telework.

DATABASES

A great many databases provide citations and/or full-text articles related to workplace flexibility. The following are the most important and comprehensive databases for research on this topic.

ABI/Inform (Bell & Howell Information and Learning)

This is the premier database for research in business, including topics related to management. In our judgement this is the most useful database for exploring all aspects of flexible work arrangements.

Academic Universe (Lexis/Nexis)

This full-text database provides international coverage of major newspapers and other sources of information, such as newswires and transcripts.

Dow Jones International

This comprehensive full-text database covers more than 6,000 business sources.

Periodical Abstracts (Bell & Howell Information and Learning)

This is a general-purpose database that indexes core journals in most disciplines. This is a good interdisciplinary starting point.

PsycInfo (American Psychological Association)

This is the premier database in the behavioral sciences. There is good coverage of topics related to organizational psychology and psychological aspects of management.

Social Sciences Abstract (H. W. Wilson)

This database provides coverage of the core social-science journals. There is little "popular" material in the database; it is focused primarily on academic literature.

Sociological Abstracts (Cambridge Scientific Abstracts)

This is the leading database for sociological research. A major subfield in sociology is the sociology of work.

Wilson Business Abstracts (H. W. Wilson)

Although not as comprehensive as ABI/Inform, this database indexes popular, trade, and scholarly journals.

USEFUL TERMS FOR DATABASE
OR INTERNET SEARCHES

Alternative work arrangements

Alternative work schedules

Alternative work strategy

Annual hours

Annual hours contracts

Annualised hours (British term)

Career breaks

Career part-time

Compressed workweeks

Corporate sabbaticals

Dispersed working

Distance staffing

Downshifting

Electronic cottage

Extended personal leaves

Family and Medical Leave Act

Family-friendly

Father-friendly

Flexible hours

Flexible schedules

Flexiplace

Flextime

Hot desking

Hoteling

Job sharing

Mobile worker

Non-territorial office

Paid time off

Parental leave

Partial retirement

Paternity leave

Phased retirement
PTO
Remote work
Road warriors
Satellite offices
Social-service leaves
Telecentre (British term)
Telecottage
Telecommuting
Telecommuting centers
Telemanager
Telesubstitution
Telework
Telework centers
Teleworking
V-Time
Virtual office
Virtual organization
Virtual work
Voluntary leaves
Voluntary reduced work time
Work at home
Work sharing
Work/family programs
Work-life programs

LIBRARY OF CONGRESS SUBJECT HEADINGS

These terms are used to describe the contents of books. Using them in library catalogs will help retrieve additional materials in a targeted fashion.

Compressed workweek
Four-day week
Hours of labor, flexible
Job sharing
Leave of absence
Parental leave
Part-time employment

Sabbatical leave
Telecommuting
Telecommuting–Europe
Telecommuting–United States
Telecommuting centers
Telecommuting centers–management
Work and family
Work sharing

Glossary

Compensatory time Also known as comp time, these are hours worked but not paid that will be used as time off later.

Compressed workweek A full-time work schedule that is completed in fewer than five days.

Core time A time period when all of a company's employees are required to be on the job.

Distance staffing A new term applied to recruiting and hiring new employees who telecommute. This suggests that telecommuting has moved beyond the stage where it is perceived as an employee benefit.

Downshifting The practice of deliberately scaling back hours at work in order to spend more time on other areas of life.

Family and Medical Leave Act Legislation passed in the United States in 1993 that guarantees American workers at companies with more than fifty employees the right to take up to twelve weeks of unpaid family leave.

Flexible work arrangements Sometimes referred to as alternative work arrangements, these are working patterns that involve adjustments in the timing, scope, and/or place of work.

Flextime The generic term for work schedules that permit flexible starting and quitting times.

Hot desking Describes a situation in which several employees use the same desk at different times.

Hoteling Shared office facilities for highly mobile employees. The office space may be used by employees who are going to be in a given geographic location only temporarily.

Intranet A term used to describe any network located within an organization that is generally using Internet technology.

Job sharing A type of regular part-time work that permits two people (called job sharers) to voluntarily share the same full-time position.

Leave banks Banks of donated vacation days that permit employees who have exhausted their own vacation time, sick leave, or the like to borrow extra days off with pay.

Leaves Authorized absences from work without loss of employment rights. Leaves may be paid or unpaid.

Nilles, Jack b. Evanston, IL, August 25, 1932. The father of the telecommuting movement.

Non-territorial office A term coined by MIT researcher Thomas Allen for any office-space allocation program that does not assign desks or workstations to specific employees.

Paid time off Commonly referred to as PTO, a policy that allows workers to pool their vacation, sick, and personal days.

Partial retirement A flexible option that allows employees to work part time prior to full retirement.

Permanent part-time work A work schedule that is less than forty hours per week. These permanent employees are on a company's regular payroll and may or may not receive benefits. These employees are sometimes referred to as career part-time workers.

Phased retirement A flexible work option that allows employees to phase into retirement over several months or several years.

Sabbatical Generally a paid leave that is offered to employees at set intervals for the purpose of study, research, or retooling. Employees are expected to return with some job-related achievement.

Summer hours Employees work after hours during the week in exchange for shorter hours on Fridays. Sometimes refers to the practice of beginning work earlier in the morning and consequently leaving earlier in the afternoon during the summer months.

Telecenters (or telecentres) Sometimes referred to as remote work centers. These are facilities that may or may not be owned by a corporation. The facilities are away from an organization's main office(s), usually in the suburbs or some location that is perceived as being more convenient to employees. The aim of telecenters is to reduce commuting times or provide a convenient location for short-term team projects.

Telecommuting A flexible work option that allows employees to work at home all or part of their scheduled hours. Some telecommuters work in telecommuting centers, where work is moved to the worker.

Telecommuting contract A document that outlines the roles and responsibilities of the employer and the employee who wishes to telecommute.

Teleworking The term generally used instead of telecommuting outside of North America (i.e., working at a distance).

Virtual office An alternative work process in which an employee has no physical location for an office, but connects electronically to resources (main office, home office, or a network) from wherever he or she happens to be.

Voluntary reduced work time Sometimes referred to as V-Time, an option where full-time employees voluntarily reduce their work hours and take a corresponding cut in pay.

Work sharing The practice of shortening work hours so work can be spread among more employees.

3/12 A variation of the compressed workweek where employees work three twelve-hour days.

4/10 A variation of the compressed workweek where employees work four ten-hour days.

9/80 A variation of the compressed workweek where employees work a week of four nine-hour days and one eight-hour day followed by a week of four nine-hour days.

Name Index

Subject Index

ABOUT THE AUTHORS

Christine Avery has been a librarian at Pennsylvania State University since 1990. She is currently the head of the Commonwealth College Libraries, which consists of the libraries at twelve Penn State branches. Prior to this she served as a social science librarian and a business librarian at Penn State. She is the coauthor (with Diane Zabel) of *The Quality Management Sourcebook: An International Guide to Materials and Resources* (1997).

Diane Zabel is a business librarian at the Schreyer Library for Business at Penn State University's University Park campus. An active member of the American Library Association, Zabel has chaired many committees relating to continuing education, information literacy, and building library collections. She is currently serving as the elected chair of the Collection Development and Evaluation Section of the Reference and Users Services Association, a division of the American Library Association. She is the coauthor (with Christine Avery) of *The Quality Management Sourcebook: An International Guide to Materials and Resources* (1997).